George Shipman Payson

All for Christ:

A sketch of the life and labors of the Rev. Charles H. Payson

George Shipman Payson

All for Christ:
A sketch of the life and labors of the Rev. Charles H. Payson

ISBN/EAN: 9783337713782

Printed in Europe, USA, Canada, Australia, Japan

Cover: Foto ©ninafisch / pixelio.de

More available books at **www.hansebooks.com**

ALL FOR CHRIST:

A SKETCH

OF

THE LIFE AND LABORS

OF THE

REV. CHARLES H. PAYSON.

EDITED BY HIS BROTHER.

TENEO ET TENEOR.

AMERICAN TRACT SOCIETY,

150 NASSAU STREET, NEW YORK.

1877.

DEDICATION.

TO THE DEAR FATHERLESS CHILDREN,

CHARLIE, SARAH, BESSIE, EDDIE, AND MAY,

THIS VOLUME

IS AFFECTIONATELY INSCRIBED.

PREFACE.

THIS little book, as will readily be seen, is not the work of any one hand. It is a mosaic of varied tributes to the memory of a good and brave man, which have been collected from many sides, and testify to the esteem and admiration with which he was regarded by all who knew him. His friends and associates, co-laborers in the field of New York city missions and brethren in the ministry, the members of his own and of his father's family, and some who only knew him casually, have joined to make this picture of his life; and however imperfect it may appear, it is hoped that it may not be without some good results of cheer, and comfort, and instruction.

I confess to feelings of great reluctance at the thought of undertaking even to edit a memorial of my brother's life, well knowing that my love for him might make me partial. But Providential events and the judgment of friends constrained me to forego these scruples, and to attempt a work which has been delightful just in proportion as it has proved laborious; and I can but indulge the hope that the intimacy of those fraternal relations in which for many years he acted towards me as a father towards his son, may have conduced to some appreciative views of his work, which might not have been secured from a different point of observation.

Due credit has been given in the book itself so far as practicable to those who by letter or otherwise have kindly contributed to its material. But it is proper to state here that the reminiscences of my brother's early home and education have been mainly furnished by his college classmate and lifelong friend, the Rev. C. D. Helmer, D. D., of Brooklyn, and that in the editorial work I have been greatly assisted by the Rev. Geo. L. Prentiss, D. D., formerly pastor of the Church of the Covenant in this city, and now Professor in the Union Theological Seminary. Dr. Prentiss was for many years familiar with my brother's labors, was warmly attached to him, and has taken the deepest interest in the preparation of this memorial. To these gentlemen my thanks are specially due. G. S. P.

INWOOD-ON-HUDSON,
New York City, Nov., 1877.

CONTENTS.

WHEN comes the hour, which now I may not know,
When from this changing world my soul must go,
Will my life's plans be broken?   Truly, no.

God placed me here ; I chose not place or name,
To do his work, his business, be my aim,
Through every day, in all the plans I frame.

My one great aim in which all others blend,
To which my work, my pleasures, pastimes tend,
Be to fill well the time my God may send.

Then when he calls, wherever I may be,
Doing the common work he gives to me,
At books, or prayer, abroad, on land or sea,

My soul will not be stricken with dismay;
A home and treasure have I far away,
Whither my Lord will guide me on that day.

My real life unbroken passes on,
Working in shadow till the night is gone,
Rising to higher service with the dawn.

I hold a mystic thread within my hand,
My little plans imbraided strand in strand,
Anchored far onward in the unknown land.

What time mine eye is single, full of light,
'T is plain and palpable, and ever bright,
A guide to lead me through this earthly night.

I see its glow away where dim wings shiver,
Above the shadows of death's gloomy river,
And on beyond within the vast for ever.   PERSIE VERE.

ALL FOR CHRIST.

CHAPTER I.

CHARLES HENRY PAYSON, whose early death is so widely and tenderly lamented, deserves a more permanent recognition than that of a transient obituary notice. From the merely human point of view, we should say that Mr. Payson's decease was untimely, for his career was ended in the very prime of his physical and mental powers, and in the midst of most abundant usefulness. But the memory of those who have illustrated the teachings and the spirit of Jesus is gold in the treasury of the saints on earth. In heaven the names of such are imperishable, and radiant with a lustre of glory that nothing will ever dim. And among those who still live to work and pray and hope for the regeneration of mankind, these names remain as sacred possessions and stimulating examples.

Mr. Payson was born in Leominster, Mass., September 28, 1831. He was the eldest child of Rev. Phillips and Elizabeth Boutelle Payson, inheriting thus a name

eminent among the most honored Christian families of
New England, and fragrant with associations of devout
piety and holy zeal.   The father of Phillips Payson, the
Rev. Seth Payson, D. D., was for many years pastor of
the Congregational church of Rindge, N. H.   His eldest
son, Edward, became a successful and distinguished minister in Portland, Me., where he died at the early age of
forty-four years, leaving behind him a reputation for saint-
liness and devotion to the Lord's work which for half a
century has been most fondly cherished by Christians
everywhere.

Phillips, a younger brother of Edward, was born in
Rindge, N. H., August 11, 1795, and died in Fayetteville,
N. Y., February 16, 1856.   Having prepared for Dart-
mouth College, ill-health prevented him from pursuing
the course of study ; but he was graduated in due course
at the Theological Seminary in Andover, Mass., 1820.
Never robust, his whole life became a struggle with the
obstacles and limitations of physical infirmity.

He became pastor first of the "Calvinistic church"
of Leominster, Mass., which grew rapidly under his ministrations.   But the failure of his health compelled him
to quit the field after several years of very successful
ministry.   His name is fragrant there to-day with some
of the most hallowed and tenderly-cherished associations
which cluster around the early history of that church.

He was afterward settled in Hadley, Mass. ; then
again in North Lyme, Conn. ; and finally in Harpersfield,
N. Y.   But finding himself physically unable to perform
the arduous duties of the pastoral office, he abandoned

the active work of the ministry, and became a teacher in Ames, N. Y., until compelled at last to give up all labor requiring mental or physical exertion. The last part of his life was devoted to the education of his children.

It is much to be regretted that none of his private letters remain which might serve to throw a light upon his character, or to reveal the holy influence which he exerted in his family. That influence was very great, especially upon his eldest son, who to the very end of life cherished and revered the memory of his father as an inspiration. Even while dying he was overheard to say, "It may be I shall meet father and mother and Jesus to-day."

Phillips Payson was a holy man, deeply and tenderly beloved by those who knew him best in the best years of his life. The late Dr. Todd of Pittsfield once said of him, that when he was settled in Leominster "he was the JOHN of their association." By the several churches of his charge his name is still remembered with affection. In the family-life, his fondness for his children, his devotion to their good, his perfect consecration to the Divine will, and above all his cheerful and unfaltering trust in God, made his presence felt as a simple benediction. His patience was complete. His faith never seemed to falter even in the darkest hours. It made his daily life a hymn of praise and prayer, so that, as one of his children reverently said, "his face seemed often lighted with glory." His strongest desire for his children was that they might be faithful followers of Christ, and his one great prayer for them, "Lord, that they all may be thine!" He saw the fulfilment of this desire in the conversion of the

youngest members of his family only a few weeks before
his death, and on his return from their first communion
together, said, " Lord, now lettest thou thy servant depart in peace, for mine eyes have seen thy salvation."
" How exhilarating and transporting the forethought," he
writes to one of his children, "that (as we have often
prayed) we as an entire family shall at last be gathered
around the throne." And his last words seem but the
echo of his life, " I die assured of heaven."

It is needless to say that the influence of such a man
upon his family was very great. Not only was it a controlling influence—for a single word or look from him was
the certain "end of strife "—but it was a most beneficent
and inspiring one. It made religion honorable in their
eyes. Such steadfast faith and true obedience to God
were seen to be the only ends of life worth living for.
And far above all gold and treasures which this world
can give, his children prize the legacy of Christian example and Christian education and Christian principles left
them by this sainted father.

Charles, the subject of this sketch, was the eldest of
the family. He inherited the high intellectual and large
moral and spiritual qualities of this cultured Christian
ancestry. He was in the line of the gospel ministry, by
birth, by the faith and prayers and training of his parents,
and by all the most potent influences that streamed upon
his young mind and flowed around his early life.

The moulding influence of a mother's character upon
her son has always been recognized, and Charles Payson
was fortunate in having a mother whose piety and intel-

ligence were remarkable. She belonged to the class of holy women who, like Hannah, devote their children to the Lord from the very beginning of their existence. In her private diary, still a rich legacy in the possession of her children, is recorded this prayer of her heart at the time of her marriage :

Oh, deny me the necessaries of life rather than take the Holy Spirit from me! Without his illumination all will be to me a dreary waste; every Christian grace will become languid, and I shall see and do nothing for the salvation of sinners.

If any mother ever realized the responsibility of maternity, surely Mrs. Payson did. Her soul yearned for the moral and spiritual welfare of her children ; and through them she hoped to glorify God in the salvation of mankind. And the fact that all her children early gave themselves to the service of God, that the three sons all entered the gospel ministry, and that one of the daughters became a foreign missionary in China, are notable evidences that God hears the prayers of faithful parents who trust his grace for themselves and for their offspring.

At the risk of intruding upon the sanctity of private records which this devout mother probably never dreamed would see the broad light of public print, it is deemed desirable to make some brief extracts from her diary, touching this very important matter of consecrating children to the Lord. Of September 28, 1831, she writes :

This is an eventful day. A young immortal, a dear and lovely son, was committed to our charge. I hope I receive it as a blessing from the King of heaven. Never did I know before the responsibility of such a pledge. May I have grace to dedicate this child *daily to God*, feeling it not my own, but lent me for a few days, to pray for and instruct in the

ways of religion. Oh that its life may be spared, and may it *now* be sanctified, *even now;* that its first moral acts may be those of conformity to the
requirements of the gospel. How solemn the thought that this child must
live for ever, either in heaven or in the darkness and misery of the finally
impenitent. And if this future destiny of my child hangs, as I believe it
does, very much on me, how ought I to tremble lest I fail of discharging
my duty. Oh my Heavenly Father, save me from the doom of an unfaith-
ful mother !

Again, some years later, she says :

March 31st was a memorable day. God in mercy gave us a daughter, whom we received as from his hand, and I hope we have consecrated
her to the Lord as long as she lives. I think I can see the hand of God in
all his dealings, and feel more than ever an ardent desire to train *all our
children* for the Lord.

After the birth of her next child she writes :

Another little son was given us. What a weight of responsibility
now rests upon me. Five children to feed, to clothe, to educate, and *pray*
for. Surely it is a great work. May it be the great business of my life
to train them up for God. Had I nothing else to do, this would be
enough.

How pleasant are the duties of a mother when we feel that we are
laboring for God. . . . May our little ones be sheltered under the wings
of the Almighty, preserved amid every temptation, and after having spent
their lives for God, be received with their dear parents to the abodes of
the blessed.

1848, *Sept.* Charles left for Amherst College. Oh that God will
throw around him those arms which keep all His children safe. For some
weeks he has hoped that he has given himself to God."

Dec. We are happy to learn from his letters that he has publicly professed Christ. He is now about seventeen years old, and it is our ardent
and united prayer that God will by *rich grace* prepare this son for the
ministry. "Knowledge is power;" and oh that *all* his *powers* may be consecrated to the immediate service of God.

Thus fervently prayed Charles Payson's mother for
her son; and as the years passed away, and he became
more and more conscious of his own mental and moral
bent, the work of preaching the gospel grew in his deepest thoughts, sympathies, and desires, to be the divine

mission for him among men. He possessed rare abilities for business, and would hardly have failed to become successful in almost any secular calling. But a nature so derived in genealogy, and a boyhood so saturated with the stimulating and purifying influences of genuine piety, hears with quick perception the call of the Master, "Go ye into all the world and preach the gospel to every creature."

Some reminiscences of his boyhood are furnished by a sister, who was perhaps as intimately associated with him as any playmate of his youth. In reply to a letter in which some reference was made to a proposed memorial of his life, she writes :

As a child I remember our dear brother to have been generous, warm-hearted, and truthful. There was nothing of sullenness or obstinacy in his disposition. Ardent and impulsive in his temperament, his faults were only those which are common to such natures, almost wholly on the surface, and such as parents and friends are ever most ready to forgive and forget.

He was a very good child in the main, but not at all one of the *pious* little boys of whom we sometimes read, who delight to sit with folded hands and meditate, while their companions are at play. He was a genuine boy, had a ringing voice and hearty laugh, was thoroughly wide-awake, and as full of enthusiasm and energy in his sports, as he was, in after-years, when engaged in work for his Master. A relative seeing him threading his way, when a lad, about the streets of New York, at a time when he was an entire stranger to the city, remarked that he never saw a boy like Charlie Payson. Let him drop from whatever height you chose, he always came down on his feet.

Though exceedingly fond of play, he read with avidity all sorts of books, had a good memory for what he read, and was quick at his lessons. His affectionate nature prompted him to be particularly fond of pets, and there were always several about the house which were his especial property. There were doves, and rabbits, a pet lamb, the horse which he took pride in caring for, and the little dog, which was his loved companion from childhood till he became a man.

2

His naturally fine tastes led him to delight in flowers, and the house-plants which frequently adorned the windows of the family sitting-room when Charles was a youth, all belonged to him, and were by him most attentively cared for.

I recall one incident of his boyhood which shows that he had, even then, a tender spot in his heart for the poor and forlorn, and, as a child, was like St. Paul's ideal bishop, "given to hospitality." All the other members of the family having left home for the day, Charlie, the boy of ten or eleven years, remained by himself in charge of the house. About mid-day, two colored women, tired and footsore with walking many a weary mile, stopped at the door asking permission to sit and rest, hoping, doubtless, to obtain also a morsel of food. But the kind-hearted boy put them off with no morsel. Spreading the cloth, he treated them as though they were "angels unawares," placing on the table every delicacy the house afforded; and of this banquet the hungry travellers partook to their hearts' or rather stomachs' content. The mother of the youthful host returning at evening was much surprised, and probably equally annoyed, to see what inroads had been made upon her cakes and jellies and more substantial viands, by the lavish hospitality of her liberal-hearted little son.

At sixteen years of age Charles had completed his preparatory studies under the tuition of his father, at that time principal of the academy at Ames, New York. The ancient and established idea in New England of a thorough education for the gospel ministry, controlled his father's plans for his children; and Charles saw before him the plain and open course of a youth devoted to the work of preaching the gospel.

He had not, however, up to this time, made a public confession of faith in Christ. A Christian lad in spirit and desire and aim, he still hesitated to take what seemed to him a most solemn and important step. His native sincerity and conscientiousness prevented him from any sudden or ill-advised entrance upon an avowed religious career.

In this state of mind and feeling he left his delightful

home, and entered Amherst College in 1848, where he was graduated with his class in 1852. A new and inspiring career was now opening before him. The duties, the pleasures, the responsibilities of college-life, all began to stimulate afresh his energies and awaken his latent powers. Thrown upon his own resources and among companions brought together from all parts of the land, his natural disposition to do well whatever he undertook, was quickened into intense activity. One of his classmates speaking of him at that early period says: " On entering college he seemed to feel that he was enjoying great privileges which he must greatly improve."

How all these new surroundings affected his thoughts and desires, becomes evident from his fidelity to duty as a student. He was always in his place, and did his work with scrupulous care and tireless industry.

A letter written to his " Dear father, mother, all," at the beginning of his second year at Amherst, furnishes abundant testimony to the fact that he made good use of all his time and opportunities. The boy had already grown to be a man. And so far from having been diverted by these new experiences from his religious desires and aims, as sometimes happens with young men in college, he had evidently been developing in spiritual character.

In the letter just referred to he writes :

I was very sorry to learn so grievous a report of things at home. To hear that one and another of those whom I so well knew were snatched away, and especially the death of dear ——, was certainly sufficient to make any one pause and think of his own condition. The night I received your letter I could not but reflect on the one that I spent with him a short time before I left. I could almost see the Angel of Death standing over us, hesitating which of us he should take. God has seen fit that he should be taken and I left, for what purpose He alone knows. Oh, pray for me that I may be kept in that straight and narrow road that leads to eternal life. It sometimes seems as though I could willingly leave this world of darkness and sorrow and soar away to the mansions of bliss. But there is one blessed consolation, that the more toils and sorrows we endure, being faithful to the end, the brighter will be our crown, and the more perfect our enjoyment in the world to come.

These are not the words of a dreamy, sentimental young man, for he was not at all of such a disposition, but of one intensely earnest to do the work of life, and deeply imbued with the spirit of religion. And they correspond strikingly to a remark made by a classmate more than twenty-five years afterward in speaking of impressions received from young Payson at this early stage of his college course : "There was a certain sad and subdued tone in his early life in college, as if some deep sorrow had recently passed over him or his. This had entirely passed away before we graduated."

The following letters were written by his mother shortly after he left for college:

DEAR CHARLIE : The adage "Out of sight out of mind," I find is not true in respect to you and your mother's undying love. On the contrary, your absence increases my interest and affection. While I can rejoice in the belief that you are a child of *principle* and *piety*, still, our wicked hearts are so deceitful and you are so constantly exposed to various temptations, I think often and much about you, lest you may yield to some sins peculiar to a student's life. How many are overtaken by pride and envy and jealousy, and various passions, and led by these to grieve the Holy Spirit. Try and live nearer to God by faith and prayer than any of your friends or family-circle ; "to our own Master we stand or fall." . . . . That you may be humble and distinguished as a man of prayer and genuine piety, is the most ardent prayer of your dear father and mother. . . . . We shall be happy to hear from you soon after receiving this. Give much love to Henry, and accept a large share from every member of the family.

From your dear　　　　　　　　　　　　MOTHER.

AMES, June 12, 1849.

DEAR CHARLIE: I was much pleased that you could take a trip east during your vacation, and hope you are now enjoying health, and what is more, the felt presence of God. Let not your studies divert your mind from prayer and other religious duties. Look well into your own heart, and while you look at sin in all its odiousness, at the same moment flee by faith to the Saviour. . . .

Whatever trials we meet in this life, may we have grace to look away from them all and say, Our Father—my own covenant God and Father—will befriend, and take care, faithful care of me and mine. I was never able to confide in God and trust all with him as I have been during the past nine or ten months. For the most part—perhaps I ought to say daily—I feel to cast all at the feet of Jesus, having the joy of calling him mine, with unswerving confidence that, while we as parents, have entered into an everlasting covenant with God, his promise stands secure that he will be a God to us, and our dear children. In all your studies set God before your thoughts, and have no other motive but a desire to honor him; and then you will have a peace and a joy language fails to express.

We are almost counting the days before you return. May we be permitted again to meet and enjoy the unbroken family circle, and honor God far more than ever in our lives.

With very much love,   MOTHER.

AMES, July —, 1849.

MY DEAR CHILD: Feel not solitary and alone; trust your covenant God, and he will provide for all your wants and lead you to feel that his watchful care will guide and protect you till you shall be enabled to say like Jacob, " The Lord is in this place, dwelling with me in my room and by the way, and I knew it not." The dream of Jacob is delightful for contemplation. To see God by living faith, to feel that he is about us, providing for all our wants and fitting us for a mansion in heaven, ought to reconcile us to every trial here below. May God ever attend you by a retinue of angels, ministering to you at all times, and restraining you from sin. May you drink largely from the fountain of living waters and be enabled to do much for God during this vacation, and show to all around you that you have the spirit of Christ.

Thus prays your affectionate mother,

E. B. PAYSON.

During his first college year he had been brought to such a stage of religious experience that he publicly avowed his saving faith in Christ, and united with the College church. Speaking of this in a letter to his parents he writes: "The next Sabbath after I received your letter I joined the church in college. Long had I hesitated, doubting whether I was a child of God or no, now hoping and believing, and again cast down and desponding."

This statement of inner life only discloses that conscientiousness which always characterized him, and the lofty ideal of the Christian character towards which he continually looked, and which he ever strove to realize. Others differently constituted would have experienced no such alternations of hope and fear.

Continuing to speak of the same matter he goes on to say, that he had an interview with President Hitchcock, who had encouraged him to make a public confession of his faith, and had stimulated his desire to do so by the fact that those who defer this duty after being converted, are liable to lose their interest in religion. And furthermore, the same wise adviser admonished him that not a few thus never became avowed Christians at all. But, on the other hand, by uniting with the church, doubts and difficulties were sure to be removed.

"This with other reasons," he proceeds to say, "induced me to join. And although I have some dark days yet, it seems as though I could say from my heart, 'The Lord is my portion, what want can I know?'"

Abundant and positive are the testimonies to his piety and manliness, given by those associated with him in his student life. One classmate says: "He always exhibited a decided Christian spirit and principle, and we always knew where to find him when a moral point was at stake. I can recall no incident which reflected aught against his Christian integrity during the whole course of college discipline." And this testimony of his classmate is confirmed by the records of the institution, which declare that his deportment while there was perfect.

These facts remind us of the Scripture, "*Against such there is no law.*" Discipline was not for him who was thoroughly controlled in desire and purpose by the word of God. So steadily from the outset did the current of his life flow toward the kingdom of God, whose interests and righteousness he supremely loved and sought to attain.

It would seem to be no slight element in making up an estimate of any man, that his associates should bear witness to such uniform Christian character and conduct in the midst of temptations that lead astray so many young men, who, going forth to the experiences of life from excellent homes, fail to return with unsullied manhood.

While, then, faithful in all his duties as a student, performing conscientiously the work assigned him by his instructors, Mr. Payson never forgot that he was to render himself useful as a servant of the Saviour of the world. The cultivation of his intellect was only a means to an end. His studies were to prepare him to accomplish the utmost for the good of man and the glory of God. His knowledge was to be an instrument employed in saving others. Never did he suffer personal culture to stand in the way of usefulness. His was not an ambition to merely excel others in the ranks of college honors. He was too zealous a disciple of Christ to yield to such a temptation. And hence, while his standing as a scholar was good, he was better known as one of the active Christians in his class.

A classmate writes :

I remember Charles H. Payson in college most for his conscientious adherence to what he deemed to be right. In the class prayer-meetings his prayers were very earnest, penitential, tender, and evidently the out-goings of a soul used to communion with God. He was always at the meeting and always in the spirit of it. So of other religious exercises. The religious element was highly developed in him. He was one of those few among the students who used to go out to teach in Sunday-school and hold prayer-meetings in adjoining towns.

Another also writes of him :

A man of great sweetness of spirit and of deep religious experience ; a shining example of the devout, consistent Christian.

And yet another classmate recollects him in the following description :

His literary productions always showed evidence of thought, and of his studious endeavor to make each performance better than its prede-cessor. This honesty of purpose was characteristic of all he did and said, and entered into every exercise, whether in the recitation room, the Liter-ary Society, or the meetings of his class. And by it he attained a good position among his fellows. . . .

Through not possessing those positive characteristics that cause one always to run against the angles of another and hasten to encounter opposition in those who do not agree with him, yet he never stood in an equivocal position, but on each question which might arise among his fellows it was known where he would stand even before his opinion was asked for. . . . His aim always was to be right, and he was sure to err if at all on the right side.

These testimonies from the best witnesses, so clear and harmonious, present a distinct outline of the character and career of Mr. Payson during his life as a student at Amherst. From the intimacies of a close friendship, enjoyed by a few personal friends, abundant evidence might be brought of his unusually ardent affection, his peculiarly warm sympathy, and unselfish devotion. Whatever he had, or could do, was always at the disposal of his friends. Self-forgetful, he was abundant in all kindly offices to others. Warm-hearted and impulsive, he counted nothing too costly for a sacrifice, in the interests of a genuine friendship.

At the same time, thrown much upon his own resources for support, he developed self-reliance, and displayed that thrift, energy, and industry, which characterized him throughout life. The eldest of a large family of children, he relieved his parents as far as possible from all care of himself; and in later years, when father and mother had gone to the joys of heaven, he as elder brother took their place in affectionate concern and aid for his brothers and sisters.

And thus, during these four important years of student life, making the most of his opportunities, he prepared himself to enter upon the work of the Lord in the Christian ministry. After graduating with honors in 1852, he spent some time in teaching, in order to obtain means for completing his studies in the Theological Seminary. Almost immediately he became principal of the academy at Pompey, New York, and the same qualities of character which he had already displayed in col-

lege were brought into even fuller exercise in this new
and responsible position.

Here is the testimony of an eye-witness and of a
Christian man who has himself since done a noble work
in the ministry :

Mr. Charles H. Payson came to Pompey Academy fresh from college, and full of the enthusiasm which always characterized him. He
could do nothing by halves. He put new life into the old Academy,
which, with the entire community, was beginning to feel the drain of large
communities on the great thoroughfares of travel. He threw himself
earnestly into the work of the church, and made himself felt as a man of
society, the Christian scholar, and the enthusiastic Christian. He and
his entire family were nothing if they were not Christian.

I was then entering my last year of preparatory study with Amherst
college in view. It was a happy thing to be thrown in with one of such
glowing temperament and Christian life, the impression of which has
never left me, and I think never will.

And I am certain he will be remembered in the long line of worthy
principals in this honored school of central New York, as among the most
successful, and in his ardent Christian devotion perhaps without a peer.

Persons of cooler temperament and age sometimes thought him a
little extravagant in statement and manner, and sometimes spoke apolo-
getically, willing to make allowance for inexperience. But the sober ver-
dict of our time sets its crown on religious enthusiasm when it flames up
in a sound mind well versed in the Scriptures, and takes side with the
man who sets things moving, so it be towards some wholesome end.
Principal Payson stands approved in both these respects. Long will he
be remembered in old Pompey.

Having passed nearly two years in teaching, Mr.
Payson devoted his time for a few months to the Insurance business. In this as in every employment he undertook, his genial manners, tact, and energy, rendered
him especially efficient. He was so prospered financially
during those few months that some of his business
friends were led to remark that if he should devote himself to business rather than to the ministry, he might in

a few years attain to affluence. And the company with which he was engaged offered him a liberal salary if he would remain.

But he was not to be diverted from his chosen work. In the fall of 1854 he entered Union Theological Seminary in New York. At last he found himself directly engaged in those special studies by which he was to be prepared for his chosen work in life. To this had he long been looking forward. And now that the time had come, he seemed to gather up all his energies to do with utmost zeal and fidelity what these three years of final training laid upon him in duty and privilege. If the opportunities of college seemed to him great, these were even greater. Studies most congenial, most inspiring, now absorbed his attention.

And yet here, as always, his desires and aims were of the most practical sort. Not to be a scholar in speculative theology or simply learned in the lore of scientific religion, but to fit himself most completely to be a worker in the pastoral office, was his solemn purpose. What he longed to do was the work of Christ in saving mankind. All his knowledge, all his discipline and culture, was only so much of preparation for that final object.

He could not therefore be content with the duties of ·the lecture-room and the labors of routine studies, but sought all opportunities to make himself useful in Christian work. A teacher by nature, he turned instinctively and sympathetically towards Sunday-school instruction. He heartily believed in the theory of evangelizing the world through the religious training of the children. And although while a theological student he did not discover the Lord's purpose concerning him in this special work, he was nevertheless being prepared for it by divine influence and guidance.

The following communication from one of the teachers in his first Sunday-school may serve to illustrate this fact :

DEAR SIR: Having learned that you were about to publish a memoir of the Rev. C. H. Payson, I have felt that it would be a privilege as well as a duty to send you some account of his first work in this city, believing that very few, if any, of his personal friends know how well that work was done and how much was accomplished. I have neither dates nor statistics, but only some precious memories, which it will be a pleasure for me to recall.

Not long after his entering the Theological Seminary of this city, he was invited, through Mr. Pardee, to take charge of a feeble Sabbath-school connected with the Bethesda Baptist Church, meeting then in Chrystie near Delancey street. It was soon apparent to that little band of teachers, that God, in his providence, had sent them no ordinary man for their superintendent. His singleness of purpose, his entire consecration, and his warm, loving sympathy, won all hearts to himself. He began his work in earnest ; he visited from house to house in that locality, and soon, where there had been but a handful, there was a roomful of attentive, interested scholars.

As I look back to those days, I ask myself wherein was the secret ? Why did those scholars attend so regularly and become so interested ? There were no prizes offered nor entertainments given, by which to attract them. No! These were not necessary. There was a stronger attraction than such things could offer. The children were drawn by the magnet of love. I believe that the smallest child felt that the superintendent loved him, and sought by all possible means to do him good.

But an earnest Christian like Mr. Payson could not be satisfied with merely a large and interested school. He longed for something more ; for the salvation of the scholars he labored and prayed. Well do I remember one Saturday night, at our teachers' meeting, how he poured out his soul in earnest desire that salvation might come to the school.

The language he used has passed from my memory, but the impressions of that evening will never be effaced. I went from that meeting with the assurance that there was a special blessing in store for our school; for God never gives such earnest desires for the outpouring of his Spirit to disappoint us, but rather he gives them because he means to bless.

Therefore it was no surprise to me, the next morning, to feel the holy hush upon the school during its opening exercises. And when during the session I glanced across the room and saw a class of young girls with their teacher in tears, I knew what it meant. The Holy Spirit had come,-in answer to prayer, and touched the hearts of those who had hitherto been indifferent to the claims of the gospel.

I need not dwell upon that day. From that hour began one of the most quiet, yet sweetest works of grace I ever witnessed. Not only was every member of the class referred to brought to Christ, but other scholars, and some of the teachers, came out upon the Lord's side. Some of these have passed on to glory, but many still remain, and bear living testimony to the genuineness of the profession then made.

It was not enough for Mr. Payson that those under his care should be converted, but having been the means of leading them to Christ, he sought to train them for Christian usefulness. For this purpose he established a children's meeting, where the young converts were encouraged to speak of their joys and temptations, and where, as one who was privileged to attend those meetings has said to me, "he became a young convert with them, entering with ready sympathy into all their experiences, and thus seeking to lead them to a *more* and *more* confiding trust in Jesus as their friend and Saviour."

But this sketch would be incomplete did I fail to speak of Mr. Payson's peculiar fitness for visiting the sick and the poor. In this department of labor he was especially blessed. I recall his visits to a widow whom he found in an upper room of a tenement-house, without relatives, and entirely dependent upon charity. The comfort and blessing that his ministrations were to that sick woman cannot be told *here*, but shall be told *there*, where the reward will be given for the cup of cold water.

One day while visiting for Sunday-school scholars, he found in a rear house in Forsyth street a little lame boy, a confirmed invalid. He could not attend Sunday-school; and one might have supposed that, amid the pressure of other duties, the lame boy might have been passed by. But no; often did Mr. Payson find time to cheer that humble home by his presence. It was not too small a service for him to carry Sunday-school papers to lame Johnny; and when he went to Germany, he made arrangements to have little Johnny visited.

Another incident is recalled of a little infant-class scholar whom he brought every morning to Sunday-school. She sickened and died, but left him the assurance, as he often expressed it, that she would be among the first to meet him in heaven.

3

These incidents may seem trivial to some, but I refer to them because they illustrate that trait so prominent in Mr. Payson's character, that no service, where he could speak a word for the Master, or let in a single ray of sunshine into an otherwise darkened life, was in his estimation small. I have reason to believe that the joy and blessing which he had in his labors in that school, had much to do with his decision to devote his life to the Mission work. That school long since disbanded. Scholars and teachers are scattered, but the work still remains. There are those who to-day can testify that there was an impulse given their Christian life *then* that is still felt. And thus began the life-work of one of whom we may now say, "He rests from his labors, and his works do follow him."

Later in his seminary course Mr. Payson was engaged in work in a mission school connected with the Rev. Dr. Potts' church. A gentleman associated with him at that time speaks of this work as follows :

If I remember aright he came to us in the fall of 1856. The mission school was then located in the Thirteenth street public school building, near Sixth avenue. It was very small in numbers and but feebly sustained. A number of the young people of the church came to the rescue, and having districted the neighborhood, thoroughly canvassed it for scholars, who soon began to pour in from all directions, and Mr. Payson's services were then secured while he was still a student at Union Theological Seminary. He was full of zeal and enthusiasm, and entered with all his heart into the work, endearing himself to all around him, and making many warm friends. He interested himself very greatly in the half-grown boys in the neighborhood, and organized a boys' meeting for debating and mutual improvement. . . . He had great influence over this class of boys, and attracted them to him by his kind and cordial manner and his sincere interest in their welfare.

On the completion of his studies at the seminary he severed for a time his connection with our school and sailed for Germany. . . . His purpose was to perfect himself in the German language, with a view to laboring among the German population of our city. . . . .

On his return from Europe, in September, 1858, he found us in our new building on Sixth avenue, near Tenth street, and very soon after was engaged as a missionary and superintendent of the school. Having lost none of his zeal or enthusiasm during his long absence, he now went to work in deep earnest, devoting his whole time to the interests of the mission, and soon gathering around him a good congregation, composed chiefly of the parents of the scholars. He held a Sabbath evening service and a weekly prayer-meeting, and for a time a daily union prayer-meeting which was largely attended. How often I have gone with him to the dingy garret or the dark cellar-home of some wretched family, seeking for scholars or bringing comfort and aid to them in their misery. His warm and sympathizing heart was always open to their sorrows, and he was constantly devising plans for their relief and comfort. For years after he left us many of these people would find delight in talking to me of the dear Mr. Payson who used to visit them and do them so much good. I have many letters from the older scholars, written at that time, in which they speak of him in terms of affectionate regard, and of his enthusiasm and aid in their hours of darkness and doubt.

Another feature of his work was the establishment of several meetings for prayer in the homes of the people. These he styled "*Neighborhood Prayer-meetings.*" They were very successful and largely attended. Mr. Payson took great interest in them, and gathered around him a large number of helpers, who would distribute themselves each week among these several meetings, Mr. Payson always attending one or another of them. This plan of holding prayer-meetings in the homes of the people has been adopted in many other missions, but I think the idea originated with him. They were kept up for several years after he left us, and resulted in much good.

In recalling these facts I have been carried back to those days of pleasant intercourse with Mr. Payson and work together for the Master. He had a noble corps of helpers around him, men and women of devoted piety and earnest zeal, some of them afterwards devoting their lives to the ministry or to the work of foreign missions. Some, no doubt, have already greeted him on that distant shore, where I trust we shall all reassemble some day. . . . . .

I met Mr. Payson on last Christmas day, and enjoyed a most delightful talk with him about old times. It seemed to give him much pleasure to hear about the old scholars and of what had become of them.

Very truly yours,   E. McJ.

An article from Mr. Payson's own pen, recently published in the "American Messenger," describes a scene which occurred at this very time.

One Saturday afternoon I was seeking scholars for my Sabbath-school in the city of New York. My search had been comparatively without success. I was wearisomely climbing the narrow staircases of a dirty tenement-house, when at last I came to a door on the upper story. A cheerful "Come in" greeted my rather hopeless knock. I opened the door, and knew I was entering a Christian home. There is a wonderful difference between that labored cleanliness which says, "Take care; no strangers wanted here," and the comfortable neatness of Christian hospitality which says, "Come in and rest." It was not the flowers in the windows, nor the simple pictures on the wall, nor the neat rag-carpet, nor the white coverlet of the bed which filled the alcove opening out of the little sittingroom, which gave me this idea, but the kindly look which shone out from the face of that cheerful-looking old woman beautifying all her surroundings. I felt at home at once, and often repeated the visit which gave me ever some new lesson in Christian life and experience.

Little by little I learned her past history. Once she had lived in easy circumstances, and rejoicing in the love of her husband and five children. One by one they died. One by one creature comforts had to be given up, till at last, broken down by incurable disease, and forsaken by all who naturally should have cared for her, she became utterly dependent. In this hour of trial she was enabled to look to God alone and ask of him the aid she could find nowhere else. Her disease prevented her leaving her little room to supply any need, however imperative. Only when her house was burned, if my memory serves me, did she leave her room for thirty-eight long years. And yet all this time she lived alone. For rent, clothing, fuel, food, and medicine, she had no one but God to depend upon. And to him she went, with all the trusting simplicity of a child to a parent, and was never disappointed.

I well remember one occasion when my own faith was greatly tried in her behalf. For some two years it was my privilege to pay her rent from the funds of the church with which I was then connected. Unexpectedly one Saturday afternoon, instead of the money, I was obliged to inform her that the allowance had been cut off. I knew that Monday the rent came due, and being unable myself to meet the necessity, was full of trouble in her behalf. I expected, as a matter of course, to see my trouble reflected in the face usually so full of peace and comfort. Imagine my amazement when, with a cheerful smile, she said, "No matter; it is all right;" and changing the subject, went on as if this matter was not of the least consequence to herself. But I could not rest, knowing as I did that she had nothing in hand to meet this claim. So I brought it up again, and asked her how she could be so composed with this new and unexpected trouble resting upon her. What should we do? Then came her never-to-be-forgotten answer: "Do you suppose that the good Father, who took care of me for eighteen years before this help ever came, is going to leave me now? Don't trouble yourself one moment about it, for I know my rent will be forthcoming just as soon as I really need it." So it proved, and her unwavering faith was triumphantly vindicated then, and thousands of times besides, before God called her to himself. By death or removal one set of Christian helpers after another passed away; but God was the same unchanging Friend all the way through. On him she leaned in prayerful trust ever, and he never failed her.

Hundreds have enjoyed the little meetings held in her room every Sunday afternoon, and often on weekday evenings besides. Many an unconverted soul has there found Christ, but more feeble Christians have been so strengthened through that poor woman's faith, that her memory will be precious to them for ever.

About a year after he entered the seminary he writes to one of his sisters as follows :

MY DEAR SISTER : I wrote you last just before I left Cleveland. I have had some very bad news since I returned. My dear chum Benjamin was very ill with the typhus-fever when I came to New York, and yesterday, as we hear, the dear, good fellow breathed his last. It sometimes seems strange that God should remove one so talented, so nearly ready to stand up and speak in his holy name. I have often wondered the last two days why it was that the angel of death, as he looked into our room last winter, chose Benjamin and left me. How truly Young says, "Death loves a shining mark." May I not hope that our Father has some good work for me, since thus he spares me ? I found my room occupied by a Mr. J—— of the Junior class on my arrival here. I think we shall get along very pleasantly, as he is a pleasant, agreeable fellow. We have things nearly righted now ; have purchased a very pretty carpet.

My happiest day was when I visited the Sabbath-school again. All the scholars acted as though they were beside themselves. The boys stamped, and all over the room it was, "Mr. Payson has come, Mr. Payson has come !" And such bright, hearty, welcome smiles ! Oh, they brought a very balm to my troubled, weary heart ! I went into the room where the infant class were assembled. We sang two or three old pieces, or rather tried to. . . . The little ones stared at me as though they could n't see enough. One of the sweetest of the little band came at last and gave me her fan, a tiny little baby fan, and then went back and wondered what more she could do. After five minutes' deliberation she came again, and put up the very prettiest little mouth for me to kiss. As a climax, little Allie said, "Mr. Payson, we 've had a little sister at our house since you went away." Ah, such prattling innocence ! Would this world held more of it.

The death of his father in February, 1856, to which some expressions in the last letter are attributable, threw

*

a great weight of responsibility upon him, not only in the administration of the estate, but in the care of his widowed mother and younger brothers and sisters. Referring to some of these things, he writes, partly upon the half sheets accompanying the examination papers of the Theological Seminary:

MY DEAR SISTER: You know not what a source of pleasure it is at last to grasp my pen and wing a few words of love to my "pet sis." I feel I fairly deserve to be disowned; but if you will give me another try, I will promise to write you within three days of the receipt of each letter from you. Just look over the other side and see what one week furnished me in the way of work. And that was but a tithe; for who shall enumerate the cares that appertain to me as to sisters and brothers, Sabbath-schools and day-schools, lessons and teachers, debts and credits, and above all, the care of souls in my Sunday-school.

Yesterday my last great burden was removed. I received a check for the money due us from the insurance company. . . . Without it I can hardly imagine how we could have gone along at all. . . . We shall go home the first part of July, I suppose. You must make your calculations to go home at the same time. I will write you more definitely before we leave.

And now, my dear sister, how is it with you? Are you *fighting* the good fight? Does heaven seem brighter? Does Christ grow precious? At times *I want to go;* but then, oh how I want to labor for souls—to do something for him. Love Christ, so that you will *LIVE* him, and your example will be a sermon that no adversary can gainsay or resist. Pray for me, and do write me soon. I am longing for a sight of my dear "little sis." May God give me the sweet privilege soon.

Your ever-loving   CHARLIE.

While he was in the seminary Mr. Payson became deeply interested in Home Missions. Gradually there was formed in his mind the purpose to devote himself to missionary work on the frontiers of the great West of our country. The moral destitution of large regions, sparsely populated by families that had gone thither from Eastern states, awakened his sympathy and roused his zeal. With a holy enthusiasm he anticipated a life devoted to his countrymen in new communities, where the institutions of society and religion were to be founded and built up. Like Paul, he preferred not to build on another man's foundations.

With these desires and expectations Mr. Payson prosecuted his theological studies. A spirit so earnest and aims so practical would not permit him to lose his religious fervor in the colder atmosphere of mere scientific dogmatism. The grand and stimulating topics of study that make up the curriculum of a theological student, did not abate his devotion nor steal from him the spirit and power of fervent prayer.

The devotional exercises of the class and the seminary found in him a faithful and zealous supporter. Always ardent in his desire for scholarship and to excel in every exercise, he still lived in an atmosphere of spiritual warmth, that kept him in fullest sympathy with all earnest and active Christians.

In the spring of 1857 Mr. Payson was graduated with his class, holding a high position in their confidence and esteem. To those more particularly intimate with him, it was evident that he possessed qualifications and abilities for great usefulness.

But he sought, in accordance with all his controlling ideas, to avail himself of every opportunity to enlarge his acquaintance with mankind ; and, consequently, having formed with one of his classmates a plan of study and travel in Europe, he sailed from New York a few days after leaving the seminary.

To an ardent and energetic nature like his, such an opportunity became extremely stimulating ; and he declared many a time afterward that the months thus devoted had been among the most delightful and profitable of his whole student life. Whether among the old cities of Europe, with their marvels of art and wealth and historic interest, or in the midst of the glories of Alpine summits or the charms of southern landscapes, he found ever something that could be appropriated to the fund from which to draw for future usefulness. After spending the summer at Heidelberg, he was matriculated in the University of Berlin in the autumn, and devoted himself to the lectures of Professors Twesten and Nitsch, men eminent for learning and piety.

Thus passed the year of university life, in the midst of scenes and associations novel and interesting, especially to a young man from the New World.

The following season was devoted to travel through Germany, Austria, Italy, Switzerland, and France. The results of that visit upon the character and mental resources of the faithful pastor in New York for many years afterward were of no little consequence. They rendered him more cosmopolitan in his ideas and sympathies, furnished him inexhaustible stores of illustration in interpreting the truths of the gospel, and added moral weight to his opinions and utterances. And through all his after life he found in these pleasant memories a rest and refreshment for which he was ever grateful.

CHAPTER II.

LETTERS FROM ABROAD.

MOST of the letters contained in this chapter are of a general nature, and sufficiently explain themselves. Some of them are descriptive, and some, in part at least, are personal; but all will be found interesting in so far as they serve to throw light on Mr. Payson's character. The letters descriptive of foreign travel might have been multiplied, but the limits of this little book forbid.

Of the first two, the gentleman who furnished the account of Mr. Payson's work in Sixth avenue writes as follows:

I have greatly valued these two letters, and now enclose them for your perusal. You are at liberty to make such use of them as may be desirable. They are strongly characteristic of him at that time, showing his deep and earnest piety, his warm friendship, and his love for souls. I have always felt deeply indebted to him for those timely counsels, and would be glad if their reproduction would aid in lighting the pathway of some others as they did mine.

The letters referred to are given herewith, and to the second of them, it may be remarked, this little volume is indebted for its title.

HEIDELBERG, Aug. 17, 1857.

MY DEAR FRIEND: In Charley L——'s last letter he was speaking of his pleasant visits to your dear home. This, of course, carried me back to my own unexpected and therefore all the more delightful acquaintance with you and yours at "Home," and the promise I made to write you from the "Fatherland." Where can I so well fulfil that promise as here in beautiful Heidelberg? Here, if anywhere, old associations will revive, and in its quiet valleys, its retired and shady paths, must come up visions of the far-off home and the friends left behind. How pleasant among such thoughts are the recollections of our much-loved Sabbath-school, and the happy hours we spent together! How strangely true that those labors which cost us most of toil and sacrifice are those to which we can look back with the greatest pleasure. The cost was paid in weariness, but the memory of them is the fragrance of heaven, cheering us in the hours of weakness; yes, and they shall tune our harps, I trust, to a nobler song of thanksgiving in a better world.

I am sure, my dear friend, that you as well as I look forward to that land with the highest anticipations. How often have I thought you were even as the "young ruler," almost in the kingdom. I know that nothing could induce you to give up the hope of heaven, and trust that ere this you have decided the great point, and resolved to be Christ's, and his alone, both in this world and that to come. How often did the words quiver on my lips. How often would I have entreated you to accept the Best of Friends, one whom I had proved and never found wanting; but, coward that I was, I feared it might be an unpleasant subject. Forgive me, my dear E——, that I loved you so little, and remember that no news would so cheer my heart as to learn from you that the great question was settled, and you were happy. I used to think I was happy; but I assure you that one hour with my Redeemer, one hour of calm communion and unwavering faith, is better than any pleasure earth ever gave me. Think not, my dear friend, that with religion you sacrifice happiness. Look at our dear Mrs. E——; yes, go and ask her when she was happier—in the days long gone by, when earth seemed to *heap* its every blessing upon her; or now, when stripped of almost all, with health impaired, she loves the religion she once only professed. And her experience is that of the world. The pleasures that earth gives are far more in the anticipation than the reality; and then the bitter days that ever remain and mar the recollections of even our happiest hours! But I will not weary you with thoughts that you have heard from your cradle. You know what joy you can have—the prize is before you. Oh come, and bring happiness to your friends; yea, even to that angel sister who has gone a little before. I wish you would write and tell me (why should you not, E——?) that you have ceased the unequal conflict, and are Christ's for ever.... Give my best regards to all your family, especially your brother F——, and remember that so far away one heart beats warm for you with good wishes and earnest prayers. As to myself, my health is excellent; my happiness is more than pen and paper can express. The hours and moments are filled to overflow with new sights and joys. Yet amid all I long to be at home and work again. Remember me, though we meet not as of old, and make happy

Your friend,   C. H. PAYSON.

ROME, April, 1858.

MY DEAR, DEAR E——: Words cannot express the emotions that thrilled my heart as I read your precious, precious letter. It was only this morning that I was encouraging myself to still wait and pray for you by those words of Jesus in Matt. 21 : 21, 22, especially the last verse : " And all things whatsoever ye shall ask in prayer, believing, ye shall receive." God be thanked that you are at last safe ; yes, safe, for if you have truly given yourself up, Satan himself can never draw you away. Does it not now seem strange that you waited so long, and strove so hard to do what was so very easy in the end? Ah, if men were not so proud, the way to heaven would not be so strait. But we insist on doing all ourselves, and thus are never nearer the end desired—nearer, did I say? rather, every day farther and farther away from that meek, humble, childlike faith that Jesus so much loved.

And now, my friend, life is before you with new ends and aims. The question, I see, is, " How shall I spend it ?" I can tell you in a few words, only three : ALL FOR CHRIST. It is a delightful thought to me, and one that I presume you have heard me express, that here in this world, where I have to an extent control of myself, and can seek what I will, I can honor Christ more than in heaven. *There* I shall desire only to praise him ; but here, where fame, riches, and honors entice, where we are surrounded by a great cloud of witnesses, angels, men, and devils—honor and glory be to God, who hath promised us the victory in our Lord Jesus Christ. You ask me for advice. My dear E ——, I hope I have been a Christian several years, and as the result of my experience, learned by many a sore trial, I can only say, *Live for Christ.* Don't do as I did at first, seek for praise and happiness, and put Jesus in the background ; but make his glory and the advancement of his cause *the* end. Yes, if you seek riches, seek them for him ; if you travel, do it to his honor ; if you become learned, let it be that you may serve him more ; thus keep your eye always fixed on him, and then pass all these side issues, these things of earth, between you and him. If they hide him from you, put away the accursed thing. If not, use them to his glory, and be ever in the light of his countenance. Oh the heaven on earth a man may live if Jesus is all and in all !

I wonder if you feel as weak and feeble as I did when I hoped I became a Christian. It was as though I was a child just beginning to walk.
. When alone, my feet would totter beneath me, my prayers were so feeble. But when with older Christians, at the prayer-meeting or at church, it was as though a stronger arm sustained me, and I could walk when I leaned on those that loved and sympathized with me. What a strange thing this fellowship of Christian hearts is. I feel it as I write you to-night. I loved you when I wrote you before, and talked with great freedom, yet I must confess not without fear that you might take offence at my freedom. But

now how changed! That "perfect love which casteth out all fear" has bound us together by new ties, even those that eternity, I trust, cannot sever. Let me mention an exercise in which I have found peculiar delight, and which I hope you too may find profitable. It is this: beginning with Genesis, trace out the account of every prayer, and the answer; consider the circumstances under which these prayers were made, the great variety of blessings desired, and the readiness with which God responded. I am sure it will encourage you to pray as never before, and convince you that "our Father" thinks of us, and loves us in all our cares and sorrows, however insignificant they may seem to us. Clouds, so dark and black as to hide heaven itself, will yet overshadow your path. Let me entreat you, then, to pray. Never, no never, turn from your Saviour, and you will always find that the darkest cloud is only a veil that, being removed, shall reveal glories never before imagined.

You ask me if I like Europe. Yes, I do; but I love America, free, happy America, far better; and I long to be at home and at work. Since I heard the glorious news from America, I must say I have been homesick, and I almost envy you who are in the midst of God's wondrous workings. My whole heart is with you, and though surrounded by all the pomp and display of Holy Week, and treading the dust of ancient Rome, I would that it were right for me to leave to-morrow for home and the work I so long to be engaged in. But duty bids me stay, and till the first of September I must still be a wanderer. I do hope that you and all my dear friends will remember me at the throne of grace, and entreat GOD to fit me for that great work which I so much fear, yet so earnestly desire to enter upon. I trust that when you write me again I shall hear that F—— too is following in your steps. I have great hopes for him, and can but believe that he too shall find the path to eternal life. Remember me to him most affectionately, as well as to your family. I often remember with pleasure my visit to your island home. Write me at Paris, (*poste restante,*) as I am now moving about. My paper is only too small. I wish to write a hundred things, but must stop. Good-by.

Your friend,

C. H. PAYSON.

HEIDELBERG, Aug. 29, 1857.

DEAR ONES AT HOME: . . . Need I tell you how grateful I am to "our Father" that he has so kindly watched over and guided everything to such prosperous results? It is perfectly astonishing that I ever doubt when I see how constantly he is providing for us all. Each day I find occasion to reproach myself for want of faith towards my best Friend.

And so E—— is off for college. . . . My dear brother, accept the advice which was given me as I entered Amherst : "Take care first of your soul, then of your health, and lastly of your studies." Make your motto,

"Not what I am, but what I am to be in Christ." Aim high, so shall your arrow higher reach. Heaven is higher than earth. My brother, set the mark *there.* . . . In my last, I believe, I had not reached Heidelberg, and now I am about to leave it. Never did a spot become so dear in so short a time. Let me describe it, and you will not wonder that I love it. You approach it from Mauheim and the Rhine across a perfectly level plain some twelve miles wide. Suddenly from that perfect level spring up two towering peaks, (at least for this country,) the Heilenberg and Geisberg, covered to their very summit with foliage of the richest green. Here are beautiful vineyards loaded with their luscious burdens. Between these peaks, on the banks of the classic Neckar, sits Heidelberg, the queen of the Rhineland. Around her the guardian Odenwald clasps his leafy arms, as if to guard her from all harm, and shut her out from the common herd. One long street stretches up the valley side by side with the petulant stream along which noble men have walked. In its university, venerable in history, Melancthon and Bucer studied. Luther slept here on his journey to that conflict at Worms which he made immortal.

Behind it, on the Jettenbuhl, stands the castle, its glory and pride. On this was lavished the wealth of princes for six centuries. Stern war, and more cruel time, yes, and the thunderbolts of heaven itself, have conspired to make it a ruin. You climb the steep ascent, and pass the long entrance to the gate and hall, from whose huge, broken windows are seen beautiful views of Heidelberg and the valley, as of pictures in glorious frames. Above is the broad stone terrace, on one side of which rises the carved façade of St. Udalrich's chapel. In front of you, and to the right of the chapel, stands half of another tower, with walls twenty-one feet thick, and so solid that a staircase has been dug through its very heart without affecting it. Behind it are numerous towers and wings, enclosing an irregular courtyard. The eastern façade, fronting on the court, is peculiarly beautiful. In the niches between the windows are three rows of most graceful Italian figures. The first is composed of heroes and warriors, who seem to be keeping knightly watch over the fair beings that occupy the second tier. Two statues on the summit are especially beautiful. They stand out against the sky so airy and lifelike, that when the evening sunlight strikes them, one seems covering his eyes with his hand, while he delights his soul with the glorious Rhine valley spread out before him. You pass through the court; you look with awe on that rough, jagged portcullis that seems as if ready to fall at any moment, should the warden sound his horn. And remember, it has stood there since 1355! Passing the drawbridge, you come into the most beautiful grove, through which wind the shadiest paths, leading in every direction, and bringing you continually upon new views that thrill you with excitement. Far away, behind and above the castle, rises the Königstuhl, or king's seat.

You can imagine something of the care and expense lavished on this pride of the "Fatherland," when I tell you that it takes some two hours to mount to the summit of this mountain, and yet paths and roads wind around its leafy groves to the very crown itself.

But perhaps you weary of the reality of stone and trees and long for a little romance. Enter then one of those dark winding vaults that leads you know not where. Pick your way cautiously with your cane—careful! careful! For aught you know a precipice yawns before your very feet. A damp sepulchral air surrounds you. Your companion declares that you approach the "Spirit vault." Darker and yet darker grows the passage. Now comes a winding staircase with rough uneven steps. It is the entrance to the Spirit hall! Now, close your eyes and walk six times around the vault; then, you are told, will the ghost be revealed! I tried it, and I must say that I was prepared for almost anything when I got through, but not for that which did appear, a large hall with huge windows (broken) opening right out into the midst of the Castle Park! Another similar passage leads you down to a vault in which is placed the old Heidelberg Tun, a huge barrel, so large that people dance on the top of it, and which contains eight hundred hogsheads, or 283,200 bottles of wine. It was built in 1751, and has been three times filled. It is 36 feet long and 24 high. In front of it stands a wooden statue of the famous dwarf of the castle, the jester, who always drank his 15 bottles of wine before sleeping. (No wonder they needed huge tuns!) You form little idea from this poor description of this ivy-covered, tree-embowered Feudal temple, of its beauty or its vastness. But this is not all that makes Heidelberg delightful. Two or three times a week skilful musicians go up into the castle garden and there discourse music almost divine!... Then it is that the city pours forth its wealth and beauty, and old and young flock to the castle. Tables are scattered here and there through the groves, and you continually meet families sitting around them, and discussing their wine, beer, and other refreshments, while they listen to the sweetest music. But I must lead you across the valley and give you a nearer view of the Heiligenberg (Holy Mountain). Upon its highest peak you will see a ruin— the angle of the wall of the convent St. Stephenas. . . . In front of this and nearer the city you find another ruin yet more remarkable, for it is nothing more nor less than the foundation of an old temple to Mercury, and a short distance in the rear is found an old vault where the Sibyl is said to have given her responses. . . . Here some years ago were the headquarters of a miserable set of fanatics called Flagellators, who were accustomed to go through the streets half-dressed and beating themselves most cruelly with sticks and straps. Hundreds of them made pilgrimages to this mountain, styled by their leaders "Abraham's Mountain," but the world at last became weary of them and their fanaticism and they passed away.

At last an old man made this peak his home. All up and down the valley he went, bringing joy to the weary and sorrowful. In good deeds he spent his life, and when he died his life had been so stamped upon the hearts of his fellow-men that his mountain home became sacred, and for his sake they ever after called it the "Holy Mountain."

Is it not strange that a poor, unpretending man has given name to a peak upon which the heathen have raised their temples, the proud Roman his fortress and noble families their monasteries? Such is the beautiful peak on which I look as I raise my eyes from my paper. . . .

I hope you are not weary, for there are other spots of which I want to tell you. Some two miles up the valley is a most beautiful little nook, shaded by luxuriant forest-trees, through which a lovely stream wends its way to the Neckar. Here once lived the enchantress Jetta, who prophesied centuries ago that this Palatinate should become famous, and who met with a sad death. She was torn in pieces by a wolf! Ever since the spring has been known as the Wolf's Brunnen. Here is a pleasant little hotel, and, if you wish, one of the maids will show you a pleasing sight. By ringing a bell she calls from the brook and reservoir large numbers of the finest brook trout to the shore, where they eat crumbs from her hand. I never saw larger trout, nor such numbers.

Just opposite the Wolf's Brunnen stands a beautifully-situated old monastery or convent, now a water-cure establishment. Back of this, along the edge of the mountain towards Heidelberg, runs a charming little path called the "*Gute Kostenweg*" or the "Path of good peeps," which well deserves the name, for at intervals, vistas have been cut through the branches and now the city, now the castle, and then the Neckar, and the Wolf's Brunnen or Königstuhl appear, a beautiful picture framed with the rich green of the overhanging boughs. I certainly never saw more beautiful views than some of these little vistas furnished.

Such is Heidelberg, or rather part of it. When I return I hope to have some engravings that will convey a better idea of its loveliness than my poor pen-sketches. One never feels the emptiness of words as when he endeavors to describe that which fills his soul. Then indeed we realize that we have that stirring and moving within us that is worthy of a nobler and more exalted life.

BERLIN, Oct. 23, 1857.

My DEAR L——: Early Monday morning, Aug. 31, we found our way to the dépôt at Heidelberg and soon were off for Frankfort and Berlin. The railroad passes through the level Rhine valley that stretches from the Odenwald six or eight miles to the Rhine. So we swept swiftly along through luxuriant fields of grain and orchards loaded with fruit, while on our right rose the far-famed Odenwald, on whose every peak—and they are many, was set some castle old and gray and hallowed with ancient story. We passed churches built by Charlemagne, and turrets where the flags of the Crusaders often waved. . . . The scenery is perfectly chaotic from this window, the forest-robed hills of the Odenwald rolling and tumbling over and upon each other like a school of porpoises, in marked contrast to that rich and level plain that stretches far away in the opposite direction. We hurried through Darmstadt . . . . to Frankfort. . . . The gem of the gallery here was a picture of Huss' trial, by Lessing. . . , We went to the Kaisersaal or Emperors' Hall where some forty-five German emperors have celebrated their coronations. . . . The walls of the room were covered with portraits of these emperors finely painted, and it is said they are mostly correct likenesses. . . .

The Jews were very numerous in Frankfort, and live in streets whose like for filth and stench I have never seen. The houses are very high, and almost meet far above your head across the narrow street. They apparently are crowded from garret to cellar; and such display of old clothes and books, rusty, worn-out kitchen furniture of every imaginable description, and in the most dilapidated condition, I never before have seen.

The geniuses that presided over these tempting displays of merchandise were worthy of their position—either old men of the toothless, hatless, shirtless order, or hags who looked as though they could, with their wiry, bony fingers, make shillings of sixpences without the least effort. Yet in these vile streets have vast fortunes been made, and at the head of the street stands the countinghouse of Rothschild himself. He is truly a money king. . . . .

After speaking of Dannecker's beautiful statue of Ariadne and of their visit at Marburg, he says :

At noon we were in Cassel—and the rain. Cassel has some very fine buildings, and, according to Murray, the infallible, the largest square in Germany. In the centre of the park stands a statue at which I could, without many compunctions, have hurled a stone, for it was that of Frederick William, elector of Hesse Cassel, who hired 12,000 of his people to fight, in the Revolution, against America. These, as you well know, were the Hessians of whom we read so much in the New Jersey battles—Monmouth, etc. He received twenty-two millions of dollars for them from England, which he expended in beautifying his city and embellishing the far-famed gardens of William's Hill or Wilhemshöhe.

You must permit me to take you up that splendid allée of lime-trees that reaches from Cassel to the "Palace of the Garden," a distance of more than three miles. Here is a fine palace, but you must not stop. The water is admitted this afternoon, (it is a "*fest*" day,) and the crowd, hurrying up the hill, admonish us that we must be quickening our steps. Up we go through the most delightfully-shaded paths bordered by flowers of every hue and form, till suddenly we come upon a beautiful sight. Through a splendid vista of trees you see a lofty temple crowning the summit of the ridge. A huge copper statue of Hercules makes the temple a pedestal. You can judge of its size when you learn that eight persons can stand in the club at one time, and the whole statue is 31 feet high. From the temple you descend to the spot we occupy by two staircases of 900 steps each, between which are the most beautiful little basins succeeding each other in regular steps from top to bottom. But hark ! a shout ! and the water springs, far above, with a mighty leap, into the air, as if exulting in its freedom. Quickly the basin is filled, and then one little stream after another carefully, quietly reaches down to the next basin, and then, as if the timid water-sprites were frightened, as quickly, quietly withdraw their silvery arms. But soon the rollicking, flashing nymphs come rolling and tumbling down on the sparkling flood, and in a few moments it seems as though one could mount from top to bottom on steps of glittering silver. It was a splendid sight, most truly; but the crowd are hurrying down the hill, and we must away, too, for soon there will be another water-scene. Yes, and here it is ! See ! how it gushes forth from the roots of those noble old limes and comes pouring down over rocks covered with velvet cushions of the greenest moss. You think it must sweep the crowd at the base away ; but no, channels safe and sound are provided, and the waters foam and bubble around, vainly striving to burst their rocky bounds. A little below is the grand fountain, the highest in Europe. We are just in time, and beyond those beautiful swans the waters begin to burst forth, a water volcano in the midst of that crystal sea. Up, up, up they go, each proud sprite stretching higher, higher, higher, till at last toppling, balancing, they fall; and oh, how spitefully, even angrily, they bury themselves, those flashing darts of silver spray. . . . . .

Continuing the account of this journey, he speaks of Eisenach and its "quaint old houses that looked as honest and contented as though nothing newer or better had ever been built," and then of Wartburg and "the emotions which thrilled him as he climbed that famous hill which, 237 years ago, Luther, in the hands of his captors, climbed."

The portal of Luther's Patmos is reached. . . . . First they led us into a chamber where the armor of famous old characters, such as Cardi-

*

nal of Bourbon, Pope Julius II., etc., was gathered. One was made of braided steel, and covered the whole body. Another was of brass and shone like gold. There was a sword four and a half or five feet long and very heavy. Hence we passed into a beautiful room, which has just been completely refitted, where was held a famous contest of the Minnesingers in 1207. If I am not mistaken, a picture in the Dusseldorf gallery represents the exciting scene. On the walls were beautiful frescoes. . . . From the windows of this hall there is a most enchanting view, where hill and forest and shaded valley mingle in wild, simple, unpretending beauty. Wartburg (wooded mountain) was so called by its first owner, who in one of his hunting excursions came with his companions suddenly upon the brow of the hill, and struck with the beauty of the scene before him, exclaimed, "This is Wartburg, and here is my home." Thence we passed through a narrow hall to the chapel where Luther was wont to preach to the inhabitants of the castle. It is a small room, but beautifully fitted up. I think, however, I would rather have seen the old wooden pulpit of Luther than the velvet-faced affair that has usurped its place. On the sides of the hall I mentioned are several fine frescoes representing the ancient lord of the castle starting for the Crusades, and also the glorious triumph of his return. Here, too, were sketched the leading events in the life of the noble St. Elizabeth of Thuringia, whose home was also in this famous castle. Among them the most striking, perhaps, was that representing the loaves in her apron turning into flowers. You remember the legend, I presume. Her husband was very penurious and cruel, and seeing her one morning going to the gate with well-filled apron for the poor, he demanded what she carried. "Flowers," she answered. Not believing her, he rudely tore her grasp away, when, strange to say, flowers instead of loaves fell to the ground.

But I must pass the other rooms to take you to Wartburg's greatest glory, Luther's room. This, I'm glad to say, is just as "Knight George" (Luther's name here) left it. It is very small, 18 by 12 feet, and the rough boards and cobwebbed timbers appear on every side. There is the same old stove, his copper wash-basin, his table too, on which was written, in addition to many other excellent things, his glorious translation of the Bible; and that huge old chest in which was contained his wardrobe. The window was as quaint as the rest of the room. The panes were very small and thick, and looked like the bottoms of broken bottles more than anything else I can think of. The table is banded with iron, that it may not suffer the fate of chair and bedstead, which have been carried away in bits by visitors! There is also the hole, the last sign of Luther's conflict with the devil, when he hurled the inkstand at his head and smashed it against the wall. Relic-hunters have dug every sign of it away, and left a huge hole in the plaster! But time is up and I must tear myself away . . .

A few minutes more and we are in Erfurt. Erfurt is a quiet old town of some 27,000 inhabitants, not more than half what it once contained. It has some fine buildings in it, but for the most part the streets are crooked and narrow enough. To us there was but one point of interest—Luther's cell in the old Augustine convent. It is no longer a convent, but has been changed into an orphan asylum, and as we approached the door we heard the sweet voices of children chanting the songs of praise where monks once told their beads and went through monotonous litanies. Is not this old building truly a type of the Reformation? That humble monk breathed a new spirit into crumbling, fallen Christendom, and now there is but one convent to be found where once they were counted by scores, and the once despised Luther *honors* this building by bestowing on it his name. (It is called Martin's Asylum.) We were taken up stairs and through a long hall, once the chapel of the monastery, lined with pictures of men active in the Reformation. From it opened, among others, that narrow, low-ceiled cell where Luther the Catholic was changed into Luther the MAN. It is a little room, only 12 by 12, that once held so much. The furniture is the same that Luther once used, and I wrote from the same inkstand that he used while here. The wall was written all over with extracts from the Bible made by Luther himself when a student of that long, forgotten book, which he by chance had found in ransacking the convent library. He had arranged the texts under various heads, as justification, condemnation, sanctification. I was struck with one passage that occupied a prominent place: "*Now the fruits of the Spirit are these, love, joy, peace,*" etc. They breathed the spirit of true reform. The wall where he wrote has been repapered and the verses copied upon it in a neat, plain hand. Erfurt and its narrow cell, it seems to me, tell more of Luther's greatness than any other point in his history. At Wittenberg, Wartburg, Worms, etc., he was surrounded by friends. He was opposed by bitter enemies. He had committed himself. He *must* go *forward* or perish. But here there was nothing of the kind to incite. Everything tended in the opposite direction; and yet year after year he struggled to learn the truth, and patiently, secretly toiled till the appointed time had come. May we, my dear sisters, learn the lesson, and ever working, ever faithful, wait God's time to bring the fruits. Those only are worthy of *high position* who know how to be equal to their low estate.

Pray excuse my many, many mistakes, for I have written in great haste and amid many interruptions. Good-by, and that God may ever bless you is the earnest prayer of your absent, but ever loving

CHARLIE.

MY DEAR MOTHER: .... God has indeed "provided wonderfully for you all," and I feel that he is doing it that I may the more contentedly remain in Europe my appointed time. . . . . If at any time my presence is necessary, send for me, and I will return immediately. . . . . G—— is my greatest anxiety just now. I do hope he is diligent and faithful. Do see that he is regular in his study-hours. . . . . They have a fine school at L——, and though you should remain but a few weeks, it is much better that he should be at work. If you really want, my dear brother, to enjoy your visit, you must do your duty first. Remember one thing, never put off till to-morrow what you can learn to-day. *To-day* is all we *own;* "to-morrow" never comes; therefore never say, " I will do this or that next year," if you can do it now. When you have time you must read Long-fellow's "Kavanagh," not for the story only, but the lessons he will teach. See how the poor schoolmaster was ever planning, planning great things, but at the end of life was no nearer the end desired than at the beginning. Especially remember these lines, so beautiful, with which he closes:

> "Stay, stay the present instant,
> Imprint the marks of wisdom on its wings;
> Oh, let it not elude thy grasp; but, like
> The good old patriarch upon record,
> Hold the fleet angel fast until he bless thee."

I am very glad, dear mother, that you have concluded to visit the East. I hope you will remember me most affectionately to all my dear friends there. Where is Uncle Thomas? I do wish he would write me if he is not too busy. I am sure he would have many words of good coun-sel to one just commencing the race which he has run so long and well. . . .

But I must tell you of my present home and pleasures. We have been here in Berlin seven weeks, and on the whole have enjoyed it very much. It cannot compare with beautiful Heidelberg, for it stands in the midst of a great sandy plain, watered by the sluggish, filthy Spree, a river by name, a sewer in reality. The streets are broad and quite clean, but the foul exhalations from the sewers, that assail you at almost every step, are only extelled by those of Cologne, far-famed as the foulest city of Eu-rope, or at least of Germany. Still, a man can accustom himself to al-most anything, and I can now endure even Berlin gutters with scarcely a wince.

As C—— wished to be at the meeting of the Evangelical Alliance, we hurried to Berlin rather earlier than I wished; but I have been amply re-paid in attending the exercises of a meeting the like of which I never ex-pect to see on earth. There were some fourteen hundred regular mem-bers; nine hundred or so from Central Europe, one hundred and sixty-nine from England, thirty or so from our own land, three each from Asia, Africa, and Australia; while Italy, Spain, France, Russia, and Sweden, were not wanting in delegates. Many of Germany's most distinguished men were present. England's noble son, Sir Culling Eardley, a prince in good deeds, was here, and with him not a few of England's learned and brave and good.

But the man whom I most rejoiced to see was the far-famed author of the History of the Reformation—D'Aubigné, from Geneva. He is a tall, fine-looking man, fifty-five years of age, I should think, with heavy eyebrows, that give something of sternness to his noble face; but when you hear him pouring forth his polished, pithy sentences from an overflowing heart, you feel that you are in the presence of a man who truly loves his God and his fellow-men. He occupied a prominent position throughout the exercises, and his remarks were always listened to with the utmost attention and respect.

The exercises of the first day I can never forget. There were gathered representatives from Christ's kingdom throughout the world, and though their languages differed, one heart and one spirit seemed to pervade the whole assembly. No matter whether the prayer or the speech were in English, French, or German, there were ever the same kindling eye and glowing face that betoken a feeling heart. Never can I forget the speech of a young German, a missionary from Australia. It was near the close of the exercises, and the speakers had been limited to five minutes each. His heart was full to overflowing, and he knew not how to crowd himself within such narrow limits. His words came forth in a perfect torrent while he described the greetings, so earnest, so heartfelt, that fellow-laborers—bishops, pastors, and churches—had sent to Berlin from the antipodes. But these were only the beginning. At each island on his journey home he received fresh messages; others must send words of encouragement and love. China, even, through her missionaries, he represented; and as he closed his thrilling speech every heart felt, "Millennial days are drawing nigh." Already they come from the East and from the West, the North and the South, to the great feast of the Lord, and the islands of the sea stretch out their hands unto the Lord. I was right glad to see our new American ambassador stand up as a delegate from the United States to honor her and the cause of Christianity. He is a Methodist, and has been an exhorter; was governor of Indiana three times, and is reported a most excellent and active Christian.

At the close of these exercises we received an invitation (for I had also become a member) to visit the king at Potsdam. Potsdam, by-the-way, is the favorite residence of the king, and is distant by the cars three-quarters of an hour, or about eighteen miles. Since you have never seen a king, I will try in my poor way to describe the trip and the ceremonies. We left Berlin about two o'clock, P. M., in cars furnished by his Majesty. There were four long trains filled with some twelve hundred guests. We were hurried through the level, sandy plain, and in a few minutes had the pleasure of gazing on the forests and hills of a beautiful, undulating coun-

try. Soon the spires of Potsdam, a city of some forty thousand inhabitants, appeared. But the palace where we were to meet the king was two
miles beyond; so we continued our journey to Wild Park. Presently the
broad allée leading to the palace was thronged by the hundreds of expectant guests, all straining their eyes to catch a glimpse of the royal dwelling, and soon it came in sight, a huge brick building faced with pilasters
of granite and sandstone, and crowned with statues innumerable. The
grounds around were in beautiful order, and many a fine walk was flanked
by noble orange-trees laden with luscious fruit. (By-the-way, this palace
was built by Frederick the Great, and cost $6,000,000.)

We first entered a hall, one side of which was lined with wines and
ice-creams of every flavor and hue, and in abundance truly regal. But we
passed immediately into the adjoining room, being allowed for the present
only to feast our eyes. This hall furnished a treat of another kind. It
was an immense room, whose walls were lined with gems, minerals, and
shells. The pillars, which were scattered up and down, were of the same
rich materials, interspersed with blocks of marble. The floors were of
polished oak set in diamond blocks, and polished so smoothly that one
had to keep his feet under due subjection, or run the risk of finding them
higher than his head. Thence we passed into an adjoining suite of rooms
opening one after another, the walls of which were lined with pictures
whose beauty was only rivalled by the splendid landscapes revealed
through the large windows opening on the magnificent lawn and park in
front of the palace. Here were spread tables loaded with every luxury in
the way of fruits, confectionaries, ice-creams, wines, etc. You would have
been amused to see the eagerness, curiosity, and pleasure, which appeared
on every face almost; and as I saw the terrible onslaught made on the
choicest viands, I was almost afraid the king would have occasion to
repeat the remark of the famous Brown of New York, who, having provided an immense quantity of oysters for a ministers' party, comforted
the astonished host by assuring him that "them religious eats awful."

Never shall I forget the expressive countenance of one good German
minister who, with mouth, hands, and eyes, full to overflowing, exclaimed,
"*Es ist alles für uns!*" "It is all for us!" giving the *us* an emphasis
which meant something when you considered the vast size of those capa-
cious pockets that already were loaded with "something for the children."

But the feasting at last was over, and every one obeyed the summons
to repair to the front of the palace. At the extreme right of the long steps
which stretch the whole length of the palace, were placed the Americans,
next the English, then the French, Hollanders, etc., by nationalities alpha-
betically arranged. Thus a huge semicircle was formed in front of the
principal entrance where the king was to appear. Here we waited for
some time, and for fear that some might yet be unsatisfied, the most deli-

cious ices were freely served by the ready servants. Soon the sound of wheels was heard through the shady avenue, and presently a liveried courier on a splendid white horse announced the presence of his majesty, who followed in a fine carriage drawn by six horses, guided by three drivers, one for each span. These coachmen rode not on the box, as with us, but each on one of the horses which he drove. The queen also accompanied him. Another carriage with six horses followed, containing a count and his lady, the lord chamberlain, I believe, while two or three carriages with maids of honor brought up the rear. They entered the palace, and in a few moments the king presented himself at the great central door in the midst of the vast assembly. Every head was uncovered, and shouts of welcome and honor rose from hundreds of warm and loving hearts. The king is a pleasant-looking old gentleman of sixty-three years of age, bald, with side-whiskers, and rather a reddish face. He was dressed in soldier costume, and wore the heavy brazen and golden helmet which is the distinguishing badge of the Prussian army. After being introduced to the committee, he descended the steps and was addressed by some delegate from each nation as he passed around within the circle of guests; and after each speech the more distinguished delegates were introduced to him. I observed that he was very cordial in his greetings to our noble missionaries, Dr. Dwight of Constantinople, and Dr. King of Athens, who were fortunately present. The king is a noble, consistent Christian, and has done not a little for Dr. Dwight and others in Turkey. He also carried out the plan of this Alliance in the face of the most determined opposition. The queen soon after also appeared and was greeted by several of the most distinguished guests. She is lame, but bears herself with much grace, and draws every heart to her by the pleasant, motherly smile that rests on her noble face.

Some two hours elapsed before the king had completed the circuit. As he ascended the steps the whole audience burst forth into Luther's noble hymn, "The Lord is our shade and our defence." The king remained standing uncovered while it was being sung, with his wife and court around him. Immediately the court preacher, the famous Dr. Krummacher, pronounced the benediction on his Royal Majesty and his house, and they departed in the same style in which they came, to Sans Souci, his favorite palace, some two miles from the New Palace.

Pleased with all they had seen and heard, the mighty assembly returned to the cars and Berlin. I wanted to tell you much more about this interesting meeting, which continued some ten days, but my room is all exhausted.

May God watch over and bless you all is the earnest prayer of your absent   CHARLIE.

My DEAR SISTERS way down in old Mississippi : .... Your last letters were charming. I have read and reread them and think them better than printed letters by far. The description of your ride was worthy of Dickens in his palmiest days, both for novelty and raciness of style. I can truly rejoice that you have been so favored as to be together. I shall feel much easier in regard to you in case of sickness. Every day it seems to me that I could not enough praise God for his kindness and love to us all ; but when I remember how rich he is and good and kind, I only won-der that I ever did distrust him. Ah! I wish my faith were always as strong as it is at times ; then I should always be contented and happy. . . Keep up good courage, my dear sisters. Trust in *our Father* in heaven and you shall never want any *good* thing. Pray often for your wandering brother that he may indeed be fitted for that *great, great* work to which he hopes he has been called. Ah! I feel at times so weak and afraid ! and were there not so much to do, so much need of workmen, would be only too glad to play the Jonah and escape to Tarshish. . . . You speak of that glorious work in America. Yes, we heard of it for the first time in Rome, and spite of all the attractions, I have been homesick ever since. Oh, I long to be at work! Pray earnestly, my precious sisters, that I may be prepared for the labor before me in soul and body. . . . Many thanks for all your words of love. Kind remembrances to all that are so kind to you. Good-by. CHARLIE.

TO HIS BROTHER IN YALE COLLEGE.

I was glad to see your chum and through him to learn more definite-ly of college interest in religion, and of your own special interest. I hope and pray that it may be a baptism of the Spirit that shall give you larger and nobler views of life than you have ever had before. Work for Jesus, for there is nothing in the wide world one moment to compare with it.

My DEAR SISTERS: I am just on the point of leaving Berlin, yet, if I recollect aright, I have said little or nothing of my home for the last eight months. Berlin is a city that never made itself. Standing in the midst of a great sandy plain, it offered no attractions to the manufacturer and few to the agriculturist, nor can the sluggish, little Spree, that serves as a receptacle for all Berlin's filth, ever become very famous for its commerce. In fact Berlin is a hothouse plant, that was forced to grow whether it wou'd or not.

When Frederick the Great came to the throne he would have a huge city in Prussia, a rival of London and Paris. He therefore opened new and broad streets in every direction, and told the people that they must fill them with houses. Many buildings were built at the expense of the government, which were known as Free houses, and furnished rent free in times of peace, though they paid proportionally high taxes in times of war. Under his skilful management Berlin rapidly increased in population until it now contains 500,000 inhabitants. The streets are generally broad and well paved but there is a sameness about the architecture that is exceedingly monotonous. There being but little stone in the neighborhood, the houses are built of brick, and almost without exception, stuccoed the same, tiresome, slate color. In order to occupy as much room as possible, they are stretched along the streets, while their height seems quite insignificant. The public buildings are much the same. Even the palace itself reveals the same melancholy hue, except where here and there, large pieces of the wall plaster have pealed off, suggesting the ass concealed beneath the lion's skin. The palace is a huge building, two or three times the size of the Metropolitan Hotel. It stands at the head of the famous "*Unter den Linden*," and commands a view of its whole length and of the beautiful Brandenburg gate through which the street is entered.

We visited the Palace the other day, and I must say, that, considering the sums of money that have been spent, it is rather a tasteless affair. There were immense sofas, covered with gold and silver brocade at fabulous prices, and mirrors whose frames were solid silver, which the guide informed us, 'were made by Berlin artists!' while the expression of his countenance indicated that we should call them very fine; but in conscience I could not, and I must conclude, from the specimens that have come under my eye that Germany must yield the palm in this line to the French. There were some chandeliers here that were truly magnificent, consisting of quartz crystals that shone and glittered in the sun like diamonds. One from London I think, consists of 700,000 crystals and has eighty-eighty lights. The floors are of oak, tessellated, and so smooth that you are not allowed to wear boots, but must slide around in huge slippers furnished at the door. The ceiling of one of the rooms was fine. It was so frescoed that the centre was apparently a tent-like canopy of blue silk, while, in the corners beautiful scenes revealed themselves beneath its pendant folds. In the Throne hall were some most beautiful specimens of plate that have been purchased or presented to the royal house in days gone by. One piece, by Cellini, is of gold, covered with the most beautiful graving, and figures in relief.

The White room, so called, has just been redecorated at an expense of $100,000, and contains eighteen statues of the eighteen electors of Brandenburg, from whom Prussia's royal house descended, also beautiful frescoes representing the different provinces of the kingdom. At both ends are galleries splendidly fitted up, while, between the stairs that rise upon each side, are two fountains with tropical flowers surrounding them in the greatest abundance. From the windows, I think you have the most beautiful views in Berlin. . . . The museums are the pride of Berlin, and they are certainly most beautiful. The Old Museum has a fine colonnade in front; beneath which are, by all odds, the best frescoes I ever saw. . . . There is one thing that would strike you singularly on entering Berlin : two fine churches with a large theatre between them. They are all noble buildings and produce a fine effect. By the way, theatres, operas, and concerts, are all the rage here Sunday evenings; indeed, the Sabbath is the great gala day, and the streets and parks are crowded with people dressed in their best.

And now I must leave the buildings, too famous and grand to be described by word of mouth, and tell you some of the peculiarities of the place itself. In the first place, you would be struck by the crowd of soldiers that throng the streets and monopolize the honors of private and civil life. Prussia, you know, has no such natural protections or barriers, as Italy, France, and Spain, find in mountains, rivers, and oceans; so it must rear as it were mountains of flesh and blood, and thus ward off the dangers that threaten it on every side from powerful rivals. Think of a nation of 16,000,000 having a standing army of 250,000 able-bodied men that can be increased at any moment to 500,000, and you have some idea of the terrible burden Prussia has to bear. If great honor and attention were not paid to those that enter the military service, the people would not endure it. As it is, a pair of epaulettes is a passport to favor and sunshine, and the multitudes readily catch at the tempting bait. But even so, it is not a willing service, for every man *must* be a soldier, at least three years, and a slave's life it is. The common soldier must, each day, go on parade, and then he is marched up and down by a corporal, singly, or with two or three in company, till he can accomplish all the maneuvres perfectly. These corporals are little tyrants. They call the privates all sorts of foul names, pull their ears, hold them by the nose, while they perform difficult feats, and if the poor soldier makes a wry face even, or dares to speak, put him in jail for twenty-four hours.

Such are the men that hold Prussia down. Slaves themselves, they make slaves of others. They stand on every corner, they hold watch day and night, they fill huge barracks in every part of the city, they know your going out and coming in; like the frogs of Egypt, they swarm on every side, and, should the people endeavor again as in '48 to rebel, they would only too sorely feel the yoke that galls their necks. From the hour an infant enters the world till, an old man, he sleeps in the churchyard, those Argus eyes are ever upon him. Does a parent wish his child baptized? he must ask the permission of the police. Is the child not baptized within six months of birth? he must pay a fine. Does a young man wish to marry or go into business? he must have passed a certain examination, gone through nobody knows how many a tedious form, and, having at last ob-

tained his license, rest (?) in the comfortable assurance that at any moment his newly-acquired rights may be taken away, should his conduct
be in the least suspicious. No rank or condition is free ; the clergy themselves are appointed by government ; and there is on every side, evidence
that the authorities think every man a traitor and a villain, and will
deal with him accordingly. Better, ay, far better, to have riots from time
to time, and suffer the inconveniences that we must in America, and yet
allow every man to feel that he is *free* and *honest* till he has proved himself otherwise, than to live under such a government.

With a vast military organization like this, we have, of course, some
grand displays. I well remember the splendid music that wakened me
every morning, as six regiments with their bands passed beneath my
window to parade. As one moved, so moved a thousand soldiers, while
from their serried arms wave after wave of glittering light flashed upon the
dazzled sight. Perhaps the finest scene I have witnessed was an artillery
and cavalry review in September. Some twenty or thirty thousand soldiers
were present. They were drawn up in battle array—two grand divisions
opposite each other, at a distance of some two or three miles. Indeed,
they formed our horizon, and we could but just discern them from the trees
by the glittering helmets and swords that flashed defiance beneath the
burning sun. Presently that long dark line began to move; now slowly,
now more rapidly, till at last it fairly flew, like some swift thunder-cloud,
upon the foe awaiting it. Suddenly the flying artillery poured its terrible
volleys upon the glittering host ; thick smoke curled above their heads—a
canopy to hide the dire conflict from heaven ! Broken, scattered by the
murderous volleys, whose fury they could not endure, like some huge wave
that vainly pours its floods upon an adamantine cliff, they recoiled to form
their ranks anew, and again to renew the assault. So in alternate waves
they swept across the plains, coming ever nearer and nearer, till at last we
were enveloped in the very dust and smoke of the battle itself : cannon
were flying hither and thither, while horsemen, on furiously galloping
steeds, threatened our lives at every moment. At last order from confusion came ; from that disordered, entangled mass gleamed out a noble
host in long array, while music burst forth in strains of victory, triumph,
and peace. This pageant is a *sham* fight, at which the king and queen,
with the royal party of distinguished guests, lent their presence, and
vied with each other in the splendor and beauty of their dress and equi-
page.

I have visited the New Museum since writing the above. It is a noble
monument that the king is rearing to perpetuate his fame. It is not yet
complete, but already there is enough to show how grand it will be when
finished. The building is beautiful in itself ; but it is only the shrine to
contain the immortal productions of a Kaulbach—frescoes which, for con-

ception, grandeur, and beauty, are perfect wonders of art. In the centre of the building is the grand hall of entrance, with a broad, magnificent staircase, lined on either side by copies of the Elgin marbles from Athens, mounting up a hundred feet to the very roof, through the liquid clearness of whose glassy covering the light streams down upon those wonderful frescoes, each of which must be some twenty-five feet long and twenty feet high. The first represents the Tower of Babel and the dispersion of the nations. It is perhaps the best of the whole. Kaulbach has the wonderful power of making interesting detached groups unite in one grand and striking whole. In the upper part of the picture the hosts of heaven surround the Lamb as he stretches his hand in wrath over the ruin crumbling beneath. In the centre, on one of the terraces of the temple, sits the proud king, his idols crumbling around him. Fire bursts from the censer at his very feet, while on either side his former parasites and flatterers are deriding him. Fierce determination sits on his brow, and while from the walls, crashing and falling on every side, terror-stricken groups are escaping, he will not move. On the right, meanwhile, the nations are going forth, and their different pursuits are indicated by their banners, arms, or other insignia. Just beneath them a crowd is pursuing the poor architect of the temple, who, fallen to the ground, wraps his mantle about his face, which is the very picture of agony, and dies amid the shower of stones and bricks coming from every side. In the foreground is Monotheism, represented by a noble patriarch, surrounded by his beautiful family, riding upon a huge wagon drawn by the noblest oxen ever painted. The sheep and goats follow on either side, nibbling the grass or sporting around; while on the gentle oxen two beautiful children ride, playing with each other as they eat most luscious grapes. Just imagine the contrast between this magnificent foreground and the terror and dismay on every side, and you form a slight idea of this wonderful creation. I have described one. Please imagine five other pictures of like size and grandeur, representing the Destruction of Jerusalem, the Battle of the Huns, the Crusades, Greece, and one not yet complete, and you have some idea of Kaulbach and the entrance hall to the New Museum. I have never seen its like. I hope you may some time have the pleasure I enjoyed yesterday. But I must close my most unsatisfactory description, and ask you to wait for me at Rome.

Upon leaving Berlin, the party passed through Dresden towards Vienna, and their visit to the famous gallery of paintings at Dresden and the "Green Room" of the kingdom of Saxony is described in his next letter with great vivacity. But we must pass these by and hasten southward.

Our railroad followed the Elbe, which, soon after leaving Dresden, locks itself in among the rocky cliffs of the so-called Saxon Switzerland. Here is to be found the finest scenery of Germany. . . . It is very peculiar, owing to the fact that, while a large part of the country is sandstone, which you know is soft, and quickly yields to aqueous agencies, there are basaltic cliffs continually occurring, too stubborn in their nature to be easily washed away. Thus there are deep gorges, or isolated peaks like Königstein, which have no high land within several hundred feet. This Königstein is Saxony's pride—her Gibraltar. It is fortified, and almost the only fortress in Europe that never was taken. You will not wonder at its strength when I tell you that it is surrounded by a precipice from one to three hundred feet high, and that the only ingress is through a gallery cut in the living rock, with drawbridges so arranged that when removed it is impossible for man to reach the fortress. There is a well six hundred feet deep within, and here are stores enough to last for years. There are fields and cattle, and even a forest on this rugged peak. In the Thirty Years' war it was the only place not taken. Napoleon himself found it impregnable.

The scenery grew wilder and wilder as we drew nearer to the land of Bohemia, and there was a certain firmness of character attaching itself to those old hills that must have rendered it a fitting home for the warlike tribes of mountain Asia who settled here—of Huss and Ziska, with their fierce followers, and of the fierce Libussa and her maiden warriors, who in earlier times held sway in "Boehm." At last we struck the Moldau and its broader plains, and in a little time Prague with its many spires and towers glittered beneath the setting sun. It was truly a splendid sight as we rolled over that long bridge. The river with its islands and bridges ; the crowded Jews' quarter on our left, bounded by gardens and factories ; and on the right the palaces of Bohemian princes, formed a beautiful picture.

How strange it seems to stand within the walls where Huss lived, to see on every side tokens and traces of the man who centuries ago ignited a train which brought ruin and desolation to Prague's proud towers, which drove thirty thousand of Prague's forty thousand students away from her famous old university, and ended, I was about to say, with his death and the peace after the Hussite war ; but no ! it is still felt ; it shakes the world even now, and will till the end of time. Here, too, is the famous bridge, fourteen hundred feet long, and ornamented every twenty feet with groups of the quaintest statuary, where in the Thirty Years' war the university students withstood the Swedes for fourteen weeks, and thus saved Prague from its enemies.

After describing the various objects of interest in this city, he says :

In searching for the old synagogue we were separated from each other, and when I next met H—— and F——, some four hours after, they told me of a rather odd experience. They had penetrated into a narrow, crooked street, and at last stumbled upon the old house where Huss once lived. They found it was now occupied as a restaurant, and being somewhat hungry, concluded to take dinner on the spot. They examined the card, and called for what they supposed was roast beef. The meat came. It looked very inviting ; but they were both struck with its peculiar sweetish flavor, and when nearly through eating, on examining the paper more closely, found they had been eating roast horse ! Imagine their feelings ! H—— smoked most vigorously the whole afternoon, and F—— ate apples, candy, and I know not what, to keep his dinner down. Even now an allusion to the subject gives rise to certain peculiar nervous affections, better imagined than described. . . .

Tired and cold and hungry, we entered Vienna, the capital of Austria, and its pride and glory. It was splendidly lighted, and as we passed to our hotel, all was bright as noonday. I liked Vienna very much. There is a life and bustle about the streets that reminds me of New York more than any place I have seen in Europe. The shop-windows are very fine indeed. They fairly glitter with jewelry, silks, fine pictures, etc. The streets in the old town, where the nobility and royalty have their residences, are very narrow, and as the carriages with their spirited horses go dashing by, you are in peril of life and limb, as there are no sidewalks. The streets are very clean indeed, and the contrast to New York in this respect (as you can bear testimony, L——) is considerable.

The church of St. Stephen is a beautiful specimen of Gothic architecture. The spire is very tall and of fine proportions. It is built entirely of stone, and with its graceful little turrets, produces a grand effect. We mounted up through the long, winding staircase till we came to the huge bell, that was cast from cannon taken from the Turks at their memorable siege of Vienna. It is perfectly immense—twelve and a half feet high, twelve feet in diameter, one foot thick, and some forty feet in circumference ! It weighs four hundred tons, and is rung only on special occasions. The view from the spire is very fine. The old city lies at your feet, surrounded by the Glacis with its gardens and fine carriage drives ; and the new city, with barracks, churches, theatres, palaces, and magazines,

stretches its arms on every side around. The Prater, some three or four
miles square, is a vast park, filled with magnificent trees and drives. . . .

But perhaps the most unique sight of all was the vault of the Church
of the Capuchins. Here are arranged side by side the splendid sarcopha-
gi of some seventy of the imperial house of Hapsburgh. Most of them
are of bronze, but a few are of massive silver. That of Maria Theresa is
the finest. It is oblong, some ten or twelve feet high, with breadth and
length in proportion, covered with fine reliefs representing important
events in her history, while two effigies (of her husband and herself) repose
on the upper surface. Her sixteen children lie around her. Here, too, is
buried Maria Louise, Napoleon's wife, as well as his son, who died at the
age of twenty-one, loved and esteemed by all who knew him.

We visited on the Sabbath the Greek church, where they still worship
according to the ancient ritual. The singing, or rather chanting, was peculiar, and very beautiful, far more so than the Roman-catholic; but I cannot now stop to describe it. We also visited the mineralogical museum in
the palace. It contains some of the finest specimens in the world. The
collection of precious stones was very complete and beautiful, as well as
that of meteors, which is one of the largest in the world. Some of these
stones were picked up while yet warm from the sky.

We were struck with the plainness of the royal equipages, churches, etc. Nowhere did we find the least effort to make display. We have
been most happily disappointed in Austria. We expected to be continually annoyed as to our passports and baggage. So far from this being
the case, a man can now travel from one end of Austria to the other without showing his passport at all; and from all I could see and learn, Austria is at present ahead of Prussia in all that regards the liberty of the
subjects.

We left Vienna, the city of palaces and parks, with regrets, and turned
our faces still southward. The country was beautiful. . . .

But our most surprising experience was just before us—nothing less
than crossing the Julian Alps by railroad. . . . This work has been for a
long time in progress, and was not completed till last year. The highest
elevation attained is some three thousand feet, and the inclination in places
seems almost as great as that of a house roof. It was absolutely frightful
to see a train descending one of these grades. You can imagine some of
the difficulties they had to contend with in building this road, when I tell
you it cost $7,500,000 to build twenty-five miles. On common roads in
America, the same distance of road would have been built for $400,000.
It seemed so strange to go winding, twisting along up the banks of a torrent, now on this side, and a half hour hence on the opposite bank a hundred feet higher. The scenery, too, was absolutely grand. Mountains covered with snow surrounded us on every side, and with every turn some

new scene of wildest beauty burst upon us. Near the summit we passed a peak which seemed to spring unsupported from the valley below, so wholly was it disconnected from the surrounding peaks. Its summit was covered with the ruins of a castle, once the key of this whole country, but now completely shattered and uninhabited, the result of lightning.

How beautifully, too, that street, with its neat little cottages and factories, wound around the base through the narrow pass, (you could not call it a valley,) while through the gigantic frame of towering peaks you looked out over the beautiful plain and glittering spires of Gloggnitz. In a moment this scene was snatched from our eyes, and we were whirling at full speed through a tunnel one mile long. It took some five minutes to pass through, and we counted one hundred and thirty-four gas lights with which it is lighted. A factory was built way up here just to supply it with gas. The language, too, was completely changed, and the peasants' gibberish we strove in vain to understand. Their vests were quite peculiar, being ornamented with large round brass buttons, such as soldiers sometimes wear with us, as thick as they could stand down the whole front.

At one of the stations we had rather an amusing scene. A perfect crowd of the aborigines took possession of our car, and among them a laughing, jolly, old woman, loaded with basket and kettle, which took up nearly the whole of the passage. Scarcely had we started before she uncovered her kettle, revealing amid the fumes of charcoal a dish of snaky-looking, steaming sausages, which she was ready to dispose of to the highest bidder. She had scarcely all prepared, before the scene changed. Unluckily for her, but most fortunately for our eyes, the conductor entered at this moment, and the way her sausage-kettle went out of the door was a caution to all meat-pedlers. The conductor was very indignant, and we all supposed he had thrown the kettle overboard. To our great amusement we saw him, some fifteen minutes after, busily devouring its contents on the platform just outside the door.

With such scenes within, and the ever-changing grandeur without, the hours did not seem long, although we rode twelve hours to-day and some thirteen yesterday. It seemed so strange crossing the Drave and the · Save, those famous old rivers in Roman history, along whose rocky banks the legions so often penetrated into the barbarous regions of the North. I could scarcely realize that I was so far away from home, amid scenes wrapped around with all the mist of boyhood days and studies. The Save valley is peculiarly wild and beautiful ; the precipitous cliffs spring up from the very shore of the stream, and the bright, blue, clear waters foam and rage against them. Rafts formed of hogsheads, and freighted with gayly-dressed peasants, added not a little to the picturesque character of the scene.

As we approached Trieste, the country grew fearfully barren. The peaks were desolate. Not a tree, scarcely a bit of moss, served to cover the nakedness of the rocks; but, finally, the last tunnel was passed, and as old Sol dipped behind the Atlantic wave, lighting up those snow-capped peaks with that beautiful rosy tint which painters love, we commenced the steep descent to the blue Adriatic and Trieste. At eight o'clock we rested our weary limbs in the busy mart of Austria, with its broad and finely-paved streets, and its harbor filled with sailing craft. I was surprised to find Trieste so busy and thriving. It is now, it seems, the tenth city in the world in its commerce. Indeed, every step of our way convinces us of the increasing greatness of Austria, and I leave this country with very different feelings from those with which I entered it. Oh, we are so narrow-minded and prejudiced; and, as we move about the world, we every day learn that everywhere there are bad and good, beautiful and homely, just and unjust, tyrants and oppressed, if we will only look calmly and candidly around us. . . . You must excuse the look of these sheets, as I have written with all kinds of ink, in all sorts of places, and with all manner of feelings. CHARLIE.

PARIS, June, 1858.

MY DEAR FRIENDS: . . . . In my last I was just entering Naples covered with the classic dust of the Campagna and the Falernian hills. Naples was all and more than I had imagined. It has nearly 500,000 inhabitants, and there was a bustle and excitement about it that took me quite by surprise; the carmen and sailors, too, are very noisy, and the cracking whip and rattling wheel warn you that things *move* in Naples. . . . . We concluded to visit Virgil's tomb. It is on the side of a limestone cliff that projects over the road on one side and into the sea on the other, and directly opposite old Vesuvius itself. Think of it! this lovely spot, looking out over the most lovely bay in the world, was the spot where Virgil lived, where he wrote a large part of the Æneid, and where, having completed his immortal poem, he laid him down to sleep, for he can never die. His tomb is a large square building, with windows and a door. It is almost completely covered with ivy. Above it waves a laurel which Petrarch is said to have planted. That was a strange place to me; every hill and tree and island, the sea itself, the very wind, told me of the great poet. Then behind was the Cumean promontory, and Lake Avernus with its dark groves, yes, and the Sibyl's Cave. There was Misenum. Far away beyond the horizon were Scylla and Charybdis. But I must stop, or I will say foolish things. This is a place sacred in itself, sacred as a Mecca whither thousands of the great and good have for centuries made pilgrimages.

The next morning early we were away by railroad for the burning mount. . . . . The crater itself is the centre of a steep truncated cone which it has formed on the snmmit of the mountain ridge. . . . . The ascent is quite rugged, the mountain sides are covered with a huge stream of cold, rough, jagged lava. It looks like a stream of thick, black tar that has dried and cracked in thousands of forms under the burning sun. We came at last to the steep itself. First we tried to ascend in the sand, but really one step up was two back, and we concluded to take to the rough lava again. Here, almost on all-fours, you could clamber up perhaps a hundred steps, and then sit down and rest. How ladies ever walk up there I can hardly imagine. Most, I presume, are carried up in a chair, (as I saw one fat old priest ascend,) and pay for their ride from five dollars to ten dollars, according to their skill in making a bargain.

The sight that presented itself as we reached the top was entirely unexpected. A large, rough plain appeared, with cracks running through it in every direction, from which smoke and sulphurous steam poured forth, while the rock itself was so hot that you could not stand, much less sit, for a moment. We felt that we were truly walking on a fiery sea as we hurried on to get a nearer view of the great crater about a quarter of a mile distant. Clouds of smoke were rolling from the horrid pit, and ever and anon, with dreadful groans and thundering noise, a torrent would be thrown far up into the sky.

Two or three of us went down to the brink itself; but while we were there one of these eruptions took place. I stood it very well till, looking up above my head, I saw the air filled with red-hot lava directly over me. I think I never did move more rapidly, for, almost before I knew, I had jumped down and was on the other side twenty feet away. F——, unconscious of danger, remained, and one of the pieces struck his shawl and burnt it quite badly. We dipped a few coin in the lava as souvenirs, and then beat a hasty retreat from this raging heat.

If the ascent had been difficult, we were rewarded for our toil by the descent. We now took to the sand, and leaping and bounding along like so many wild horses, fairly plunged down the steep. In five minutes I was at the bottom of this cone, that three-quarters of an hour's hard work had scarcely sufficed to ascend. . . . .

The next morning we concluded on a trip to Pompeii, Salerno, and Pæstum.

Pompeii has not its like on the face of the earth. Buried beneath a shower of moist ashes, every object retained its original position and shape, being hermetically sealed up about the time of Christ—to astonish the world of the nineteenth century. So many feet was it buried that its place was for centuries forgotten. And now it is again opened to the light of day; and as we walk its streets, and see the stores and houses, the theatre, temples, and forums, yes, and mark the deep ruts in the pavement, we can but believe that yesterday Pompeii fell. The old Hippodrome, or amphitheatre, is the most perfect ruin I have seen. There were the entrances for the higher and lower classes, and the seats rising tier upon tier far above the arena. There, too, were the cells in which the beasts and the gladiators themselves were placed, ready for the conflict, and the bloody avenue through which they drew the dead after the conflict was over. All was there ready, and we almost waited for the sleeping thousands to come again and take the seats they filled that last fatal day when Pompeii was blotted out. A temple in the midst of the city attracted our attention. It was dedicated to Iris, and there, beneath the floor, was the well in which the victims were purified. The altar still remains, and ashes and bones were found upon it. A statue of Hippocrates stood in the wall, with his finger on his lips enjoining silence. But the most interesting spot was the oracle itself, where, behind a large marble slab, you could see the narrow staircase and door through which the priest could enter into the statue and deliver the oracle which the multitudes supposed came from the god himself.

The private houses were mostly one, rarely two stories high. Their walls were generally frescoed, and many of the pictures are as fresh as though just painted. It seemed strange enough to see the wine jars standing in the cellars, and the machine at the mills ready for grinding, and stranger still, to find coffee, wheat, beans, figs, and nuts perfectly preserved. But I cannot describe what requires hours for even the most hasty review. Towards evening we took the cars again, and were soon rolling through a country rich in historic incident, and beautiful enough, with its towering hills folded in fleecy clouds and valleys cultivated like gardens, to made another Eden......

Bright and early we were off the next morning for Pæstum. Our carriage seemed an ancient chariot of victory, as we drove four magnificent horses abreast in a style that brought back classic scenes as never before. The road was perfectly level, and part of the country very thinly inhabited. Our twenty-six miles' ride was accomplished in a few hours, and we stood within the pillars of the oldest existing temples in Italy, one of which was built at least 600 B. C. The infallible Murray says that, "With the exception of those of Athens, they are the most striking existing records of the genius and taste which inspired the architects of Greece." Pæstum was an old Grecian colony founded long before Rome. There are three temples remaining, and the central one is one of the most simple, yet grand and beautiful buildings I ever saw. The columns were short and thick, but the broad capital, surmounted by a cornice in proportion, made this appropriate. The façade was very simple in its ornaments, but the whole building, while easily comprehended, produced the effect desired and contrasted finely enough with the huge Basilica adjoining, with its hundred pillars and toilsome architecture. Those were strange old ruins standing in the midst of the flowery meadows, with scarce a habitation of man for miles away. We wandered around, finding vaults and ruined walls here and there, and endeavored in the tangled grass and weeds to trace the line of ancient fortifications that once surrounded the city.

One of our company sprained his foot sadly, and as we had offered sacrifices, viz., sacrificed an excellent collation to our hungry stomachs in the very *sanctum sanctorum*, we reluctantly tore ourselves away and returned north again.

Our southernmost point was reached, and in the long vista that stretched before us, we saw Naples, Florence, Switzerland, Paris, London, and last, not least, *Home.* The sun had long been set, when, tired out, we entered Naples. In fact, we had accomplished a pretty good day's work—56 miles by carriage and nearly as much more in the cars. Our invalid was soon safely stored away, and in a few days was moving around again as usual.

The next Monday was devoted to the valuable museum here, especially interesting in the treasures gathered from Herculaneum and Pompeii, and other ancient cities. I found my pride in our great Nineteenth Century considerably humbled, when I saw that two thousand years ago they possessed nearly every article of convenience or luxury of which we can boast. Planes, hoes, shovels, edged-tools of all kinds, glass-ware in every variety; kitchen-ranges furnished in a style that would make a Parisian cook's eyes glisten from their perfection and variety. But in the higher arts they were also proficient, and in a case of silver instruments belonging to a physician of Pompeii, was found a peculiar kind of forceps, the exact copy of one that was patented in England a few years since as a most valuable invention. . . . . .

I was much interested too in the old manuscripts that were found in Pompeii, and especiallly in the very ingenious manner in which they are unrolled. For many years no one could imagine what those little black masses of charcoal could be. Under a powerful microscope the truth was revealed, and since then philosophers have been all alert to discover the treasures thus concealed, and unroll the charred mass without destroying the characters. This had at last been most ingeniously accomplished, and several books have been deciphered, although the process is, of necessity, exceedingly slow and tedious,

I fear you will weary with my long delay in Naples; but I cannot close without giving you a short account of our visit to Lake Avernus, Solfaterra, etc. Early in the morning we took carriage, and were soon rattling through the famous old tunnel leading out of Naples through "Virgil's promontory." It is at least half a mile in length, and yet nothing is known of its construction. It was in existence hundreds of years ago, as it is described by Pliny and others; but it was much smaller then, and you can see where the hubs of the wheels once rubbed against the wall high up on the side. It is miserably ventilated, and we were almost stifled from dust and stench as we rolled along through. We soon came to Solfaterra, the crater of an old volcano. It still fumes a little, and in 1198 quite a torrent of lava poured down its sides into the sea. To reach it we passed through Pozzuoli, the once famous post Puteoli, where Paul landed on his eventful journey to Rome; and we mounted up the same steep hill, by the same Appian way he once walked.

A short distance hence is the famous temple of Jupiter Serapis, which may well be called a geological chronometer, and which has excited more attention and speculation from learned men than perhaps any other existing ruin. It consists of a fine large open court, surrounded by walls of marble, and in the centre are three fine marble pillars, each some forty feet high, and cut from one piece of marble. The floor is now entirely covered with water to the depth of some three or four feet, and the whole building is gradually sinking into the sea at the rate of perhaps an inch yearly. Twice before has it sunk in this way, and then again risen to its former level. These changes can be traced on the pillars as at each descent they have been pierced by the sea-borers, which have left their marks as high as the water rose. Just beyond is Mount Nuovo, which is very interesting from the fact that it has entirely risen within the historic period. It was formed in three days, and is about fourteen miles in circumference, and some five hundred feet high! The ashes from the eruption were carried one hundred and fifty miles. You could hardly imagine that a spot so blooming with vegetation as this beautiful conical hill could ever have been the scene of such fiery visitation. Ruins are here on every side, so many that the land cannot hold them, and beneath the sea you can trace the streets and temples of bygone days.

The most beautiful spot in Italy, it is not strange that the voluptuous Romans filled every nook with their marble palaces. All the great and learned of Rome had their villas here.

But the interest in all these fades, for we are approaching the Avernian gulf and the awful cave of the Sibyl. Lake Avernus, with its beautiful shaded banks, is really not such an awful place, and to tell the truth, I saw a good many birds fly over the placid surface with perfect impunity. Yet it did seem a little bordering on the marvellous to see stones floating on its surface. I could hardly believe my eyes, and taking a stone, hurled it far out into the lake, where it danced about like a duck. The enigma was solved when I took the stone in my hand. It was lava pumice, something like glass slag, very porous and light. We now lit our torches and made ready to enter the cave of the Sibyl. . . . At last we came to a little side passage, where, on account of the water, it was necessary to mount the guide's back, if you would reach the cave itself. The rushing of the waters against the sides of the cave sounded in the pitchy darkness truly infernal ; and when the voices reverberated through the passages, it seemed as if old Cerberus himself was loose. It was really quite a relief to get back into daylight and pure air. . . . Delighted with our excursion, we returned just at sunset along the magnificent road that skirts the cliff high above the bay. It is lined with fine villas, many of them romanticly situated, with crooked, winding paths and roads along the cliffs to their portals. And then the blue, blue sea, with gay-colored craft, and beyond, Naples glittering in the setting sun, while above them all rose Vesuvius, with his forehead wreathed in mystic vapors. As I looked on that scene I did not wonder that the passionate Italian loved Naples, even though it seems built in a crater itself, and exposed any moment to destruction. Indeed, since our visit, the very path by which we ascended has been swept away, and the fiery torrents are rolling again into the plain from five or six new craters. . . .

Our stay in Florence was comparatively short, yet it was long enough to teach us that it is one of the most delightful cities of Europe for a residence. The city itself is neat and clean, the streets broad and fine, and almost entirely free from beggars, while one can live extremely cheap. It cost us only one dollar a day at the hotel, and we were as well provided for as any man could wish. The country around Florence is full of splendid drives and views. One can best appreciate the beauty of its location from the summit of the Campanile. . . . This Campanile is famous in architecture, being considered by many (Ruskin among the number) as a most perfect piece of architecture, almost the most perfect extant. It belongs to the cathedral, although it stands a few feet from it, and is entirely independent of it. It is seven stories high, and each story differs from its neighbor. The work in many parts is exquisitely beautiful, fine enough for a lady's flower-stand.

But Florence has yet higher claims in the magnificent collections of fine arts she has gathered. Here is the world-renowned Pitti Palace, and here I found that gem of paintings, copies of which I have seen a thousand times, Raphael's Madonna and child, with John the Baptist standing at her knee. It is a small oval painting ; but there is an ease and grace about the mother as she sits with her child in her arms, and a delicate harmonious blending of color in the whole that I cannot describe—but to me makes it one of the most perfect of pictures. And this is but one of a thousand ; for the whole upper story of this magnificent palace is devoted to pictures, and most of them from the most famous pencils of history. Here, too, are some splendid specimens of Florentine mosaics. Among them is a table covered with fruit, vines, and flowers, most exquis-

itely wrought, and so perfect that you could almost take them in your
hands. You can imagine the time and pains necessary for its construction when I tell you it cost some $40,000.

There is here too another equally famous collection of paintings in
the Uffizi. I spent most of the few hours I could here bestow in the Tribune, where are collected the gems not only of painting but of sculpture.
Here is the world-renowned *Venus de' Medici* as well as the Wrestlers,
Apollo and the Whetter. I suppose it is very presumptuous in me, but
I never can like the Venus. The body and limbs are almost faultless in
their execution, and are truly beautiful; but the arms and hands, by their
awkward position, mar the whole. They are stiff and unnatural, and the
wrists seem too long. I have always felt this in the copies, and it is no
better in the original. But it is almost wicked to find fault in such a
sacred place, for here are gathered the St. John of Raphael, the Loves of
Titian, the Sibyl of Guercino—in fact one masterpiece from each of the
famous masters of antiquity. The room is worthy of the gems it contains.
The ceiling is of mother-of-pearl, its floor of precious marbles of varied
hues ; the hangings of the doors of crimson velvet, and the furnishing of
the whole in the same style of grand yet simple beauty. The frame is
fine, but it is the pictures that command our reverence in spite of all other
attractions. . . .

The next morning we visited the Westminster Abbey of Italy—the
Church of Santa Croce, famous for the noted dead who are buried there.
Here are the tombs of Michael Angelo, Danté, Alfiero, Galileo, Macchia-
velli, and a host of others. It is a fine church, with its monuments and
beautiful pictures and dome. I was happily disappointed in Pisa. It is
one of the gems of Italy, so quaint and unique in the architecture of its
famous tower and cathedral. I know not how, but I had previously
formed the idea that the tower leaned on account of some accident, but
when I came to see the cathedral the whole was explained. No two pillars, capitals, entablatures, façades, or cornices, were alike. One part
was higher than another, and arches with unequal legs abounded. This
was the most elaborate Corinthian, that the sternest, simplest Doric. It
is truly a miracle of art, and I cannot conceive how any human genius
could make so great irregularities, yes, almost deformities, into one grand
whole. Yet this is the case ; and as you take the whole in at one view
scarcely one of these peculiarities strikes you. It is only when you examine it in detail that they appear to amuse and astonish. The tower is
built on the same principle, and as you study it, you can see where the
nicest calculations have been made to counterbalance the unnatural inclination. We ascended to the summit, where we had one of the grandest
views, stretching away up into the Alps on one side, to the Pyrenees on
another, and to the Mediterranean on the other. It was really frightful

to look over the railing and see how much the building varied from the perpendicular.

Delighted with our Pisa visit we turned our faces toward that dreaded Mediterranean. Fortunately, the night was calm and beautiful, and about one o'clock in the morning, amid the crowing and cackling of innumerable fowl that covered our deck, we entered the port of Genoa. I could not sleep, so I walked the deck and looked at the same hills, yes, and counted the same bright constellations that four hundred years ago greeted the humble Genoa pilot, the far-famed discoverer of my own dear native land. What changes since then! The land that to him was a possibility is to me to-night a bright, living reality; and the dreams and visions that visited his pillow here, drawing him forth on his adventurous journey, are fulfilled. I cannot sleep, but visions fair and beautiful draw me towards the same West, the same golden end. May God grant them fulfilment in his own good time. Till then, farewell.

CHARLIE.

CHAPTER III.

HIS FIELD OF LABOR.

THE field of work to which Mr. Payson was called soon after he returned from Europe, and in which he continued to labor all his life, was in some respects peculiar. Its relations to the church were anomalous. No name has yet been found by which it can be truthfully represented in the records of the Presbyterian body. The duties of a pastor in this field are those of every Christian minister, and are simple and familiar, but the position which he occupies is unparalleled, and no official recognition of it upon the records of the church has yet seemed possible.* The following terse and clear description of the general features of the work has been kindly furnished by the Rev. Howard Crosby, D. D., LL. D., and will be found especially valuable to those who are not acquainted with the field :

MISSIONS IN NEW YORK CITY.

" The city of New York, with over a million of inhabitants, nearly the half of whom are foreign born, has long presented an interesting problem to the church of Christ in the matter of its evangelization. The churches of the city conserve and foster piety among their members and their families, but in their own regular services make no direct impression upon the vast numbers who never

* See Appendix, Note A.

enter a church. The New York City Mission has labored for nearly a half century to meet this want, and by its mission-stations in destitute quarters has done much. It now has four churches fully organized, under its care, besides its numerous mission stations, where much fruit is rewarding its wise and energetic labors.

"Not many years ago, the different denominations of Protestant Christians began to work on the unevangelized masses in the city by denominational societies, establishing and supporting denominational missions and churches, thus leaving the "City Mission and Tract Society" more largely to be supported by Presbyterians.

"These denominational societies have done an earnest work. The Methodist Society has established sixteen churches and chapels, of which one has become self-sustaining and independent. The Baptist Society has established five churches, all still dependent upon it for support. The Episcopal Society has organized no churches, but has established seven chapels.

"A third form in which general city evangelization has been carried on, is by the effort of individual churches, the Baptists having two missions of this character, the Episcopalians seventeen, and the Presbyterians ten. This form of the work has these advantages. 1. The members of a particular church become personally interested in the work. 2. They are ready, therefore, to contribute to the full support of the work. 3. The wants of the work are fully known to them, and the supply of these wants becomes a natural action of the church life. 4. The missions thus created furnish an admirable field of labor where the church members are strengthened in their graces.

"While the ultimate hope regarding these missions is that they may become independent churches, yet the difficulties in the way have not thus far been surmounted. The chief difficulty is, the inability of the members worshipping at these missions to furnish pecuniary support for the sustentation of independent churches. To the question, 'Why do not the parent churches furnish the means?' the answer is, that if these mission churches be cut off from the parent church, the special interest of the parent church fails, the members seeking other fields of labor, into which they throw their strength. On the other hand, the reason why the mission church cannot support itself pecuniarily, is in the fact that as its members become increased in wealth, they naturally gravitate to other parts of the city, and become connected with other churches. New York is so built, that the poorer classes are geographically separated from the richer classes, a fact which makes the mission problem peculiarly difficult. It is this fact that also prevents the members of parent churches from going to the mission churches and casting in their lot with them, thus enabling them to bear the pecuniary burden of self-support. It might be added, that it would be doubtful whether the children of a family that may be brought up away from evil sights and sounds, should be exposed to the contamination of degraded parts of the city, as would be the case if such a family should cast in its lot with one of the mission churches.

"It is true that some of these missions are not in degraded quarters, and of the future independency of these there is a fairer expectation.

"The Rev. Charles H. Payson was one of the most devoted laborers in this mission field that our city ever saw. With sound judgment, indefatigable industry, quenchless zeal, administrative ability, sympathetic soul and fine pulpit talents, he for seventeen years presided over the Third Avenue Mission of the Madison Square Presbyterian Church, receiving the hearty and liberal aid of that efficient church. Under his ministry the mission became, in everything but self-support, a strong and useful church, sending forth its blessed influences in every direction in that important part of the city. He so taught the people to give, that they were able to raise from $4,000 to $5,000 a year among themselves. This has been a mission church raised in the best neighborhood and under the very best auspices, and yet its self-support is at present impossible. Under wise management, we may ere long see this consummation reached.

"But now take another instance at the other end of the line. Grace Mission of the Fourth Avenue Presbyterian Church is situated in Twenty-second street, near First avenue, a neighborhood pronounced by the police captain of the precinct in 1866, when the mission was founded, one of the worst in the city. The Rev. Mr. Cummings, a most able and laborious minister, who was pastor of the mission, has testified that it must *always* remain a dependent chapel, because (as we have before stated) of the removal of its members to more central churches, as soon as their personal reform and Christian progress have raised them in the scale of society. In this way not only the money is taken away, but also the material out of which to make the church officers. It seems then that in New York we must expect to have this anomalous mission system as a necessity, only now and then, under most advantageous circumstances, a chapel of this sort becoming an independent church.

In point of fact these mission churches act like independent churches. They have their own pastor, their own communion seasons, their own auxiliary societies; the only points of contact with the parent church being in the sessional action at the reception of members, and in the Sunday-school work of the members of the parent church.

" The appointment of the pastor is made by the session, according to the wishes of the actual workers in the field. Of course there is no installation or recognized ecclesiastical connection ; and perhaps here is a point (a matter mostly of name, however) which should be regulated in a judicious way, so that every body of Christians worshipping together and their virtual pastor, may appear before the churches in their true light.

" In a memorial of Charles H. Payson, this sketch is appropriately placed as indicating the wide and important field to which he gave the flower and strength of his life. No one knew all the merits of the mission question in New York better than he, and no one has done more to inspire courage and faith in his fellow-laborers.

" He now rests from his labors, and his works do follow him. Through all ages will results testify to the faithfulness of this man of God, and in the history of the evangelization of this great and wicked city, no name will shine brighter than that of Charles H. Payson."

The special field in which Mr. Payson labored was the Third Avenue branch of the Madison Square Presbyterian Church. The following outline of its early history is taken mostly from the official records of the chapel as prepared by the Rev. Mr. Hough, its first pastor.

In the autumn of 1856 it was determined by several members of the Madison Square Church to attempt the establishment of a Mission Sabbath-school. Some steps towards the accomplishment of this end had been taken in the fall of the preceding year through the influence of a benevolent lady then living in West Thirty-fifth street. A few scholars were gathered in the basement of her own house, but the place soon becoming too straitened for the numbers in attendance it was determined to put the work under the care of the Madison Square Church. It was found that the district lying east of Third Avenue between Fourteenth and Fifty-fourth streets was not provided for by any Presbyterian church or chapel, and the work was accordingly transferred to this locality. A rough uncomfortable room, which during week-days was used as a carpenter shop, was obtained upon the north side of Twenty-ninth street east of Third avenue. Mr. James Morris was elected superintendent, and Mr. Theodore Morris librarian. The first scholars were mostly wild, unmanageable children, who, upon, the first and second Sabbaths, tore up and destroyed many of the Bibles and singing-books, rendering the presence of a policeman necessary to the maintenance of even tolerable order. Mr. Theodore J. Holmes became connected with the school in December as secretary and visitor; Mr. J. W. Hough as visitor in January, 1857.

On the first Sabbath in February the school was removed to the public school building in Twenty-seventh street. The seats were uncomfortable and the room ill-adapted for Sunday-school purposes, yet a great gain was thus secured upon the arrangements in Twenty-ninth street. In April Mr. Morris died, and in May Mr. William E. Dodge, Jr., was elected superintendent. Two sessions of the Sunday-school were held, one in the morning and one in the afternoon; but it was found after some experience that the classified session in the afternoon was impracticable on account of the difficulty in providing teachers. Accordingly this was changed in October to a "boys' and girls' meeting," at which the time was chiefly occupied in singing and general exercises.

On Sabbath morning, Jan. 10, 1858, the school took possession of the new and commodious chapel which had been erected by the Madison Square Church on Third avenue between Thirtieth and Thirty-first streets. On the following Sabbath evening, January 17, was held the first church service for adults. Mr. Hough supplied the pulpit from March 7, 1858, till May 1, 1859, performing the duties of a pastor at the same time. A prayer-meeting was also organized by the aid of several young men from the Madison Square Church. The first morning service was held Oct. 17, 1858. About one hundred were present, the majority being children from the school. The morning congregation seldom reached more than one hundred; the evening congregation steadily increased from one hundred to about three hundred; and the prayer-meeting ranged from thirty to sixty. Meanwhile the Sunday-school continued to prosper. During the summer of 1858 it was placed under the care of Mr. Theodore J. Holmes, who succeeded in holding about two hundred in regular attendance. A Young Men's Bible Class, was formed under the instruction of Mr. Spencer W. Coe, which was afterwards divided and a portion given to Mr. George W. Lane.

After the resignation of Mr. William E. Dodge, Jr., Mr. Nason B. Collins officiated in his place till May 3, 1860, when Mr. David Wetmore was elected superintendent and from that time till this he has performed the arduous duties of that position with a zeal and faithfulness which are above praise.

Mr. Hough was ordained as an evangelist at the Madison Square Church by the Fourth Presbytery of New York, Sabbath evening, March 13, 1859. "*It not being thought best to organize a distinct church, steps were taken to bring together those from the Mission Chapel congregation who desired church membership as members of the Madison Square Church worshipping at the Mission Chapel, with power to receive additions to their number and to observe the ordinances of the church at the chapel.*"*

* These are the precise words of the official record.

Accordingly the session of the Madison Square Church met at the chapel, Saturday evening, March 12, 1859, when twelve candidates were examined and accepted, three being also received by letter. At a second meeting held on Wednesday evening, March 16, six other candidates were examined and received. On Sabbath evening, March 20, 1859, the sacrament of the Lord's Supper was administered for the first time. Twenty-one persons were received into membership. The nucleus of the present organization was thus formed.

May 17, 1860, Mr. Hough left for a vacation of six weeks, hoping thus to recruit his exhausted strength. But finding still farther rest necessary he tendered his resignation, which was accepted.

It was at this time that Mr Payson, who had supplied the pulpit during the temporary absence of Mr. Hough, was invited to take his place, and accepted the call. He was ordained as an evangelist at the Chapel, Sabbath evening, Nov. 25, 1860, by the Fourth Presbytery of New York. The large and pleasant room was filled by an eager and attentive audience, a great proportion being composed of regular attendants upon the Sabbath services.

The opening exercises were conducted by the Moderator, Rev. James H. Dwight, and the sermon preached by Rev. George L. Prentiss, D. D., now Professor in the Union Theological Seminary, and formerly pastor of the Church of the Covenant in this city.

" The discourse," as reported by a contemporary paper, " was an able and eloquent exposition of the true, practical nature of Christian beneficence. This was shown to be nothing less than an entire consecration of the life to Christ, and a faithful, persevering work for Him. Energy, enthusiasm, and clear judgment must enter into such a life. The true follower of Christ should go, as He did, among the poor, the forsaken, and the outcast, not fearing the contact or the taint of the vile and suffering. He must be willing to study with patient care the best means of doing good, and with the joy of working for his Master bear with cheerful self-denial the hardships and toils so blessed a work may impose."

If the sermon had been inspired by a prophetic spirit it could hardly have been a more fitting inaugural to such a ministry.

"The consecrating prayer was offered by the Rev. Henry B. Smith, D. D., Professor of Theology in the Union Theological Seminary, accompanied by the laying on of hands by the Presbytery; after which a very touching charge to the pastor was made by the Rev. William Adams, D. D., his peculiar relations as the head of the parent church giving it an additional force and interest. He congratulated Mr. Payson on his taking charge of so interesting a field, after long years of preparation and labor. He alluded feelingly to his ancestral honors and inherited fitness for such a work, Mr. Payson's father and grandfather having been faithful ministers, and his near relation, Rev. Dr. Payson, of Portland, whose praise is in all the churches. Dr. Adams exhorted him as one who would now take the charge and responsibility of so important a part of his own church work, to great faithfulness and prayer, to enthusiasm in life, to careful study, and to faithful adaptation to the great variety of hearers who form the congregation at the chapel. The remarks concluded by an affectionate appeal to the people to receive their new pastor with love and confidence, and to use the same care and preparation in hearing the word of life as would be necessary in preaching it faithfully.

"The services were closed by music, and a benediction by the new pastor."

It is quite impossible to estimate the indebtedness of this enterprise to the cordial sympathy and material aid of the Madison Square Church. Its origin and financial support, and the spiritual growth of its people through all the years of its remarkable history, are very largely

attributable, under God, to the zeal and fidelity of the
members of that church, of which the Rev. William
Adams, D. D., was for so long a period the distinguished
and honored pastor. His successor, the Rev. William
J. Tucker, D. D., has manifested no less deep an interest
in the work of the Memorial Chapel; and under the able
ministrations of these eminent men, the Madison Square
Church has continued unremittingly for twenty years its
generous support of the work undertaken in this field.
At the commencement it furnished all the funds necessary for the conduct of the mission; and during the past
nine years (since the people at the chapel began to give
part of the amount) its annual expenses here have averaged from $4,000 to $6,000, besides the private contributions to the poor and sick, which have in all cases
been considerable—probably several thousands of dollars
per annum. Then, too, the "Snowflake Offering" for
the erection of the Memorial Chapel in 1874–5 amounted
to more than $40,000; and $50,000 had been paid for
lots in 1873–4.

But these generous contributions of money were by
no means all nor the greatest share of the support most
cheerfully provided for this enterprise by the parent
church. Many of its most efficient and capable workers
engaged in active labors here. In the Sabbath-school,
the Employment Society, the Industrial School, the
Neighborhood Prayer-meetings, at the annual Christmas
festival, and in almost every department of religious
work connected with the chapel, the zealous and devoted
Christians who worship in the Madison Square Church

took part with an enthusiasm and fidelity which merit the highest encomiums.

Mr. Payson's field was all prepared for him. The members of the large and influential Committee to whom the management of this enterprise was intrusted from the first were among his constant and cordial friends. Although they disagreed with him at times with reference to the conduct of the "Mission" (as it was called at first and for many years) Mr. Payson had abundant opportunity to recognize their uniform courtesy, and untiring interest in the work. He often spoke of them in terms of the warmest appreciation, and both in public and private gave frequent expression to the deep sense of gratitude he felt for having been called, in the good providence of God, to labor with the members of a church whose sound judgment and financial ability were inspired by such steadfast zeal. Some of these gentlemen were identified with the chapel almost from the very first, and were the "pillars" of Mr. Payson's work, as he himself often styled them. Humanly speaking, their aid and that of those connected with them, also from the parent church, were indispensable to his success. In season and out of season, by night and day, both summer and winter, these noble Christian men labored, as they still labor, with a faith and patience, and indefatigable devotion to their work, which moved the admiration and stimulated the zeal of all who knew them.

It is especially worthy of note that the members of the Madison Square Church who engaged in this field, carried light and life to dreary homes, not by the dole of charity or the cold unsympathetic aid of money lavishly bestowed, but, as their Saviour did, by the personal contact of loving hearts. The poor felt the comforts of their bounty, bounteously bestowed ; the cheerless were gladdened by their love; and many a weak and desolate soul of whom the Judge may say at last, "It is one of the least of these my brethren," was not only succored in distress, but saved from sin as well, through their kind ministry.

There is one man in particular from that church of whom we can only speak with the most affectionate and kindling admiration of his character. He is loved and honored as a father in the chapel. The poor all know him as their friend. He goes from house to house and from child to child with every want upon his heart and every name upon his lip. He is as loving and gentle as a mother, and as wise and prudent in advice and thoughtful of the interests of all as any man should be who is called to administer counsel to twelve hundred clients. As a simple matter of fact, this Christian layman has been a co-pastor of the church. He has never borne the title, but he has done a vast amount of visiting and ministering, and waiting and sympathizing, such as few ministers ever do, and in those favored years not long ago, when business did not press too heavily upon his time, accomplished quite as much as any pastor does. And all from love for souls. He is perfectly simple. No such thing as affectation or display appears in anything he does. He seldom "speaks" in meeting, but when he prays, prays with such fervor and humility, that every waiting heart goes out with his to worship at the throne.

And still another, with equal zeal and extraordinary powers of endurance, in spite of multitudinous engagements and engrossing cares such as throng upon the path of every business man in this metropolis, and in the very face of obstacles which ordinary Christians plead at times as reasons for neglect of public duty, consecrated every Sabbath-day, and at least two evenings every week, to the cause of Christian service here. Scarcely a Sabbath-day for seventeen years has seen him absent from his post. The prayer-meetings held each Wednesday and Friday evening through the year witnessed his constant devotion and indefatigable zeal. Few laymen ever spent more thought and care, or sacrificed themselves more cheerfully for the promotion of the cause of Christ in any field. And it is hardly possible to overestimate the indebtedness of this particular enterprise to the benevolence and fidelity of this one man. Almost from its very inception it has felt the beneficent influence of his life.

Nor have these Christian workers stood alone to represent the parent church. Others engaged in different and most important branches of the work with equal devotion and faithfulness. Many others made equally noble and generous sacrifices, possibly even greater. "Every man shall have praise of God." And it cannot escape our notice here that the same philanthropic and Christian spirit of love pervaded all the efforts in this field from the very first. Personal comfort, time, and money, were freely given up by those whose highest inspiration is the cross.

He would be a strange servant of Christ who could assume the care of souls under such auspices as these, and not find his zeal enkindled by the very atmosphere in which he stood. But Charles Payson brought to this field a heart already enkindled by divine grace, and already aglow with love for souls. He brought an enthusiastic nature, warmed and inspired by grateful memories of a Christian home, a Christian ancestry, and Christian training through all his life; and he needed nothing more to draw him into instant sympathy with all these earnest workers for the Lord.

During the summer of 1860, the same year in which Mr. Payson assumed the care of the mission, it became evident that the accommodations furnished by the chapel were insufficient for the growing demands of the work; and accordingly additions were made to the chapel building, consisting of an extension of the main edifice some twenty-five feet in the rear, together with two wings, the one fronting on Thirty-first street, forty by twenty feet, the other, on the opposite side of the chapel, twenty by twenty feet, each two stories high. These furnished rooms for the infant-class on Sunday, and for social prayer-meetings during the week, as well as for a large and well-arranged Sunday-school library.

The religious life of the new organization received a great impulse at this time; and during the following year between forty and fifty united with the church, most of them on confession of their faith. The Sunday-school rapidly increased in numbers and interest, and during the winter of 1860–61, the average attendance at the morning session was six hundred and fifty, as many as seven hundred and fifty frequently being present. The prayer-meetings also grew very fast, till the room used for this purpose was crowded with from one hundred to one hundred and fifty; and without any excitement the work of grace continued through the year. Several were added to the church upon confession of their faith at every communion season; and this peculiarity of the work, marking the very commencement of Mr. Payson's ministry, characterized it to the end.* It is a noteworthy fact that, throughout the sixteen years in which he labored with this people, there was not a single month in which some case of hopeful conversion did not occur. The spirit of revival was constant in the church, and a deep tone of active piety pervaded all its services.

This may be well illustrated by the following request, which is only one of many, presented to the pastor at one of the weekly meetings by a lady member of his church:

> "Oh, to be nothing, nothing,
> Only to lie at His feet,
> A broken and emptied vessel,
> For the Master's use made meet:
> Emptied, that he might fill me,
> As forth to his service I go;
> Broken, that so, unhindered,
> His life through me might flow."

MY DEAR FRIEND AND PASTOR: I most deeply feel that I need your prayers and the prayers of our brethren and sisters in Christ. I want to be what the lines above express—nothing, nothing, that I may see the glory of Christ in the conversion of precious souls to whom I stand very nearly related. I have long prayed in secret for a heart single to God's glory, but something in me seems to hinder the possession of the full blessing I crave. Perhaps I should not so present myself for prayer

---

* The only exception (in September, 1870) was caused by a misunderstanding on the part of applicants for admission as to the time for meeting the Session.

when so many unconverted souls demand our earnest intercession ; bu¹ I
feel deeply burdened in spirit. I hope that you are better again, and that
you may be thoroughly furnished to every good work.

Most truly your friend.

Mr. Payson very often received letters of this character. His life was so devoted to the highest good of those
he served, and was so genuine a life of prayer, that no
one could remain long under its influence without ac-
knowledging the power of holiness to kindle holiness,
and of a pure, self-sacrificing love for Christ to awaken
longings after just such love in other hearts. He possessed in a marked degree the graces of self-sacrifice,
humility, and simple faith in God; and these, above all
other gifts with which he was endowed, contributed to
his success. They led him on to labor for the poor and
destitute, the outcasts of society, the lepers of to-day,
the desolate and heart-broken and hopeless men and
women of the great metropolis, with a zeal and self-devotion which have borne their golden fruit in hundreds
upon hundreds of emancipated souls, the full measure of
whose blessedness will not be known until the harvest
home. It was the predicted glory of our Lord's public
ministry, to which He himself more than once alluded,
that he was "anointed to preach the gospel to the poor,"
and that the "poor had the gospel preached unto them ;"
and it was the joy of Mr. Payson's life that he was privileged in just this way to follow Christ.

It is not generally known that during his long and
patient ministry to this people of the eastern district of
New York, Mr. Payson received urgent invitations to
leave his field and become the pastor of other churches,

in any one of which, as the world judges, he would have
occupied a far more eligible position, and wielded a much
more coveted influence. These invitations were never
sought in any way ; and yet, through all his ministry,*
they were repeatedly presented to him by large and flourishing churches in Toronto, in Montreal, in Bridgeport,
and in other towns and cities of the Middle and Eastern
states, as well as in New York itself, in the vain attempt
to change his purpose and win him from his chosen
field. He invariably preferred to stay "where," as he
often said, "the Lord hath called and blessed him in his
work." But he never dismissed any one of these calls†
hastily or carelessly, invariably seeking rather by earnest
prayer—as he did indeed concerning every event of his
life—to know what the Divine will might be.

It was the opinion of one of the leading clergymen
of New York that "in every respect Charles Payson humbled himself to this work." But with that rare sympathy
which springs from unaffected love for men, for all men,
even for the worst, because of the possible good which
may be wrought in them, he stooped to the very lowest
whom he met, so generously that no one ever thought
him condescending, and so entirely, with all the wealth
of his overflowing heart and vigorous mind and prayerful life, that more than a thousand men and women still
bear the impress of his character as members of the
church of Christ on earth, and as we hope, of that great

* The last call, of the most flattering and honorable nature, was presented in 1876.

† The invitations were sometimes presented with, and sometimes
without, the formality of a regular call.

household in the skies of which the Saviour says, "These are my own." Indeed it has been truly remarked that " Mr. Payson never knew any distinctions between men." His love was catholic. His life was like his Lord's in this, that both the rich and poor, the great and the ignoble, the educated and the ignorant, alike found sympathy in him, and learned that when he gave himself to men he gave himself without reserve.

The brief sketch of his labors to which we shall soon turn, confirms the testimony which another city pastor, his associate in the parent church, bears to his self-sacrificing love for his people. "Our brother," he said, while speaking to the large and tearful assembly which thronged the church at Mr. Payson's funeral, "had a spirit of brave, grand, simple, honorable consecration to his Master. . . . But it seems to me that his life was more than consecrated. He had the rare gift of putting himself completely in another's place, and of throwing himself without reserve into everything he did! Whatever the work, he gave to it his best energy and thought. With him there were no distinctions between what we call little and great. . . . Duty was alike important in any case. . . . He would not spare himself. What was said of Christ might be said in a large measure of him : '*He saved others, himself he cannot save;*' and so truly did his heart go out towards the real good and happiness of his flock, that this deeply-bereaved people can say '*We love him, because he first loved us !*'"*

* From a partial report of the address of Rev. J. W. Tucker, D. D., by a lady friend.

In the same strain of thought and feeling, the Rev.
E. F. Burr, D. D.,* whose reputation as a scholar and
brilliant writer has made him so widely known, writes,
under date of February 12, 1877, to Mrs. Payson :

From the outset of my acquaintance with Mr. Payson I conceived
the highest opinion of him, both as a man and as a Christian minister.
The sermons from him to which I have listened were such as to make me
wonder that the great audiences to which he preached were not still
greater.   While admirably suited to his own congregation, they were quite
as well suited, as to all the elements of effective speech, to the most
scholarly and critical assembly in the land.   If New York has in her pul-
pits any man more gifted with comprehensive faculty and robust eloquence
than Charles Payson, she is greatly to be congratulated.

But to me the crowning thing in the man was the splendid devotion
with which he gave himself to a work usually not much coveted among
men of his large ability.   The Master, who himself so pitied the sheep
which had no shepherd, knows how to appreciate a spirit so like his,
own. . . .

And here it may be proper to mention a fact which
will perhaps place in a still clearer light the "splendid
devotion" to which Dr. Burr refers.   In the "*Minutes
of the General Assembly of the Presbyterian Church in the
United States*," the form under which church work is reported rendered it impossible, in the peculiar position
Mr. Payson occupied, that any separate record of his
work should appear.   Thus to one unacquainted with
the facts he would seem to be there represented as little
better than an idler in the Lord's vineyard.   During the
sixteen years in which he toiled so faithfully and with
such blessed effect as one of her pastors, these records
tell almost nothing about his work.   Sixteen empty col-

* Author of "*Pater Mundi*," "*Ecce Cœlum*," "*Ad Clerum*," "*Ad
Fidem*," "*Work in the Vineyard*," etc., etc.

umns follow his name in these official pages year after year, and the same silence is observed in the case of his devoted fellow-laborers in the field of New York City Missions.* Take, *c. g.*, the record for the year 1873, given on the next page, and it is substantially the same for every other year from 1860 to 1877.

During the past two years the forms have been so changed that the *contributions* of the Memorial Chapel stand opposite the name of its pastor; but from first to last no records of the numbers admitted to the church, of the children connected with the Sunday-school, or of any other proofs of its Christian life and growth are associated with his name. This strange anomaly is perhaps the result, in part at least, of our present system of Presbyterian church mission work as carried on in New York. In some cases it may well be questioned whether the effect of this system has not been to repress and keep in the background rather than to develop those free, self-supporting virtues which are the strength and beauty of any church. And it is to be feared that under this system the mission chapel, its pastor, and its labors may be to the eye of the church at large almost wholly absorbed and lost sight of in the parent body.†

But without discussing the point, it is enough to say here that Mr. Payson himself was not unconscious of the false position in which he, together with his fellow-laborers in the same field, was placed anew every year by the

* See Appendix, Note A.
† Compare upon this whole subject the very interesting and important papers furnished by the Rev. Drs. Hastings and Tucker of this city, and published in the Appendix, Note A.

8

EXTRACTS FROM MINUTES OF GENERAL ASSEMBLY FOR 1873.

MINISTERS AND LICENTIATES.	CHURCHES.	Added on Examination.	Added on Certificate.	Whole Number.	Adults Baptized.	Infants Baptized.	S. S. Membership.	Home Missions.	Foreign Missions.	Education.	Publication.	Church Erection.	Relief Fund.	Freedmen.	General Assembly.	Minister's Salary.	Sustentation.	Congregational and Miscellaneous.
	P.*	75	45	1,440	5	67	1,100	18,877	10,840	857	1,728	4,558	908	335	161	14	8,000	---	12,101
	P.	19	23	796	2	18	603	803	266	200	440	300	113	169	28.44	5.000	109	5.146
	P.	5.7		350	2.5		650	212	122	37	53	10	30	30	2.37	2,500	10	1,300
Charles II. Payson,	S. S.* Mad. Sq. Mission.	57	43	1,052	1	15	1,285	1,825	775	250	128	272	229	274	47.39	8,000	276	20,682
	P.	8		344		5	410	3,927	3,251	54½	321		524	631	66.35	5.000	500	17.551
	P.	23	8	450	4	74	320	12	8.10		5	10	8		4.74	1,000	7	1,730

* P stands for Pastor; S. S. for Stated Supply. P when affixed to the name of a church, signifies that it has a pastor. The names of Pastors and Churches are purposely left blank, as being unnecessary; but it will be noticed that strong and weak churches are alike represented in the Minutes. Only the Missions are left without a record.

Minutes of the General Assembly. He would have preferred not to be designated, or to see his brethren designated there as " *S. S.*," when to all intents and purposes
he and they were true Christian pastors, wedded to their
flock by the tenderest and holiest ties. It was a wrong
which he thought should be righted, a wrong which he
did not hesitate, on suitable occasion, to protest against.
But still he laid no inordinate stress upon this matter,
knowing full well that the only record worthy of much
solicitude is that kept by the Master himself.

The extract from the Minutes of the General Assembly, given on the opposite page, is in no way exceptional.
The same contrast might be shown in other years as well,
and, with the exceptions above noted, it exists in every
year of his ministry from 1860 to 1877. This, however,
may serve to illustrate the facts.

In this connection the contemporary record of a judicious and competent critic, Rev. Lyman Abbott, D. D.,
will be found both pertinent and interesting. In 1872, Dr.
Abbott wrote a series of letters for " The Advance," upon
" Popular Preachers of New York," of which the following is that devoted to Mr. Payson.

Of all the thousands who daily pass up and down Third avenue in
the neighborhood of Thirtieth street, there are probably very few who
know that they are passing a church which every Sunday contains one of
the largest Protestant congregations in the city. And if the reader, stopping at one of our fashionable hotels, or entering into the more select circles of our polite and refined society, were to inquire for the names of the
most popular preachers in the city, it is certain that Rev. Charles H. Payson would not be described as one of them. Nay, if he were to ask for
Mr. Payson's church, it is doubtful whether he could learn where it is situated. In fact it is not a church, but only a branch of a church. It is a

"mission" established by the Madison Square Presbyterian Church, (Dr. William Adams',) which defrays its expenses, provides its pastor, administers in the last resort its government, furnishes the Sabbath-school with many of its teachers, and to which those who are converted through its instrumentality become united when they make a profession of religion. Indeed, Dr. Adams' church has for several years received larger accessions of members through the instrumentality of its mission than directly through its own services. In a sense it may be said that Mr. Payson is the colleague and copastor with Dr. Adams, though they work in entirely different fields, and minister to entirely different congregations.

Mr. Payson's church is built, to use Mr. Beecher's expressive, though inelegant phrase, in "the belly of a lot." Its unpretentious front is hardly to be discriminated from the block of stores in the midst of which it stands.

Entering and ascending a flight of stairs to the second floor, the visitor finds himself in a large hall capable of seating 1,000 or 1,200 people, and perhaps more. It is perfectly plain. The pews are movable settees. At your right as you enter is a large box labelled "Building Fund," for this congregation have become incited with the laudable ambition to become independent and self-supporting, and secure a church home which they can truly call their own. It is slow work, for it takes many pennies to build a city church, but the work goes bravely on. At the farther end of the hall is a low, broad platform, with a simple reading-desk in front. On one side stands a grand piano, a substitute for an organ. Experience shows that it serves a better purpose as a leader alike for church and Sunday-school; and there is no choir. None, did I say? Rather, every hymn is sung by a choir of a thousand voices, a choir which compensates for some discords in music by the grand harmony of feeling which animates it.

It is half-past seven. The hour of service has arrived. The congregation are in their seats. They are prompter than some of their fashionable neighbors. There are no empty pews, and but few empty seats. There are not many Protestant ministers who address larger Sabbath evening congregations than Mr. Payson. It is a congregation composed for the most part of those whose meagre incomes, varying from $600 to $1,500 a year, debar them from churches whose pew-rents are from $50 to $300.

The preacher rises in his place. Without being handsome, he strikes one as being a fine-looking man. He is, perhaps, a little above the medium height, with dark hair, keen and at times piercing eyes, and a nervous, but self-possessed action. He throws into his reading of Scripture a dramatic fire which fixes the attention of his audience, many of whom follow him with open Bible in their hands. His prayer is simple, earnest, but not oratorical, and is the utterance of one who knows the wants of the people whose petitions he conducts to the throne of grace. He joins in the singing, being precentor as well as preacher. He announces his text. If his sermon is written, it is only before him as a reminder. He refers from time to time to his notes ; but as his discourse proceeds, warms with his subject, leaves the desk, addresses his audience now from this, now from that side of the platform, throws aside the tone and manner of a minister, and appears more like a platform speaker than like a pulpit orator. He abounds in illustrations. His sermon does not lack continuity, but its power consists in the spiritual warmth which characterizes it. His action is sometimes perhaps too fervid, and his tones too intense for our taste, yet he rarely breaks the bond of sympathy which unites him to his congregation.

The sermon over and the benediction pronounced, you rise decorously to go forward and introduce yourself to the preacher. But he is not there. With a celerity that is somewhat astonishing he has rushed down the aisle and is standing at the main entrance submitting to the American handshaking with his congregation—blacksmith, glazier, milkman, butcher, and their wives and children, with a kind word of personal inquiry to old friends and with a cheery welcome to strangers. Though we account Mr. Payson among the popular preachers of New York, it is perhaps this personal and unaffected interest in his people which, more than his preaching, is the secret of his popularity; and we place his name here because he is a type of a class of preachers unknown to fame on earth, though not unknown above, who are consecrating their lives to the fulfilment of Christ's mission in laboring that the poor may have the gospel preached unto them.

The tables upon the following page, prepared from the official records of the Madison Square Chapel, exhibit some of the fruits of his ministry. The figures, it will be seen, are not altogether complete, especially in connection with the Sunday-school, but they are sufficiently so to furnish a brief and summary description of his labors; and the attention of the reader is the more particularly invited to them, because, as has been said, this is the first and only tabulated statement of his work ever published. The pastor of the German branch, it should be noted, was the Rev. Martin A. Erdmann.

CHURCH MEMBERSHIP OF MADISON SQUARE CHAPEL.

	May 1, 1859	1860	1861	1862	1863	1864	1865	1866	1867	1868	1869	1870	1871	1872	1873	1874	1875	1876	1877	TOTAL.
Whole number from the first ----	21	39	84	121	160	195	251	297	333	387	444	535	615	696	771	851	916	986	1051	1051
Whole number added during year	18	45	37	39	52	46	36	57	91	80	81	75	80	65	70	65	70	65		1030
No. added on certificate ----	18	10	30	27	30	33	33	43	62	60	62	65	52	54	56	54	54			796
" " confession of faith	3	8	7	12	19	13	4	17	14	20	19	10	11	11	14	11	11			234
" " to the English branch	13	45	37	39	39	52	46	36	54	51	60	59	50	46	64	55	55			878
" " German "	1	2	8	3	6	14	13	20	29	39	6	31	31	8	19	6	10			152
Whole number dismissed ----	3				13		20	21	21	23	27	37	43	92	114	126	136	156	156	156
" " that died ----		1		2	6	14	9	21	21	23	27	43	45	56	62	71	78	91	91	91
" " left on the roll	21	38	82	112	148	184	224	256	281	321	364	437	493	559	617	670	719	772	804	804

CONTRIBUTIONS FROM MADISON SQUARE CHAPEL.

	1860	1861	1862	1863	1864	1865	1866	1867	1868	1869	1870	1871	1872	1873	1874	1875	1876
Missionary objects ----	$79	$144	$218	$216	$204	$411	$395	$305	$400	$463	$233	$308	$733	$308	$340		
Sunday-school pennies --			70	110	152	233	272	208	341	531	473	283	302	334			
Special purposes ----		206	63	275	508	250	741	92	458	856	130	490	120				
Miscellaneous ----			280	110	300	282	1973	2000	2497	129	3181	3255	286	2950	59361	3924	
Congregational ----																	
Total ----	$79	144	494	669	1041	1434	2890	3254	3450	4638	4822	3450*	4115	695651	4726		

SUNDAY-SCHOOL RECORD.*

	1871	1872	1873	1874	1875	1876	1877
Largest attendance ----	1236	1221	1228	1211	1107	1031	1150
Average attendance ----	507	526	537	544	699	438	495
Dismissed† ----	382	356	342	353	399	214	271
Died ----	3	5	9	5	9	7	5
Added ----	443	370	362	334	254	332	340
Joined the church‡ ----	14	11	14	5	10	38	22
Whole number of teachers	70	62	71	56	54	54	69

* The records of the Sunday-school previous to 1871 were not kept with sufficient accuracy to warrant their publication here.

† Those were dismissed who were found attending any other Sunday-school.

‡ The whole number admitted to the church from the Sunday-school from 1859 to 1877 inclusive was 220.

CHAPTER IV.

METHODS AND MEANS.

In his annual report of the chapel work for 1876, Mr. Payson says, " There are from twenty to twenty-five services of various kinds held every week in connection with the chapel, an average of ten each Sabbath and two to three each week day. Together with the Sabbath-school teachers, over one hundred are employed in one way or another each week. This does not include the forty volunteers who have canvassed the neighborhood of the chapel, inviting all non-churchgoers to God's house, nor the various works of love and mercy performed by individual members of the church on their own responsibility.... You will be interested to know that some gathered from off the street fifteen or eighteen years ago are to-day among our best Christian helpers. One occurs to me now who every Sabbath, rain or shine, takes a journey of two miles to bring an impenitent friend and his wife to church. She has done this for two years, and still prays and hopes for their conversion. This is but one illustration of her untiring zeal for Christ..... Most of our enlarged space is already occupied. Four Bible-classes occupy the upper story of the building, at the same time that the two lower stories are occupied by the infant-class and Sabbath-school proper."

The methods and means which Mr. Payson chose to

enlist the members of his church in active work were such as long experience proved to be best adapted for his field. It was an invariable rule with him to give every Christian some work to do for the Master. If one had a talent for singing, he was placed in the singing-class which met each Tuesday in the year. If another showed promise for usefulness as a teacher in the Sabbath-school, or a leader of the Young People's Meetings, or a visitor among the sick, he was employed, if possible, in one or another of those fields. The Temperance Association, the Society of Christian Workers, the Committees on Strangers, Invitation, Family Prayer-Meetings, Employment, and the Sick, and other such agencies, enrolled a very large number of the members of the church, and furnished fields of Christian activity for almost every one.

In illustration of the efforts Mr. Payson made in this direction, the organization effected in 1867–8 may be mentioned, only as an illustration, however. Work did not begin nor end with this. It was continued by means analogous to those then employed from the very commencement of his pastorate to its end. But this will serve to illustrate.

In the year 1867–8, under the efficient leadership of Mr. S. Tyler Williams, the "*Society of Christian Workers*" was organized by Mr. Payson for the purpose of securing effective coöperation in Christian work. It was composed of five committees: "The Employment Committee," "The Good Samaritans," "The Committee on Strangers," "The Family Prayer-Meeting Committee," and "The Committee on Invitation." A "*Pastor's Circular*" was distributed through the congregation, in which, after quoting the words of the apostle in Romans 12 : 5–8, he says :

In accordance with these God-given principles, there is work for *every member* of our church. May your pastor ask your *earnest, prayerful attention* to the following questions ? They may suggest your work. All responses are confidential, to aid him in classifying his helpers.

Name, ---

Address, ---

DEVOTIONAL.

Will you daily remember your church and pastor, by using our printed Prayer Register ?*

Will you select one or more unconverted persons and daily pray for them till they are brought to Christ?

Will you endeavor regularly to attend any of the following services ? If so, indicate it by an X opposite such meetings. If willing to take part, make two XXs.

CHURCH SERVICES, morning and evening?

SABBATH-SCHOOL, or ADULT BIBLE-CLASS?

YOUNG PEOPLE'S PRAYER-MEETING, Sabbath evening, 7 o'clock ?

CHURCH PRAYER-MEETING on Wednesday evening?

SABBATH-SCHOOL PRAYER-MEETING on Friday evening?

Any FAMILY PRAYER-MEETING (they are held on Monday, Tuesday, and Thursday evenings)?

FEMALE PRAYER-MEETING, Friday afternoon at 2½ o'clock.

GOOD SAMARITAN WORK.

Will you sit up with the sick, if called upon, one night each month ?

Will you visit the sick ? If so, what day ?

VISITING DEPARTMENT.

Can you take a district, and see that all its families are invited to church services?

Will you try to bring children to our Sabbath-school ?

* See page 98.

STRANGERS' DEPARTMENT.

Will you, at our various religious and social gatherings, welcome strangers, and endeavor to make them feel at home?

— —— • ———

☞ No one of course is expected to work in *all* these departments; if you have any preference, please indicate it on this line.

- - --

When you have filled out these Circulars, please keep one and return the other, through the boxes, to the pastor,

CHARLES II. PAYSON.

The *Committee on Strangers* was appointed, as the Circular indicated, "to welcome strangers at all religious and social gatherings and to make them feel at home." This committee was greatly assisted in its work by the fact that the chapel seats were free.

The *Committee on Employment*, at the close of the first year, reported twenty or thirty individuals for whom work had been secured.

The *Good Samaritan Committee* was appointed to provide watchers for the sick. It was composed entirely of volunteers from the chapel, who engaged to take their turn in sitting up at night with those who might be ill and unable to provide suitable nurses for themselves in any other way. More than twenty persons volunteered at once to undertake this most exhausting and self-sacrificing work; and during the first year of its organization more than one hundred nights were spent by the faithful members of this noble band beside the sick-beds of the poor and destitute. Each member of this committee held himself or herself responsible for at least one night in every month, and most of them, it must be added, were poor, hard-working women. Nor is this work a transient one. Nine years have passed away since the organization of this committee, and yet we are told that eighteen out of the twenty or thirty still remain, who can be called upon at any time to "watch" and nurse the sick. There is no other organization, perhaps, connected with the chapel that can more effectually perpetuate the memory of its self-denying pastor than the "Good Samaritan Committee;" and there certainly is none other whose work lies more directly in the line of the Master's eternal reward and exalted praise, when at the last He shall say, "Come, ye blessed of my Father, inherit the kingdom prepared for you from the foundation of the world."

Thirty or more in the same year united with the *Committee on Family Prayer-Meetings*, and proved both faithful and efficient laborers in this field. These meetings were a peculiar feature of the work and deserve especial notice. They were established by Mr. Payson in various districts among his congregation, and were held in private houses, where from six to thirty individuals would assemble for prayer and conference on such evenings as were not occupied by services in the church. The average attendance was ten, and, in some years at least, one hundred and fifty persons were thus actively employed in what has proved to be one of the most effective and fruitful agencies connected with the church. In the year 1866, *c. g.*, fifteen such meetings were held in various localities on four different evenings of the

week, eight of which were conducted by gentlemen and
seven by ladies, some having been appointed exclusively
for ladies. Mr. Payson during many years was most effi-
ciently aided in the oversight of these services by members of the Young People's Association of the Madison
Square Church, and the responsibility for them at all
times necessarily devolved upon others than himself.
But from 1861, when first established here,* these "Family Prayer-Meetings," or, as they were sometimes called,
"Neigborhood Prayer-Meetings," were among his favorite means of reaching the masses and employing the
workers of his church.

The work of the *Committee on Invitation* is also worthy of special remark. The vicinity of the chapel was
thoroughly districted, and all families not attending
church were invited to do so. A large number of the
chapel people, who had not previously found any field in
which to labor, were thus successfully engaged in Christian work. In the winter of 1869–70, 1,446 visits were
made, 153 adults induced to attend church, and 65 children gathered into the Sabbath-school. In 1870–71, for
the first and last time in the history of Mr. Payson's pastorate, there were no accessions to the church at one of
the regular communion seasons.† This roused the
members to new activity. District visitation was pushed
with vigor. Prayer was offered without ceasing unto
God, and in January, 1871, the largest number (29)

---

* See the letter on p. 27.

† The sacrament of the Lord's Supper, at which applicants were admitted to the church, was celebrated every second month throughout the
year.

ever received at one communion were admitted to the church. One man is reported to have visited regularly seventy of the chapel families, making for himself a little parish within a parish.

In 1860 a *Young People's Prayer-Meeting* was established, which has been continued ever since. The *Female Prayer-Meeting*, begun in 1864, has been faithfully sustained.

In 1869 the *German Congregation* was organized. Mr. Payson's visit to Germany had been by no means thrown away. It served to bring him into active sympathy with a large and most interesting part of our city's population ; and the facility in the use of the German language which he there acquired enabled him to wield an unusual influence over the Germans in his vicinity. For the sake of retaining their children in the Sabbath-school, it was found desirable to organize a separate service for the adults, and for this purpose to secure the assistance of a German pastor who should preach to the people in their own language. This arrangement was consummated in 1869, and the Rev. Martin A. Erdmann was invited to take the pastorate. Since that time he has worked most faithfully, except when failing health rendered it impossible, and the German branch under his efficient ministry has steadily grown in strength and numbers, as will be seen by reference to the tables on p. 90, until now, in 1877, there are 132 members.

A very effectual means of creating an *esprit du corps* among the members of the chapel, and at the same time promoting the spiritual interests of the church, was the

Prayer Register, introduced early in 1865. It was Mr. Payson's own device, and illustrates perfectly the love he bore for every member of his church, and the strong desire which he felt that all should be united in the firmest bonds of Christian sympathy. It originated in his own practice of praying individually for each member of his church at home, and has been productive of great good, not only among the members of his congregation, but elsewhere as Christian people have adopted it. The following extract from the Register in use during 1872-4 will serve to illustrate its form. The cover and first two or three pages are here transcribed, and it will be noticed that, after the pastors, elders, and chapel committee, each member of the church is assigned a day in which to be remembered in the prayers of the people at home. It may be added, that after the names of church members, were appended those of other Christians "*worshipping with us,*" and of the "*children of the church.*"

PRAYER REGISTER
OF THE THIRD AVENUE BRANCH
OF THE
Madison Square Presbyterian Church.
1872, '73, '74.

Without ceasing I make mention of you always in my prayers. Rom. 1 : 9.

God forbid that I should sin against the Lord in ceasing to pray for you. I Sam. 12 : 23.

Again I say unto you, That if two of you shall agree on earth as touching anything that they shall ask, it shall be done for them of my Father which is in heaven. Matt. 18 : 19.

DIRECTIONS FOR USE.

I. Fasten this Register in your Bible, so that you will see it every time you read and pray.

II. On Sabbath-days pray for the church as a whole.

III. On week-days pray for the person or persons whose names stand opposite the day of the month, with the exceptions mentioned in the next direction.

IV. The exceptions are the dates against which stand the names of deceased members in *italics*. On these days render thanks to God for their victory.

V. Besides the subjects above mentioned, carefully remember the special topics for each day of the week, given on the next two pages.

TOPICS FOR EACH WEEK.

MONDAY.

For our rulers, national and state, and all in authority and places of influence.

TUESDAY.

For a blessing on the missionary labors of Miss Payson, in China, Mr. Easterday, in Michigan; and on the missions in Zulu-land and Syria, towards which we contribute. Also on our own efforts and gifts, and on missions in general at home and abroad.

WEDNESDAY.

For the children of our church and Sabbath school, that God will bless parents and teachers in their efforts to bring them speedily to know and fear the Lord. The same blessing for the children of our whole land.

THURSDAY.

For a blessing upon Rev. Mr. Erdmann's labors among the Germans, and that God will raise up a truly evangelical ministry for our whole German population.

FRIDAY.

For our church—for the sanctification of its whole membership, for God's direction of our future, for the parent branch, and for Christians of every name and place.

SATURDAY.

For the reformation of the intemperate, and a blessing on all efforts to promote the cause of Temperance in this city and throughout our land.

SUNDAY.

For a blessing upon our pastor and his ministry, and on the preaching of the gospel and the reading and study of the Bible everywhere.

DATE—1872.   NAMES.
Monday, January 1 ------------------ William Adams, D. D.
Tuesday, January 2 ----------------- Charles H. Payson.
Wednesday, January 3 --------------- Martin A. Erdmann.

ELDERS OF THE CHURCH.

Thursday, January 4 ---------------- { Robert M. Hartley.
Tredwell Ketchem.
Oliver E. Wood.
Ezra M. Kingsley.
George W. Lane.
John F. Trow.
Charles Collins.
William E. Dodge, Jr.
David Wetmore.

CHAPEL COMMITTEE.

Friday, January 5 ------------------ { Theodore Roosevelt.
D. S. Egleston.
George W. Lane.
William E. Dodge, Jr.
David Wetmore.
Joseph Gillet.
S. W. Coe.
Z. S. Ely.
Thatcher M. Adams.
William C. Martin.
S. T. Williams.

Saturday, January 6 ---------------- James Goodliff.
Monday, January 8 ----------------- (*Henry G. W. Cannon.*)
Tuesday, January 9 ----------------- Mary Cannon.
Wednesday, January 10. ------------ Mary M. Belger.
Thursday, January 11 --------------- (*George K. Butterfield.*)

In the Prayer Register for 1875, for the sake of con-
densation, since the membership had now become so
large, instead of appointing a separate day for each individual, a single day for an entire family was used.

Mr. Payson was also very deeply interested in the subject of Temperance, as in every other practical subject which Christian workers meet. He began at first to favor moderation as opposed to total abstinence, but before many years was convinced that the only effective way to save intemperate men was to practise and to preach Total Abstinence. All efforts for reform in this direction, however, he believed would prove in vain unless controlled and inspired by Christian faith ; and the Temperance movement in his congregation assumed from the first the form of a church movement. In 1870 the *"Church Temperance Society"* was organized, and the following Circular, accompanied by a Pledge, was sent to every member.

YE are the salt of the earth :.... ye are the light of the world. MATT. 5 : 13, 14.

If meat make my brother to offend, I will eat no flesh while the world standeth, lest I make my brother to offend. 1 COR. 8 : 13.

"Before God and man, before the church and the world, I impeach intemperance. I charge it with the murder of innumerable souls. In this country, blessed with freedom and plenty, the word of God and the liberties of true religion, I charge it as the cause—whatever be the source elsewhere—of almost all the poverty, and almost all the crime, and almost all the ignorance, and almost all the irreligion that disgrace and afflict the land. 'I am not mad, most noble Festus. I speak the words of truth and soberness.' I do, in my conscience, believe that these intoxicating stimulants have sunk into wretchedness more men and women than found a grave in that deluge which swept over the highest hilltops, engulfing a world of which but eight were saved." REV. THOMAS GUTHRIE.

Under the leadership of Rev. Mr. Payson, a Temperance Society, on the Total Abstinence basis, has been organized in connection with the church to which you belong, and is called the CHURCH TEMPERANCE SOCIETY. All are cordially welcomed into its membership ; but it was specially designed to enlist church-members, of whom more than two hun-

dred have already enrolled themselves. You, as a CHURCH-MEM-
BER, are earnestly invited to connect yourself with the Society, and to
engage heartily in the promotion of its objects. If you are prepared to
take this step, please sign and return this Pledge without delay, in the
envelop herewith enclosed. If you are in doubt as to duty, will you not
seriously consider the matter and decide it now? Whether, on reflection,
you sign the Pledge or not, be kind enough to return it, in order that there
may be no doubt as to your having received it. The figures in red ink will
indicate whence it comes, though it may not bear your signature. Members are not subjected to taxes of any kind.

S. T. WILLIAMS,

SECRETARY.

The results of this movement have not been fully
reported. Up to August 12, 1874, when the society
numbered *one thousand and seventy-two members*, it had
had a constant growth, and we doubt not is as efficient
and useful to-day as ever. The amount of good accomplished by such an organization is of course incalculable.
One illustration may be given.

"When I first united with the church," writes one of its members, "I
was in the liquor business, and thought it all right. I saw other people
drinking, and reasoned with myself that some one must sell them liquor
if they would drink, until one Sabbath morning our pastor spoke to me
about the Temperance Pledge, and told me to pray over it and see if the
Lord would have me sign it. I prayed over it and saw no way to get out
of it. I was convinced that I should sign it, and did, and have kept it,
and shall, by God's help, till I die. Mr. Payson took great interest in me
and helped me greatly, not so much in pointing out the evils of intemperance, as by showing me the power in prayer and that Jesus cared for me,
to keep me and help me at all times and by all means. I must say that
Satan comes many times and makes the way *so* smooth to go back to the
business, not to drink, but to sell; yet the Lord is strong, and he will keep
me to the end. Much may have been lost from a worldly point of view,
yet the Master says: 'In the present time joy, and in the world to come
life everlasting.'"

The *Woodlawn Association*, organized November,
1871, was most wisely designed by Mr. Payson to meet

very great need of his growing congregation. The number of deaths among its members was becoming larger every year, and it was found that the parent church could not always provide that aid which was sometimes necessary on occasion of burying the dead from families connected with the chapel. Accordingly, to relieve the poor and protect the rich, a church mutual life-insurance company was devised, which was governed by the following by-laws, among others :

(1.) Adults may become members by the payment of fifty cents, children twenty-five cents.

(2.) On the death of an adult member, the Association will pay $50 ; of a child, at least $25, towards the funeral expenses.

(3.) At each death an assessment will be made on each member not exceeding fifty cents for an adult, and twenty-five cents for a child.

(4.) Any member failing to pay the assessment within three weeks of notice forfeits all the privileges of the Association, and can be restored only upon payment of arrearages and by vote of the managers. . . .

(9.) No person shall become a member unless he or she is a total abstainer from intoxicating drinks. . . .

The affairs of the Association are conducted by a Board of Managers elected annually, and consisting of nine adult members, who elect from their number a president, secretary, and treasurer. They meet once a month for business. If a death occurs, they vote an assessment. They receive all propositions for membership, and decide upon them by vote. The assessments thus far have averaged a little less than three a year. At the commencement there were 197 members, of whom 39 were minors. During the first two years the Association increased rapidly in numbers, and since then has gained (net) only three or four each year. The present membership is about 260, of whom 60 are minors, so that an

assessment raises about $115. It has proved a very great
help to those in trouble. It comes with relief when this
is most needed in the families of the poor. Just when
they are in deepest want of sympathy and aid, this simple but most efficient agency provides the indispensable
assistance which they seek. It has already commended
itself for adoption in other churches in the city and vicinity, and is admirably adapted for the good designed.

Another very efficient means of doing good is the
*Employment Society,** which has continued its efforts unremittingly for seventeen years, since October, 1860,
when it was organized to furnish sewing to the needy
who cannot obtain it otherwise, and to provide substantial clothing for the poor at cost. The expenses are de-
frayed by various members of the church. The plan is
to purchase cloth, and pay the women for making it up
into garments, which are then sold very cheaply to those
whose occupation is such as forbids their making them
for themselves, and who can buy them for less money
here than elsewhere. Some wealthy and benevolent
families have frequently had their sewing done by this
society. In 1870, $700 were expended for material, and
forty women provided weekly with employment; in 1865,
$360 were laid out, and forty or fifty individuals furnished
with at least seventy-five cents' worth of work to do each
week for several months. These facts may serve to illustrate the work of the society.

* The *Employment Society* and *Industrial School* did not originate
with Mr. Payson, but were conducted and supported from the first by the
generous efforts of ladies from the Madison Square Church. This brief
description of their methods of work may be found useful in other fields.

The *Industrial School*, organized in 1857-8, and faithfully continued every Saturday in the winters for nineteen years, is justly considered one of the most practical parts of the work. Its object is to instruct the girls of the chapel Sunday-school in sewing, and, if possible, to fit them for self-support with the needle—a result which in some cases has been attained. In 1865, two hundred scholars and twenty teachers were in regular attendance, and four hundred and sixty-three garments were made by the children and given to them at a cost of $527 for material. The largest attendance has been three hundred ; but during the past three years the numbers have been considerably less, as many of the older scholars have been compelled to aid in the support of the family during the general depression in business.

For the purpose of instructing the children in the doctrines of the Bible, Mr. Payson had a *Catechetical class*, which for several years, towards the close of his life, met each week at the chapel to study the Westminster Shorter Catechism. His remarkable power of adapting himself to children, which rendered his monthly addresses to the Sabbath-school most entertaining and instructive, enabled him also to deeply interest even the youngest of this class in the dry technicalities of that admirable formula of faith. A large number of expectant children were sure to be found awaiting him at the appointed hour on Thursday afternoon ; and though the record of the other years is not complete, we may accept the statement of his journal, that in 1873--4 " there was an average attendance of eighty out of a total membership of one hundred and twenty," as affording a glimpse of the amount of work accomplished in this way. It was Mr. Payson's custom, at the close of the year, to present each member of this class with a potted plant or flower, or a picture, or Testament, and the attachment between the pastor and this little group in the nursery became oftentimes very strong.

The *Bible readers*, connected with the chapel almost from the first, have been very useful. Ladies can sometimes gain access to families where even the best of pastors fail, and the amount of pastoral work required in a mission field so large as this is at all times far too great for any one person to perform. Mr. Payson was ably assisted by some of the most faithful Bible readers New York has ever known; and although he made pastoral visits every afternoon* in the week, he found the assistance rendered by these judicious and excellent Christian women of very great importance in his work. They carried aid and comfort to many homes, where, owing to the multiplicity of his engagements, the pastor could not go, and at a time when just such aid perhaps was indispensable. It is a humble and a hidden work, this noble work of Christian Bible women in New York; but though it has no record here upon the books of men, the Master has recorded it above.

Besides the means and methods now enumerated, some of which deserve a more extended notice than can be given here, Mr. Payson brought into frequent use all

---

* Except Friday, when he was at the chapel to meet any who might wish to converse with him.

those innocent social influences which prove to be the handmaidens of the church, and serve to make a people at once more sympathetic and efficient. Sociables and tea-parties, fairs* and festivals, singing schools, lectures, concerts, readings, stereopticon exhibitions—everything of the kind which could instruct or edify while it amused, found cordial sympathy and active support with him. Indeed, it was on such occasions that Mr. Payson was most thoroughly at home with his people. His sympathetic nature and hearty enthusiasm for every innocent enjoyment "contagiously inspired all he met." There was the most thoughtful consideration for every one with whom he spoke—a kind word, a winning smile, or a sparkling witticism, which threw new life into every social gathering of the church.

"The poorest and the most forlorn," it has been truly said, "were as thoroughly assured of his effective sympathy as were the most virtuous, intelligent, and wealthy. No one could be too poor or too ignorant, if there was room in his heart for Christian love. . . . Though his power in the pulpit was truly winning and commanding, it was preëminently great in social intercourse with his people."

And this was perhaps nowhere more apparent than in the weekly meetings for prayer and conference. They were very informal. Every one was encouraged to speak or pray; even the ladies at times took part, by sending a written note to the pastor, although this was not frequently the case. One of the members of his church writes:

He was the life of the prayer-meetings. His prayers were wonderful. He would enter into the service with deep feeling, as though he had

---

* At which there was *no raffling.*

come straight from the throne of grace, and each heart would be warmed by his good influence. Many, indeed, have come to the meetings time and again, feeling unhappy because the burden of sin or care weighed heavily; and a few words from our dear pastor helped to lift the weight from every heart, for he always taught us the words of Christ, "Come unto me, all ye that labor and are heavy-laden, and I will give you rest." After meeting he would stand at the door and personally greet each one as they passed out ; and then would wait on those remaining to see him, and administer to them spiritual comfort such as they might need. His remarks upon the subject of the meeting were very refreshing and instructive. I believe that God always gave him the right words to utter, for his heart was continually overflowing with a feast of precious truths for his people. Oh, how many times have I left the prayer-meeting with feelings which I did not take into it—precious thoughts about the Saviour's love and mercy, and resolutions to strive more earnestly to love and honor the dear Lord. If anything he suggested to us appeared difficult to perform, he always led the way ; and in the neighborhood prayer-meetings our dear pastor would call in unexpectedly (for on some evenings as many as three were often held) to give a word of advice, comfort, or cheer. When the dreadful news of his death came to us, we felt cast down and bewildered, for we have lost one who loved our souls' welfare better than his own life.

But there was one service at the chapel which was peculiarly his own. The exercises on *Thanksgiving day* were unique. They were of the simplest possible nature, and so full of prayer and praise, that no man not a misanthrope could fail to have his heart enkindled by attending one. The pastor carried his loving Christian enthusiasm into this meeting more cordially, if possible, than into any other of the year. There was no formal sermon. Experience had shown that it was of little use. The people would not come to hear it. But they came very eagerly to such a service as this. There was a hymn of praise, a prayer of thanksgiving, the reading of a few brief written testimonials of what the Lord had done in blessing one and another, and then in rapid succession twenty or thirty individuals would rise and tell what favors Providence had given them, their families, and friends, the church, the Sunday-school class, their home, their own souls, until the spirit of praise was seeking utterance in every heart, and the entire congregation turned away reluctantly from such a feast of good things.

These meetings were always full. They were eagerly anticipated, and gratefully remembered for many a day. The fervent faith of humble souls, the glowing love of thankfulness, the sincere joy of gratitude, the tearful penitence for misspent days, unkind remarks, ungracious thoughts and ways, all found a free expression in these yearly meetings of the church, when, like a Christian family, pastor and people met to tell their joys and raise memorial stones of praise. It is impossible to gather up again and reproduce in formal words the sweetness and gladness of those bright hours. To more than one weary heart they were like a boyhood's vacation. They broke the fetters of dull routine, and opened a whole summer of rest and sunshine through the hour of simple faith and thankful recollection.

One member of the church kept a " Thanksgiving-book," in which he recorded whatever he had to be grateful for throughout the year, and on Thanksgiving day would read from this diary of his best things the answers to prayer, the unexpected blessings of Providence, and the bright, glad days which threw their sunlight on his path.

Another, last Thanksgiving, thrilled the meeting by his simple tale of want and thankfulness.

10

"One year ago," he said, "the days looked bright and fair, and I hoped for a prosperous year in my business. But these have been hard times. I have had no work to do, and I cou'd not find any to do, though I looked for it everywhere. My wife was taken sick, and then the baby was taken sick, and we thought it would die ; and I had to stay at home and walk the floor by day and night with that child in my arms, praying that the Lord would spare it, if it was his will. And he did spare it, and I believe it was in answer to my prayer. And I want to thank the Lord to-day for this great blessing. I never knew before how dear my home is to me, and how sweet and good my children are. I do n't say this to boast. I dare say I have no better things than others of us have ; but I do thank God that he has let me be at home so much this year, and given me my child again in answer to my prayer."

Those who could not "speak in meeting"—the ladies who observed the Presbyterian injunction so often attributed to St. Paul, and other members of the church whose diffidence or inexperience deterred them from taking other part—sent letters to the pastor on that day, from which he chose the most appropriate to read. The writers all were known to him, and he never failed to give the letters as he read them the life and fervor of that grateful love in which they had been penned. The meeting would be often thrilled by these brief testimonies to the good and loving providence of God.

A poor old washerwoman whose son was miserably vicious and dissolute, wrote :

I can thank God this Thanksgiving day for all his kind mercy to me during the past year. I do thank him, for he has given me health and strength and many blessings, and he has answered my prayers in so many ways. I would ask you to help me to pray for my son that he may be brought to Christ and be saved. I have faith to believe that the Lord can and will save in his own good time.

Another, whose early life was very vain and frivolous, but who had been disciplined and sobered and made use-ful in her home by severe trials, writes :

I can thank God for this Thanksgiving day, and I do praise and thank him for all the blessings he has bestowed on me and my family this past year. Although I have had trials and losses, yet the Lord has blessed me through them all, and wonderfully blessed me. The Lord's promise to his children is, "When thou passest through the waters I will be with thee, and through the rivers they shall not overflow thee; when thou walkest through the fire thou shalt not be burned, neither shall the flame kindle upon thee." Isa. 43: 2.

A very poor widow, whose long life of sixty years has been spent in constant poverty, sent the following:

Better is a little with righteousness, than great revenues without right. Better is the poor that walketh in his integrity, than he that is perverse in his lips. I thank thee, O Lord, for all thy blessings.

"My dear pastor," writes another, "help me to render thanks that I have the sweet hope that my dear husband and my six children are travelling with me to our better home. . . . . I thank God with all my heart for the many blessings received, the prayers answered, and especially that he has so increased my trust in him within the past few days."

One, whose family and herself had been converted from a Sabbath-breaking, irreligious life, says:

I cannot express in words the gratitude I feel in my heart to my Heavenly Father for his great love to me and mine. We were once walking in darkness, but I now rejoice that we are an undivided family, travelling in the narrow way that leads to everlasting light. My prayer is that we may all prove faithful, and be found among the "multitude whom no man can number" around the throne.

Still another says: I fear all the people together cannot praise him as I would like to, for our new church, our many blessings as a church, the deep religious interest in the church for which I have longed and prayed, and above all, that God has been so good as to allow me to help to bring souls into his kingdom. Pray that he will use me yet more to his honor and glory. For the kind friends he has given me, and for his help in *peculiar* trials, and—if I should go on to mention my causes for thankfulness, I should take up the whole time.

> " I travel on, not knowing,
> I would not if I might;
> 'T is better to walk in the dark with God,
> Than by myself in the light.
> 'T is better to walk with him by faith,
> Than to walk alone by sight."

Please accept the small sum enclosed in silence. I wanted to do a *little* for Him who has done *so much* for me.

The allusion in this last is to the habit of the people of contributing from their poverty toward the wants of others yet more needy than themselves, that the Lord might help them all to keep Thanksgiving day. Nothing could have been farther from their mind than that these facts and words should ever reach a public eye. They gave as unto the Lord and not as unto men, and the spirit of the whole is illustrated by the spirit of these few. But no other way seems open of clearly showing what those bright Thanksgiving days became to them. Under the inspiration of their pastor's leadership, whose life was full of thankfulness and faith, they made those hours "conjubilant with song." No other meeting seemed so near to heaven, except perhaps the glad and solemn service of communion. But here they learned the secret of that truth which Christians far too often overlook, "The joy of the Lord is your strength," and here Thanksgiving day began each year.

In illustration of the way in which the various agencies referred to were employed it may be interesting to glance at the following

SUMMARY OF ONE WEEK'S WORK, 1868.

7. SUNDAY.
1. Sunday-school Prayer-meeting.
2. Sunday-school.
3. Church Service.
4. Children's Singing Meeting.
5. Boys' and Girls' Meeting.
6. Bible Class and Monthly Teachers' Prayer-meeting.
7. Church Service.

4. MONDAY.	Four Family Prayer-meetings.*	
4. TUESDAY.	1. Young Ladies' Prayer-meeting.†	
	2. Employment Society.	
	3. Service of Song.	
	4. Church Prayer-meeting.	
4. WEDNESDAY.	1. Young Ladies' Prayer-meeting.†	
	2. Three Family Prayer-meetings.*	
2. THURSDAY.	1. Female Prayer-meeting (afternoon,.	
	2. Church Prayer-meeting (evening).	
4 FRIDAY.	1. Young Ladies' Prayer-meeting.†	
	2. Three Family Prayer-meetings.*	
1. SATURDAY.	1. Industrial School.	

26 Services.

In the next year it will be remarked the German services were added—two preaching services on Sunday, and two prayer-meetings during the week; also the Young People's Prayer-meeting Sunday evening before church, and the Catechetical Class on Thursdays, making in all six services not enumerated above.

The Rev. Wm. Hutton of Philadelphia, who during his seminary course, was for a time associated with Mr. Payson as visitor in this field, writes :

He was truly consecrated to his work—the work of preaching the gospel to the poor. Difficult, indeed, it was in many respects, but how consistently and conscientiously did he perform it! How much of physical endurance, patience, sympathy, and faith is demanded of those engaged in the self-denying work of a New York missionary pastor, none can comprehend unless familiar with the work. . . . As a preacher he was eminently practical. His preaching was adapted to his hearers. He fed his people, not upon "happy turns" of thought or expression, but upon the sincere milk of the Word. He was little exercised about "rounded periods," but very anxious about reaching souls. And God gave him goodly wages—how many souls were led by him to Jesus! His prayers were remarkable. Critics might say they were too *familiar*. A man must live very near the Master to offer such prayers. By them he led his people to regard Jesus as a very dear and sympathizing friend—just what He is. At

* The number of family prayer-meetings varied from year to year.
† Three different services of this kind were held each week.

0

the last interview had in New York during the progress of the Moody and Sankey meetings, he was rejoicing in the return to home, to temperance, and to God of certain ones for whom he had been specially laboring.

The following reminiscences by an intimate friend may also be interesting in this connection, as serving to illustrate the truthful remark of the preceding writer that he was little exercised about "rounded periods," but very anxious about reaching souls.

Mr. Payson had, I think, an excellent command of language and a lively imagination, so that, if he had been greatly ambitious to obtain celebrity as a writer, or had made it his chief aim in life to secure literary renown, he might have attained considerable eminence in " the world of letters." But desire for the applause of men was very far from being uppermost in his thoughts. His heart was so busied always with " adding to his virtue brotherly kindness, and to brotherly kindness charity," so overflowing with sympathy for the unfortunate and unhappy and tempted ones who crossed his path, that it would have been impossible for him to be satisfied with immuring himself in his study, and devoting his time to the preparation of elegant discourses. How could he sit there quietly choosing felicitous expressions for next Sunday's sermons, rewriting and rearranging a sentence here and a passage there, choosing fine flowers of poesy and beautiful rhetorical figures, when the messenger from some poor, forlorn member of his flock, a washerwoman, perhaps, with a sick husband and a dying babe, who begged him to come and pray with her, was waiting for him just outside the study-door !

And next day perhaps it was a bright-eyed boy, the baker's son, who needed consolation. Three days ago he had fallen from the cart and broken his leg, and when the sermon was only half finished, there was a timid knock at the door, and the boy's sister appeared, who told how, ever since the accident, the boy had done nothing but moan and beg to have Mr. Payson sent for, declaring that no one else could comfort him as the minister could. And he must go ; be the discourse a polished and elegant one or not, there must not remain uncomforted a single sorrowing or afflicted one among his congregation, if any word or act of his can bring them consolation.

Hardly has the happy sister left the door, bearing the good news that the minister will call and see Johnny that very afternoon, when it opens again and admits that poor inebriate, who signed the pledge last week for the third time, and who means to keep it now, if it kills him. That very morning he had been most sorely tempted to join his boon companions in just one more social glass, and he had almost yielded—was suffering still from the agonizing conflict through which he had passed, and there seemed no haven of refuge for the tortured soul like the pastor's study. And was the door of that to be closed upon him? By no means! This large-hearted, loving-hearted man forgets that he has a sermon to write—has no thought of anything but the forlorn and sorrowing brother-man who sits by his side, struggling so heroically with the demon of a depraved appetite. An hour passes—two hours perhaps; they take no note of time those two -the one eager to impart help and strength and consolation, the other so intensely eager to secure the needed help and strength. And secure it he does. You saw him enter perhaps pallid, weak, and trembling; he goes forth looking almost like a different being, dignified, erect, and manly, and trusting, not in himself, but in the Lord, for strength. And it was the pastor who uttered the words of encouragement, who gave the kind advice, who offered the fervent prayer, which were the instruments in God's hands of bringing salvation to that poor man's soul. Already had the angels who were hovering over the hallowed spot flown heavenward with the glad tidings that another sinner ·had become repentant. But the sermon that might have been so polished and finished a discourse—the sermon which was neglected that the feet of a sin-stricken wanderer might be set to walking the heavenly road—that is still uncompleted. The pastor must extemporize the rest. He will finish the arrangement of it in his mind to-morrow, if he is not interrupted before he goes to officiate at the funeral of the washerwoman's baby.

And what if men did not applaud! What if other men's sermons were more carefully and elegantly written, and brought more fame to those who penned them! His saved men's souls; and that is enough. His at least told the simple story of the Cross in words that touched men's hearts, and won them to the truth; and for what better or higher results of preaching can we ask? The thought was doubtless often in his mind,

> "The Master praises! what are men?
> Go labor on—enough, while here,
> If he shall praise me—if he deign
> My willing heart to mark and cheer;
> No toil for him shall be in vain."

One other fact deserves brief mention here. In preparing his sermons for Sabbath morning, Mr. Payson for many years previous to his death followed a "course." Fully two-thirds of his sermons were prepared either upon some book of the Old or New Testament, or upon a topic, such as *The Life of Christ*, or *The Life of the Church.* Beginning in 1862 with the Old Testament, he preached—

25	sermons upon the book of			Daniel.
16	"	"	"	Ezra.
13	"	"	"	Esther.
8	"	"	"	Nehemiah.
76	"	"	"	Ephesians.
22	"	"	Parables.	
14	"	"	Confession of Faith.	
25	"	"	Names of Christ.	
293	"	"	Life of Christ.	
98	"	"	Life of the Church.*	
41	"	"	various topics, Baptism, Easter, etc.	
631	Total	"	special subjects.	
473	"	"	general "	
1,104	Total number of written discourses in seventeen years.†			

The remarks with which he prefaced his last sermon upon the Life of Christ, July 19, 1874, show his own estimate of this method. "It is seven years to-day," he says, "since we began the study of the Life of Christ.... How well I recall the fear and hesitancy with which I entered upon this work after weeks of prayer and deliberation. How could I hope to interest and instruct in studying themes familiar from your childhood? But each succeeding year has more and more impressed me with the inexhaustible richness of God's word. To-day I should not fear to begin these very books again, and feel sure that at every step through the Holy Scriptures we should find new revelations to stir and gladden our hearts.

* He was engaged upon this course when he died, and was following history in the book of Acts.

† Extemporaneous or unwritten sermons are not included in this list.

"But if with hesitancy I began, it is with greater reluctance that I close. How have I found myself instinctively clinging to these last verses, and wondering if ever I could give them up! And the steady attendance and attention through all these years assure me that you have sympathized with me in my feelings about this precious history. Thank God, it is of this same Jesus we shall study wherever we turn in the Bible. The same Holy Spirit who has blessed us in the past, will he not help us in the future?"

In closing this chapter, we may call attention to the appreciative words of the Rev. E. P. Roe, the celebrated author, who, in a recent communication to the "New York Tribune," says concerning Mr. Payson:

He was one of the most efficient and successful workers among the masses that it was ever my good fortune to meet, and I am far from being alone in the belief that the labors of only a few others in his calling have been crowned with results more pleasing to God than his. He was one of whom the world heard little; but if it be true that the angels rejoice "over one sinner that repenteth," his name, as that of one of God's most faithful and zealous servants, was honored in heaven. For many years he made his chapel a home, a refuge, a place where thousands found the courage to enter upon the Christian life. But the power and success of his ministry did not consist alone in his vivid and fervent appeals, nor in his broad, warm sympathies. He was a scholar in the best sense of the term. Having received a thorough preparation for his calling, he remained a close, careful student to the end, and his strong, practical mind had the rare gift of working over the truth gathered, and of imparting it, not in a weak, diluted form, but in simplicity, brevity, and illumined by apt illustration, so that the plain laboring people who chiefly formed his audience, could see its bearing upon their vital interests and daily life. His large chapel in Third avenue grew so overcrowded that a commodious church became necessary, and among the shifting population of that region of the city he has maintained a numerous and ever-increasing congregation. The number of humble homes that he entered in obedience to the command, "I was sick and ye visited me," the number of the sad and of the guilt disquieted that he has cheered and led to peace, cannot be estimated even by those who knew him best. Possessing a vigorous mind in a vigorous body, he devoted all his time and energy to the accomplishment of practical results. He sought to make his people self-respecting and industrious; he taught them how to make the most of their tenement-house life, and in the case of no poor creature did he ever stand afar off or "pass by on the other side," but he ever came directly where the sin-wounded were, and in the spirit of the Good Samaritan. If the city's welfare depends at all upon the reform and virtue of its citizens, then such wise and untiring workers as Mr. Payson, who are steadily bringing the best of influences to bear upon thousands of lives, are those whose loss is most severely felt.

CHAPTER V.

METHODS AND MEANS—SYSTEMATIC BENEFI-CENCE.

EARLY in his ministry Mr. Payson was brought to feel that contributions from his people towards the support of the gospel was a necessary means to their own growth in grace. By a series of providential experiences this conviction was deepened and strengthened until he was led to take such steps towards the promotion of systematic beneficence in his own church as form a most important era in his life-work. Indeed, so profound was his conviction that no true Christian development is possible for those who do not practise self-denying and systematic beneficence that he was willing to let his pastoral relations with this people stand or fall with the maintenance of that principle.

It was for many years his opinion that the remarkable development of the members of this church was attributable under God in no slight degree to their cheerful obedience to the Bible precept, "*It is more blessed to give than to receive.*" Certainly it is a remarkable* fact that those whose fortunes grew apace and who thus had been lifted in the social scale, when self-respect and manliness were roused did not desert the chapel as the corresponding classes so often desert the "Missions" of the city.†

---

* Compare the remarks of Dr. Howard Crosby, page 67.

† In a sermon delivered March, 1875, Mr. Payson says, "In 1862

Many of those who moved away from the neighborhood moved nevertheless with reference to the chapel and sought as long as possible to retain their connection with it. And it is no less remarkable that the middle classes* of our population, who, as a rule, are pushed from the wealthy churches by extravagance, and pushed from the "Missions" by an honorable self-respect, were being more and more drawn towards this enterprise as the principles which Mr. Payson advocated secured recognition and made themselves felt in the conduct of the chapel and became more widely known. Should those principles now be carried to a successful issue, as with the favor of Divine Providence we can but hope they may be, it is not too much to say that the problem of "how to reach the masses" will have been solved.

Beginning with a people, who, when he came to them, gave absolutely nothing towards benevolent operations, and absolutely nothing towards self-support, and who, moreover, (on account of their extreme poverty at that time,) were not encouraged to give in either of these directions, Mr. Payson with most persistent energy and faith and steadfast zeal, through seventeen years of ministry, maintained the Gospel principle that every man should give and give systematically and give "according as the Lord hath prospered him." The spirit of his teaching upon this subject may be gathered from the

our contributions amounted to $79, now they are over $6,000; *and this contrast reflects a like prosperity in many a home connected with our church.*"

* The congregation for many years has been mainly composed of the better classes of the poor, (compare Dr. Abbott's remarks, page 88,) so that it might even now be called "*A Workingmen's Church.*"

following extract from a sermon delivered October 30. 1870.

"Some people," he said, "will perhaps think that my sermon to-night has not much gospel in it, for it is to be almost entirely about money. And yet, if I study my Bible aright, there is no better method of judging our religion at its real value than that afforded by a man's account (if I may so speak) with the Lord. How much has been received? how much given? Abel gave of his lambs, and God loved and blessed him for it. Noah took ' *sevens* ' of the clean animals with him into the ark that he might have to offer unto the Lord. There was no happier hour in the desert than when those poor people gave one million to build the Tabernacle. . . . Israel never gave as in the days of David and Solomon, and never were they so prosperous. Iron became like stones, silver as iron, and gold as silver. But when they began to withhold the tenths, the least God allowed from any Jew, then the land suffered. Cf. *Haggai* 1 : 9–11. ' *Ye looked for much, and lo it came to little, and when ye brought it home, I did blow upon it. Why? saith the Lord of Hosts. Because of my house that is waste; and ye run every man unto his own house.*' The same law holds in the New Testament. 'Covetousness is idolatry.' ' The love of money is the root of all evil.' The alms of Cornelius entered in with his prayers before God as a memorial of his life. To make to ourselves friends of the mammon of unrighteousness, is to have some who shall receive us into everlasting habitations. And it is not too much to say, that, as the hands of a watch are the

11

index of the movements within, so the pocketbook is the
index of the soul. As you are sure enough that the
movement is all right when the hands keep correct time,
so you have in your benevolent account one of the best
tests of the state of your soul."

He refers to the common plea against free-will offerings, that it is better to employ plates and subscription
papers because shame will then compel the selfish to
give who otherwise would not give at all, and adds:
"What does this mean? That the fear of man is a
stronger motive than love to God. It may be for once,
but it certainly is not for continuous and faithful giving.
And, such gifts do not spend well. God loves a cheerful giver, but such giving is anything but cheerful. Nay
more, is it not contrary to the Master's rule, ‘Let not
thy left hand know what thy right hand doeth’? Therefore, it is written, ‘When thou doest thine alms, do not
sound a trumpet before thee as the hypocrites do in the
synagogues and in the streets, that they may have glory
of men.’ I would rather my people would never give at
all," he adds, "than feel that this is the highest motive.
But it is not necessary. Look at Müller's hundreds of
thousands in answer to the prayer of faith . . . Look at
the Harpoot Missions ; . . .* nearer home, at Roe's work
in Lowell ; . . . J. O. Adams' in New York ; . . . nay look
at your own past experience in which the benevolent
contributions of this church from scriptural motives have
already risen from $70 a year to $3,500. . . . Let me tell
you an easy way. Take one-tenth of all you earn each

* These examples, of course, were enlarged upon in the address.

week and put it aside for the Lord. On Sunday morning take out of this that portion which you feel you
should give to this work and another for that, praying
over it, and consulting with the Master about it; and I
know that it will not be long before our contributions
will be doubled and even trebled."

In an article prepared for the press within a few
years of his decease, upon "*Nineteenth Century Illustrations of the Master's Rule of Giving*,"* after speaking of
the ostentation which too frequently accompanies the
gifts of the church, and criticising the prevalent method
of plate-collections, he says: "A congregation composed
so largely of the poor that they have always been sustained by the parent church, resolved to try and do
something themselves. That this might prove no ob-
stacle even to the poorest in the enjoyment of the privi-.
leges of God's house, boxes were placed near the entrance in which deposits could be made at any time.
The amount contributed by each individual was known
only to God and himself. The motives urged were those
of gratitude to God, and the method advised that laid
down so plainly in the Scriptures, Let each one of you
lay by in store on the first day of the week as God hath
blessed. He that had received nothing, it was added,
was of course to give nothing; he that had received
little, was not to give a great deal; and he who had
received much was not to give little.

"Eight years have passed since that resolution was
taken During that time no plate or subscription-paper

* Matt. 6:2-4.

(with a single exception) has been passed. This people have given of their poverty, on what they regard a scriptural basis, each one responsible to God and God alone for the use or abuse of his opportunities. The result may perhaps best be shown in figures:

First year	$80	Fifth year	$1,040
Second "	140	Sixth "	1,400
Third "	490	Seventh "	2,800
Fourth "	700	Eighth "	3,200

"The people love to give, and the Lord is most evidently bestowing his blessing. If these facts shall help others to better understand and practise the Master's rule, our purpose will have been fully attained."

In 1862, under the influence of their pastor's ministry, the people began to contribute to missionary objects, and as early as 1864 we find a record of missionaries helped in India, Syria, and in the West of our own country, as well as of some gifts sent to the soldiers in the field, by those who previous to 1862 had been accustomed to give nothing. In 1867 they began to give systematically towards their own church-work, and so constant and rapid was their development in systematic beneficence, that having begun with the small sum of $79 the first year (1862), they were led to give more and more until in 1875 their contributions, regular and special, amounted to $6,978.*

---

* Compare the tables on page 90. It is noteworthy that from the very commencement there was an annual increase in the gifts from this branch of the church. In 1862-3 this increase amounted to only $65; in 1874-5 to $2,843; *i.e.*, the sum contributed in 1874-5 was larger by $2,843 than that contributed in the preceding year. The only apparent exception to this rule occurs in 1875-6 (see, however, footnotes on page 90),

The emphasis which Mr. Payson placed upon this means of grace, may be sufficiently illustrated by the following brief extract from his annual review sermon for 1876. "Two eras in the history of this church," he says, "are worthy of special mention in connection with its gifts to the Lord, which are peculiar in that they have been *wholly voluntary*—no collection ever having been taken in this congregation. I. The first dates from October, 1867, when the church, after silent prayer, rose and resolved with God's help to raise $10,000 towards a new building, if possible within three years. The *way* in which the people rose, no man looking right or left, but each doing it as unto God, is something rarely seen in any church. Our contributions as a result of this consecration of ourselves to God, doubled in a single year from $1,500 to $3,000. That was the beginning of this church edifice.* II. The second era was when in seven weeks we collected for the Memorial Fund and paid in almost $3,300—in seven short weeks! Oh, what zeal, love, and self-sacrificing devotion marked those days."†

and that is accounted for by the fact that the efforts made in the preceding year, when the chapel was being built, were extraordinary.

It may be added here that during the last year of his life, Mr. Payson announced his determination to depend for his salary upon the chapel people, and they would have raised the $4,000 necessary before the year was past. So important did he consider it that some beginning should be made in this direction, that he himself stood ready to contribute $200 or even $500 towards it, if necessary.

* The contributions of this people toward the Memorial Chapel amounted to about one-ninth of the whole sum necessary. (*Cf.* also the letter on page 141.)

† Some details of this effort are given on page 142, *et seq.*

A single illustration of the beneficent influence of these efforts upon the spiritual development of his people may be admitted here. Many more might be given, and others will be furnished by the narrative; but one is here enough to show that the sacrifices which his people made were not without rich fruits of faith and love. The following article is from his pen.

GIVING LIKE A LITTLE CHILD.

Not long since, a poor widow came into my study. She is over sixty years of age. Her home is one little room, about ten feet by twelve, and she supports herself by her needle, which in these days of sewing machines means the most miserable support.

Imagine my surprise, then, when she put three dollars into my hands and said:

"There is my contribution to the church fund."

"But are you able to give so much?"

"Oh, yes," she exclaimed. "I have learned how to give now."

"How is that?" I asked.

"Do you remember," she answered, "that sermon of three months since, when you told us that you did not believe one of your people was so poor, that if he loved Christ, he could not find some way of showing that love by his gifts?"

"I do."

"Well, I went home and cried all night over that sermon. I said to myself, 'My minister do n't know how poor I am or he never would have said that.' But from crying I at last got to praying. And when I had told Jesus all about it, I seemed to get an answer in my heart that dried up all tears."

"What was the answer?" I asked, deeply moved by her recital.

"Only this, 'If you cannot give as other people do, give like a little child.' And I have been doing it ever since. When I have a penny change over from my sugar or loaf of bread, I lay it aside for Jesus, and so I have gathered this money all in pennies."

"But has it not embarrassed you to lay aside so much?"

"Oh, no!" she responded eagerly with beaming face. "Since I began to give to the Lord I have always had money in the house for myself, and it is wonderful how the work comes pouring in. So many are coming to see me that I never knew before."

"But did n't you always have money in the house ?" I asked.

"Oh, no! Often when my rent came due I had to go and borrow it, not knowing how I ever should find means to pay it again. But I do n't have to do that any more, the dear Lord is so kind."

Of course I could not refuse such money.

Three months later she came with three dollars and eighty-five cents saved in the same way. Then came the effort of our church in connection with the Memorial Fund, and in some five months she brought fifteen dollars, all saved in the little mite-box I had given her. This makes a total of twenty-one dollars and eighty-five cents from one poor widow in a single twelvemonth. I need hardly add that she apparently grew more in Christian character in that one year, than in all the previous years of her connection with the church.

Who can doubt that if in giving as well as other graces, we could all thus become as little children, there would result such an increase in our gifts that there would not be room enough to contain them ?

In the maintenance of these principles of Christian beneficence, Mr. Payson, as is well known, met with some discouragements. From the very first the policy of the parent church was different. The large and influential Committee to whom had been intrusted the management of the chapel, generously contemplated giving to this people the bread of life without money and without price. They sought to provide a spiritual home for even the poorest of the poor, and they did not wish to have the rest and comfort of that home disturbed by any sense of pecuniary obligation. They endeavored according to their means, and to the very utmost of their ability, to carry out the spirit of our Lord's example so beautifully expressed in his own words, "The poor have the gospel preached unto them ;" and while they wished in every possible way to discourage pauperism and to reprove the disposition which looked towards abject dependence on the rich, they were determined, if possible, to provide for all God's poor committed to their care in such a way as to make them feel at home, although they did not pay a cent.   This was the principle which underlay the very names " Mission " and " Mission Chapel " as at first* applied to this enterprise.

It is possible, too, that it may have been this, at least in part, which led them not wholly to approve of the action of Mr. Payson when in 1867 he called upon his people to give $10,000 towards a new church edifice. There was no intention on Mr. Payson's part, in doing this, to oppose the wishes of the Committee, and, so far as we know, such a design was never imputed to him. The object presented to his people at that time was not strictly in the line of self-support, and therefore not in direct conflict with the views of the Committee as he understood them.   The whole truth is, that an extraordinary impression had been made upon his mind at the meeting of the American Board, from which he had just returned, by the report from the Harpoot Mission ; and his long-cherished and earnest convictions as to the duty of even the poorest of the Lord's people to give something to the Lord's cause, could no longer be suppressed.

For reasons which Mr. Payson did not foresee,† his plan failed to receive the approval of the Committee ; but the guiding hand of Providence should be recognized‡ in the use made of this movement to demonstrate the practicability and wisdom of the views which he had so

---

* The name has since been changed to Memorial Chapel, and the word " Mission " dropped.

† See Appendix, Note B.   ‡ *Cf.* the letter on page 141.

carnestly and patiently advocated. Any doubts which may have existed among the members of the Committee as to the ability and readiness of the people to give, were dispelled by their spontaneous and hearty response to this appeal ; and the result was that finally all objections to the receipt of contributions for self-support were withdrawn, and in due time Mr. Payson had the satisfaction of seeing the plan introduced and in successful operation among his people.

These facts will serve to explain some statements of a judicious and discriminating writer in a recent communication to the "New York Evangelist." Referring to Mr. Payson's work, he says,

His congregation continually increased, and conversions were numerous. But not satisfied with introducing new disciples into the Christian fold, he taught them it was alike their duty and privilege to strive for self-support, and to be helpers in works of charity. Joyfully conscious of the advantages he had early gained by self-reliance, he desired his people to know how much more noble and blessed it is to give than to receive.

Yet while his aim was thus elevated, an epoch was reached from which his ministry, before marked by a happy routine of usefulness, was suddenly lifted to a plane of bold endeavor and fearless enterprise. He greatly enjoyed the annual meetings of the American Board, and on his return from one of these in the autumn of 1867, where he had been especially quickened by what he had learned of the wonderful liberality of a church in Western Asia,* whose numbers were pitiably poor as compared with his own flock; without taking counsel with any one, he resolved to urge his people to contribute freely and systematically to raise money for building a larger and more attractive place of worship. On a certain Lord's day evening he preached a sermon with unwonted earnestness and enthusiasm in pursuance of his plan.

That plan having been duly unfolded, and their privilege and duty having been eloquently enforced by weighty arguments, he called upon all who were willing to coöperate in raising $10,000 for the purpose specified to rise.

* The church at Harpoot referred to in the Annual Report of the A. B. C. F. M. (1867.)

His appeal, it should be said, was based on scriptural grounds. He recognized the poverty and destitution of some of his people, and the need which all of them might feel of close economy. "But," he said, "this matter is a vital one for you and for me. To give from her penury was the privilege even of the widow in the gospel whose two poor mites were 'all that she had;' but the ages crown her memory with benedictions since the Saviour's blessing rested on her act. They were not all rich to whom Paul wrote, 'Upon the first day of the week let every one of you lay by him in store according as the Lord hath prospered him;' but the claim which he then made on those poor members of the church is the scriptural claim the church should urge to-day on every man who seeks to grow in grace. 'Let every one give'—such should be the language of the church—'let every one give according as the Lord hath prospered him.' And now I want to lay this obligation on your consciences. Give as unto the Lord, and not as unto men. Give from the fulness of your love and gratitude to him. Give to promote his glory and your highest good. . . . We will have a moment of silent prayer, and then all those who are ready to pledge themselves to do their utmost towards securing $10,000 within the next three years will please to rise."

The hush which fell upon the audience at once was wonderful and thrilling. Those who were present will never forget the hour. Each head was bowed in silent prayer, and over the whole assembly the stillness of a reverent and humble "waiting on the Lord" was felt;

and when the pastor rose at last, the entire congregation rose with him, and pledged themselves by doing so to give, as God had prospered them, each Sabbath in the year. "Doubtless," as has been said, "some of these people were surprised that night at the change that had come over them. They were to be no longer aimless dreamers." They were to realize in their own experience the wisdom of the words,

> "Do noble things, not dream them all day long,
> And so make life, death, and the vast Forever,
> One grand, sweet song."

And as the work to which they now had pledged themselves was one which called for energy, they began at once to move. A system was devised by which, without burdening any one, all might have chance to give. Envelopes were procured, marked " For the Building Fund," in which the contributions could be sealed and left in a box provided for this purpose near the door. The amount collected in this way varied from $25 to $50 a week, and within the next three years $6,000* were placed at interest for the "Building Fund," which, together with subsequent contributions to the "Memorial Fund," finally

---

* Mr. Payson's report of the Building Fund, in his sermon of October 30, 1870, is as follows:

From box collections, 1867–8	$1,240
" " " 1868–9	1,370
" " " 1869–70	864
" Special gifts	692
" Concert	154
" Interest	682
" Bonds in hand (conditional)†	880
" Deposit in savings-bank†	120
† See foot-note on next page (132).	$6,002

amounted to more than $12,000, of which sum, it is proper to state, Mr. Payson gave $1,225.* The entire $10,000 would doubtless have been secured within the specified time, had it not become evident that the church would not then be built, and had not the contributions been diverted early in the spring of 1870 from the erection of a new edifice towards self-support.

One or two of the incidents which occurred in connection with this effort, may be mentioned here.

The sum of $50 was given by a poor washerwoman " whose heart the Lord had opened." Another poor woman on her dying bed gave Mr. Payson four silver half dollars for the new church which he kept as a sacred legacy for several years until this edifice was built.

Mrs. —— drank beer every day before this effort was begun, and especially on Mondays when the washing was likely to be hard. But she concluded after some deliberation that she would give up this luxury and save nine cents a day for the new church, which she did, until at last she brought $9 90 and told her pastor that she was now so convinced of the folly of drinking that she had determined to abandon it altogether. Still another, living in a hall bedroom and earning but fifty cents a day, put the pennies which she saved at the grocery from " change," after buying a pint of milk or a loaf of bread,

* The last two items in the report given on the preceding page represent in part Mr. Payson's own contribution towards the new church, which was to be given " if other $9,000 were raised." It is mentioned here only to show that he was not unwilling to join his people in whatever he asked them to do. When some one remarked, " This is too much, and the church does not want to take this gift from you," he replied, " I have given my life to this work, and it is a small thing for me to give my money."

into a savings-bank for this fund, until at last she brought
$9 35 with thankfulness that God enabled her to do so
much for him. One year she brought $2 50, the next
$3 10 and the third $3 75. And this she did against the
judgment of her pastor who thought it all needful for
her own comfort.

A year or two of this kind of effort had passed, when
Mr. Payson was led to take a step, which, whether viewed
in the light of possible or actual consequences, was of
too much importance to pass over in silence. For reasons which he gives in a sermon to be quoted from
presently, he resigned his pastorate in the month of
March, 1870. There was much feeling among his people
when they learned that his resignation had been accepted, and it was not long before several of the leading members of the church and congregation waited upon the chairman of the chapel Committee to make known the general
regret occasioned by the fact and to inquire if there could
not be a reconsideration. This visit opened the way for a
conference between Mr. Payson and the Committee, and
very soon views which seemed at one time irreconcilable
were harmonized and the resignation was withdrawn.*

In reference to this matter Mr. Payson himself says,
at the close of his anniversary sermon May, 1870:

" This evening affords me the proper opportunity to
explain to you all why I felt I ought to leave. Naturally, churches grow by colonies. But the centrali-
zing policy of Presbyterianism during the last twenty-
five years has put a stop to this. Pastors here and in

* See Appendix, Note B.

12

Brooklyn complain that in these cities the colonization system is impracticable. Their people will not go away. As the next best thing mission chapels like this were organized. Some of them—this, at least, as all of you will testify—were put under the care of as intelligent, capable, and devoted a body of men as any one could ask for. Money, prayers and efforts have been lavishly bestowed, and under the blessing of God, a large success has been secured.

" Warned by the failures of other chapels which at the end of a short period have been cast off to struggle for themselves, it was resolved that this should form a branch of the parent church with the ordinances however administered in each at stated periods. That every one might feel at perfect freedom to attend here, all expenses have been borne entirely by the members worshipping in Madison Square.

" For a time this has worked well, especially since plans for encouraging and developing the resources of this chapel have been year by year provided. But as I have studied my Bible more, and have seen how the apostles required their churches to support themselves as far as possible; as I have seen dependent chapels year after year failing to do any great work for the Master; as I have heard of missions in Scotland and even in heathen lands, advanced to a noble pitch of prosperity by self-sacrificing, earnest efforts, under circumstances far less favorable than our own ; as I have studied your growing means and willingness ; and especially as one and another have come saying, ' We date our greatest spiritual

and material growth from the hour when we began systematically to give ;' I have felt that it was high time that
you did your best to meet the expenses of this place.
Until now everything has been done for you and many of
you have felt as uncomfortably in regard to it as myself.

" It was on this point that the Committee could not
agree. Some were persuaded that if such burdens were
laid upon you, many who now feel at home in the chapel
would be driven away. How to avoid this and yet to
develop the best energies of this congregation has been
the burden of the last three years. With each year it
has increased, and I had resolved that if it could not in
some way be relieved I should leave this spring. This
and this alone was the sole cause of my resignation.

"Your earnest request that I should reconsider my
resignation, sustained by the kind assurances of the Committee of the parent church, have led me to hope larger
and better things for the future, and I have resolved to
remain with the people and the work I so dearly love.

" What then is our present outlook, so far as financial
matters are concerned ? It has been resolved that all
those who wish to contribute towards the support of this
place of worship are to have the opportunity to do so.
The only condition is that these gifts shall be voluntary,
and so bestowed that none shall feel that they are not
perfectly welcome to this place. A committee chosen
from your own number* is to devise some plan by which

---

* With reference to this committee Mr. Payson says in his official
record of the chapel work for 1870 : "In the spring of this year an arrangement was made by which the congregation at the chapel appointed

these purposes can be carried into effect, and it is to this end you are invited to meet here next Wednesday evening. Am I too sanguine in believing that those whom God has blessed in this place will most gladly avail them· selves of this opportunity of bringing their thank-offerings and laying them down each week at the Saviour's feet?"

In October of this same year, in connection with his report upon the Building Fund, after glancing at the past and referring to the progress they had made, Mr. Payson said, "But some, disappointed, will ask, ' What of the new church?' To this I would answer: twice since we commenced, special efforts have been made to secure the proper lots, and a committee is now organized for this very work. Should the spirit manifested here among ourselves warrant the undertaking, I should not be surprised if the ground for our new building were broken within a twelvemonth. . . . . And while we await more light, let me ask if there is one here that feels poorer to-day for what he has given the Lord through that box? I know not a few that feel richer, for (1) they have learned to give and the blessedness of giving. They never had given before, and they have received so much pleasure from it that it has made their faces to shine with a heavenly light I had never seen there before.

a committee to raise funds for the support of the chapel and such objects as they might deem best. This committee was to coöperate with the committee from the parent church in all important matters relating to this branch of the church." In this connection the attention of the reader is especially invited to fuller statements concerning the matter of his resignation given in the Appendix, Note B. And it should be borne in mind that the coöperation above spoken of is not yet coördination, though it may eventually become so.

"(2.) Some have learned to give systematically who hitherto were accustomed to give at haphazard. Then, every time they gave there was a conflict between their conscience and their covetousness. Now, they have only to take the Lord's money already laid aside and give. The minister who had not a dime to buy a barrel of flour, gave $5 to one object and $10 to another before the day came when he was to receive his salary, and when asked how he could do this, replied, 'That is the Lord's money.'

"(3.) All of us feel a new strength in ourselves and our cause. We have now $6,000 at interest. This church has so much in store for the future, and we have learned in giving that how it may be doubled and trebled. If each one of us lays by him in store according as the Lord hath prospered him, no financial embarrassments or monetary crises will stand in the way of progress."

Afterwards, in the same sermon, he refers to the generous assistance afforded by the parent church, and says, " Twenty-six thousand dollars were subscribed in a single week, and the rest of the forty thousand dollars necessary would have been forthcoming at once if ground for building could have been secured. Are these dear brethren," he adds, "under greater obligations to help us than we to help ourselves? .... How is it in your families? You take the tenderest care of the most helpless and dependent—the little babe. As he grows older you expect him to take care of himself, to run on errands, to watch over the younger children, and at length to work and help support himself. So it is with these dear friends. With much prayer, with efforts continued

through fourteen long years, with many sacrifices cheerfully met, which will never be fully known till the last
great day, they have watched over this work and cared
for it from the first. When it began in the carpenter-
shop they cared for it ; so, too, in the public-school building ; and so, when there was need, they built this chapel.
And we are using property worth not less than forty
thousand dollars. At every call made upon them they
have responded with large generosity, till their gifts to
us amount to scarcely less than one hundred thousand
dollars. Their whole management has been characterized by a liberality shown to no other chapel in this city.
They have intrusted the management of affairs largely
to you, while they still pay at least five-sixths of the expense ; and if we were able to assume the responsibility
to-day, and it seemed the wisest and best course to pur-
sue, would at once give everything into our hands.

"Shall not such confidence and generosity be met
with a like spirit on our side? Next spring some of us
will have to report what this branch of the church has
done in twelve months. And are we who have gloried
in your generosity in years past, and who have asked
that you might be allowed to do for yourselves, doomed
to be disappointed in our hopes and expectations ?"

The next year (1871) brought a very happy disappointment to the pastor of this church and to every other
friend of the congregation who had "gloried in their generosity." It afforded ample ground, too, for justifying
that most honorable and praiseworthy action of the Committee, whereby they have lifted the people of this chapel

up to a plane of liberty and privilege such as is not enjoyed perhaps by any similar organization in the Presbyterian church.

The manner in which this people engaged in the effort to secure the *Five Million Memorial Fund*, designed by the General Assembly to commemorate the reunion of the dissevered branches of the Presbyterian church in America, reflects the greatest credit upon their energy and faith, and proves them worthy of the confidence reposed in them by their pastor and the Committee of the parent church. The name, "*Memorial Chapel*," which has been given to their new edifice, was derived indeed from its connection with this special memorial contribution, and a brief review of what they did at this time may not be found uninteresting.

When, by advice of the General Assembly—which is the highest authority of the Presbyterian church in the United States—each church was to have a share in raising this Five Million Fund, and to determine the object towards which it should be contributed, Mr. Payson's congregation chose to devote their offerings to the enlargement of their "*Building Fund*" and the erection of a new edifice. Accordingly, several clergymen were invited to address the people one Sabbath evening upon the general objects contemplated by the action of the General Assembly, and to commend this special effort to the prayers and hopes of the church. Immediately after, circulars were distributed through the congregation, in which the causes and occasion of such an effort were briefly stated and the following appeal subjoined:

YOUR OFFERING.

This sub;ect appeals to every Presbyterian in the land, whether old or young, rich or poor, and YOU are invited to give it your prayerful consideration. For the encouragement of those whose means are small and who are disposed to undervalue the importance of their coöperation, the committee mention that the first money received by the treasurer towards this great fund of five millions was a single dollar, the pious gift of a poor woman.

Remember that the call is for a THANK-OFFERING to the Lord. Let whatever you do be done cheerfully, for the Lord loveth a cheerful giver.

The General Assembly is to meet the 18th of May next, and their committee wish to close the subscription-book on the 10th of May, to give time for the preparation of a Report. It is necessary that you decide upon the amount of your contributions soon, and that it be in the hands of your pastor on or before the 7th of May, otherwise it cannot be included in the Report to the General Assembly. . . . .

Your friend and pastor,   C. II. PAYSON.

NEW YORK, March, 1871.

The result of this effort was, that within seven weeks $3,300 were collected and paid in, and a conditional offer made the amount more than $4,000.* Of this amount one young man, who began life as a boy in the mission-school, gave $200. Another, who has been saved by its influence from drunkenness, gave $25. Five others gave each $100. One gave $225, and another $83. But when it is remembered that the great majority of these gifts were from poor people, it will not appear strange that

$40	were given in sums of			$1 00 each.
60	"	"	"	2 00 "
54	"	"	"	3 00 "
12	"	"	"	4 00 "
800	"	"	"	5 00 "
18	"	"	"	6 00 "
42	"	"	"	7 00. "

* Four thousand dollars was the sum which had been asked for.

490	were given in sums of			10 00	each.
160	"	"	"	20 00	"
350	"	"	"	25 00	"
300	"	"	"	50 00	" etc.,

and that one gift was as small as ten cents.

An interesting confirmation of Mr. Payson's statement,[*] that the resolution of the chapel congregation in 1867 to give $10,000 towards a new building "was the beginning of this church edifice," appears in the following note, which directs attention to the overruling hand of Providence in this matter. It bears the date of September 6, 1877; and the writer, having spoken of the Memorial Fund, says:

"I think attention should be called somewhere to the unexpected opening made by the Memorial undertaking. Remember that when Mr. Payson proposed the 'Building Fund,' (1867,) the new building had no place anywhere except in his imagination; and at the date of his resignation, (1870,) when the contributions had almost ceased, and he hardly knew what to say to his people about the prospect, the Madison Square Church had given no sign. 'Daylight was all gone.' After a while the 'Memorial Fund' enlisted the Madison Square Church, and in view of the splendid beginning made at the chapel, it was natural and easy for the church to decide that their offerings should go towards a new building. It illustrates the old proverb that 'God helps those who help themselves.'

"My belief is, that had it not been for the 'Memorial Fund,' the new chapel would not have been erected, and

* See page 125.

this was not dreamed of when Mr. Payson propo:ed to his people to raise $10,000."

Some incidents connected with this effort were deeply interesting. One note, enclosing $20 for the fund, makes touching reference to the death of a child tenderly beloved, and then says,

Before our daughter left us we had spoken of contributing to the "Memorial Fund" as a family, recognizing our responsibility according to the measure of ability. We have found that H—— had in the savings-bank about $40, the gift of a friend; and in filling up the blank, we have pref rred to insert her name among the living children, and opposite to a sum which we cannot doubt that she, if also living, would heartily contribute to that church in which she was born, was baptized, and taught the truths which, we trust, had made her wise unto salvation.

A'l her associations with the sanctuary have been with the Presbyterian church, and had it pleased God to spare that gentle life with its dawning Chr stian graces, we feel assured that she would have early united with this beloved and honored church, and in the joys, cares, and labors have found she prized its heavenly ways,

"Its sweet communion, solemn vows,
And hymns of love and praise."

Again wishing complete success may crown this renewed effort for the new chur h, and make the work truly *memorable*,

Very truly.

Rev. C. H. Payson.

Many of the sacrifices made in connection with this effort in some of the poorest of these homes will never be fully known till the last great day. Some of them were heroic, and all of them were inspired by faith. A few must be given here.

One poor woman, who kept a candy store in a very small room on —— street, and who depended for her living upon what she could make in this way, became so deeply interested in this Memorial effort for a new building, that she sold her watch and chain and other jewelry, amounting in all to $115, that she might honor the Lord with her substance. Another, Mrs. ——, a sewing-woman, resolved that she would give something towards the new church even when she had no money in the house to give, and could not see where any was to be obtained. But she had a confident assurance that "in some way or other the Lord would provide," and in the bravery of her humble faith began to pray for work. And work came, "faster," she said, "than ever before," and in such abundance, that within the seven weeks allotted for this fund she collected and paid from the proceeds of her needlework $20 into the Lord's treasury! and this at a time when needlework was not remunerative.

A poor washerwoman, whose husband was in the army, and who was struggling hard with three children to make ends meet, promised one day that she would give $50 towards the new building "if the bounty-money came in." Her pastor disapproved of her giving so much, on the ground that she needed it herself; and really did not expect to receive it, knowing that people are apt to be far more generous when they have money in prospect than when they have it in hand. But the good woman was very much in earnest in the matter, and when the first payment was received from the government turned over $50 to the new church.

Another very interesting illustration of the genuineness and simplicity of this people's faith is afforded by the conduct of a member of the church who was engaged as housekeeper for a gentleman residing on Fifth avenue. She had managed by strict economy to save a considerable sum of money, and thought it her privilege to give at least $100 towards the Memorial Fund. But she hesitated to take it from the savings-bank "before the first Sunday of May," as would be necessary, for then she must lose the interest on it for six months; and thrift had made her conscientious. But she considered that unless the money was paid " before the seventh of May " it could not be counted in the " Memorial Fund;" the Lord called for it at once, and it should be paid ; He would take care of the interest, she thought. And so she drew it from the bank, and deposited it in the little box "at the inner door of the chapel," with which, it need hardly be said, she had already become familiar. The next day her employer sent word to her that " he wished to see her at the office, as he had something special to say;" and when she went, fearing lest for some reason she might be discharged, she found that he had been so much pleased with her services, that he had determined to advance her wages for the following year, beginning with the first of January, then already three months past ; "*and so,*" as she said to her pastor in the joy of her simple faith, " *the Lord has not only paid me back all my interest, but twice as much besides, and is going to keep me in mind of it all the year through.*"

It would be easy and delightful to multiply these illustrations of that people's faith, who, through the deepest poverty and darkest griefs, have "trusted and obeyed;" but their record is on high, and the limits of this little book forbid our dwelling more upon them here.

CHAPTER VI.

ARMY LIFE AND TRAVELS IN THE EAST.

WHILE Mr. Payson's whole soul was aglow with zeal in religious work, he always felt and exhibited the most lively interest in public affairs. Whatever tended to promote social and civil welfare ever found in him an ardent friend and supporter. As an illustration of this fact may be mentioned an incident that occurred during his seminary course.

" It was in 1856," writes a friend, " when the exciting and momentous Presidential canvass was in progress, with 'Fremont and Freedom,' for the watchword upon the one side, and James Buchanan as the leader upon the other. Many felt that the very salvation of the republic was involved in the issue. This political excitement stirred even the quiet retreat of the theological seminary, and during the summer vacation, Mr. Payson, in company with a classmate, set out upon a campaign in one of the interior counties of New York. They went from place to place, addressing the people night after night, upon the vital questions of the great political issue. Large and attentive audiences listened to those volunteer politicians, who for the time entered heartily into the work of doing their part to uphold freedom of speech for the press, and for all the people of the land.

" Into this work Mr. Payson put his entire energies,

with that contagious enthusiasm which always charac·
terized his labors. Nor from that day onward did he
ever cease to be profoundly interested in the material
welfare of his country, and ready always to do his duty
as a citizen. As Paul, though an apostle, never forgot
that he was a Roman citizen, so Mr. Payson, though a
minister of the gospel, never forgot that he was an
American."

During the progress of the war also he took an active
interest in the welfare of the Union army, not only encouraging his people to send contributions of clothing
and money, but volunteering himself to serve in the
field and hospital as a member of the Christian Commission. A brief account of this experience appears in
the following letter to his brother:

> NEW YORK, July 5, 1864,
> No. 95 East Thirty-sixth street.

DEAR G——: . . I have been down with fever and ague since my return
from the White House, so that on Sunday I could not preach, and the
rest of the time could only crawl about . . . I do n't know how much you
know of my Washington trip, but will only say that I went under the care
of the Christian Commission, stayed in Washington one week, working
in hospitals, storehouses, etc., then down to the White House, where I
stayed another week—suffering all the time from fever and ague, and so
much that I could not make an effort to get to the army and hunt out
E——.* I was, it seems, within eight miles of him, but returned without
seeing him. We had to take care of 450 sick and wounded soldiers on
our return to Washington, and a hard time we had. It was a perfect
pest-house. It used me up, and though I am much better this week, I
need rest. . . .

A letter to Mrs. Payson at this time is dated

> WASHINGTON, May 30, 1864.

MY DEAR WIFE: You see by the date of my letter I am still here in
Washington. Grant's changes have prevented us from moving. He has

* A brother then serving as chaplain of the 146th Regiment, N. Y. S. V

already had two bases, Fredericksburg and Port Royal. He is now receiving his supplies through West Point and White House, whither we expect to go to-day. I looked for a letter from you on Saturday and Sunday, but none came on either day. I was sorely disappointed, for I feel anxious about the child. I had to work hard Saturday, not getting through till eleven o'clock at night. We had a nice time Saturday morning opening boxes from the different churches, of which I will tell you more when I see you.

In the afternoon some twenty of us paid our respects to the President. He made a characteristic speech to us, shook hands all round, and gave us several autographs on the spot, of which I secured afterwards a due share. That night I went out some two and a half miles to Emory Hospital, after working a couple of hours in putting up a tent to sleep in when I returned. Returned at eleven o'clock, and laid down on the boards with about thirty others to sleep. Being very tired I rested better than you might have imagined. Yesterday morning I attended Dr. Gurley's church where I heard a very good sermon on our life being hid with Christ in God. At four o'clock went out to the Stone Hospital and talked—was back at eight o'clock, tired enough to camp down for the night. I suppose we shall have to work hard to-day getting our vessels loaded. It is only about six o'clock, and I hope to get two nice letters when the postoffice opens at eight. I wish I could run in and see you a few minutes before we start off. Take good care of yourself and the baby. How does he enjoy the new baby-carriage?

I have just received your welcome letter of Saturday, and am so rejoiced to know that you and baby are so well .... We shall leave here in a few minutes for the White House landing—shall go down by steam. Probably you will not hear from me for two or three days at least. Be of good courage. May God take good care of you all. Many kisses and love in quantities to wife, baby, and all. Pray for me. I read in Acts every morning—I have no Psalms. Any word from E——?

Yours ever,   C. H. PAYSON.

WHITE HOUSE, June 31, 1864.

MY DEAR WIFE: On a wet morning, under a dirty tent, surrounded by a talking company, I will try and describe a little of what I have gone through since I sent you my unsigned letter.

We arrived at White House at three o'clock, ... reported immediately, and were soon on shore pitching our tents. In an hour an order came for me to go and get our steam-tug and bring it down, so that the delegates could go over and make ready to relieve the wounded men coming in. We had a fearful time reaching our destination. First our tug got aground, and it was some time before we were free. It was dark—

nine in the evening you must remember. No one on board knew the way . . . . In five minutes more an eddy caught us, and smash! crash! we went into a gunboat. I did not know for a moment but we were lost. But we grappled the gunboat and found after all that we were safe. Then we took to the little boat, rowing a long way, and going four times back and forth to land our stores; then a walk along the edge of the railroad bridge and the sand bank, coming every few steps to a narrow pass where we ran the risk of plunging into the river. In this way we passed to the other side where with lanterns dimly burning, we pitched our tents, kindled fires, and at twelve o'clock laid our weary bodies to rest, as the train of wounded men had not yet arrived.

At three o'clock we were up and had some crackers and coffee. Then we buried a poor fellow who was found on the beach drowned, no one knew how. It was really sad.

We had come back to the other side of the river and had just lain down to sleep, when another order came that six hundred wounded men had arrived and that every man must proceed to the other side. As you can imagine I was hardly fit to go, but back we went in the broiling sun. You must know that the bridge across the Pamunkey was burned a week or more since, and so all those poor fellows had to stay over on the other side—in sight of the steamboats—crowded in the supply wagons, where they had lain for two days and nights already. We were soon distributing coffee, tea, wine, bread, cordials, etc., among them. One lady, a Mrs. H——, rendered invaluable aid, getting into the wagons, washing the faces of the sick and caring for them tenderly. At twelve o'clock I was completely exhausted and had to go into the woods and rest.

During the afternoon six hundred more wounded men were received, making twelve hundred in all. A heavy thunder-storm came on, and in the midst of it the poor fellows were brought over and put on board the steamers for Washington. I slept splendidly last night and had a good breakfast.

Do write me every day, and direct care of Christian Commission, Washington, or I shall get nothing. Ask Mr. —— to supply my pulpit as he proposed, a week from next Sunday. Send me the *Times* every morning, please, after you have read it. S—— can run to the postoffice with it. I can get hold of no papers here. Much love to all. How much I want to hear from you and see you. Ever yours,   CHARLIE.

Some additional light is thrown upon this brief chapter in his life by the following reminiscences of an associate.

PORTLAND, May 25, 1877.

DEAR SIR: Your note of the 22d was received last night. My acquaintance with Rev. Charles H. Payson was too brief and too long ago to enable me to make any satisfactory reply to your inquiry.

It is almost thirteen years, (May 30, 1864,) since I first met him on a steamer, bound for the White House, with a party of volunteers in the service of the Christian Commission. But for one incident we might have parted as great strangers as we first met. Outside of the prayer-meeting there is little social Christian fellowship under such circumstances. The wounded and dying absorb all sympathy as well as time. Human sufferings monopolize every thought, despite the clatter of army wagons, the bray of mules, the shriek of steamers, and other paraphernalia of war.

The continuous battles at Cold Harbor had so multiplied the number of the wounded that the immense hospital provision at the White House proved insufficient. Orders came to send the wounded soldiers to the North. A steamer was loaded, and eight members of the Christian Commission were selected to accompany this living cargo of *four hundred and fifty-two* sick and suffering men to Washington! At midnight brother Payson and myself were aroused and asked to take the places of two of the delegates who had failed. We arose, and went on board the boat Utica at about one o'clock Sunday morning. This transport had discharged a load of mules the day before and there had not been time to have it properly cleaned. A generous quantity of straw was provided, to afford bedding, and to cover the dirt ; but the air was offensive.

The soldiers were put on board the night before. Some were taken from the army wagons, directly from the battle-field, and were suffering from undressed wounds as well as from the fatigues of the journey, and all the wants common to the sick and suffering. They were distributed over the decks, in the cabin, and wherever room could be found for a man's body. This temporary hospital was divided into eight wards, allowing fifty patients to a "nurse," as we were called. My assignment was between the wheel-house and cabin ; brother Payson had charge of the cabin, so that from our juxtaposition we were closely associated for two long days and nights. We were on board but a few hours before we were summoned around a dying man, who was in my ward, but lay at the door of brother Payson's companion way.

One sick in our families at home taxes the time of the entire household ; here were more than fifty men to one nurse. It required four pailfuls of water to make one round ; then were distributed coffee, beef-tea, pork and beans, lemonade and medicines as the various patients required ; the spare moments being filled up with drawing water for wounds, stirring up the straw pallets, changing bandages, etc., besides taking messages and writing letters to be forwarded from Washington. Such was our work during the forty-eight hours of this "middle passage"—a labor that engaged the active hands and sympathetic heart of Mr. Payson to the utmost. His great executive ability, quickened by religious principle, rendered his services invaluable. This close though brief communion of heart with heart awakened a friendship to be obliterated by death only. But the great Captain of our salvation knows best where and how to occupy his soldiers. When they are summoned to the front it is for good reasons. "What thou knowest not now, thou shalt know hereafter."

Very truly yours, but in haste,   C. A. L——.

After his return from the army, Mr. Payson did not leave his field again, except for the ordinary summer vacations, until February, 1873. In fulfilment of a long-cherished plan, he then sailed for Europe, in company with his brother, for the purpose of visiting the Holy Land. His first letter is dated "Feb. 12, 1873, two hundred miles from Ireland," and is, in part, as follows :

MY DEAR WIFE : Here we are, still at sea. . . . . We shall be at least fourteen days on our passage. This is partly accounted for by the storm we encountered, which compelled us to lie to for twelve hours, and delayed us more or less for five days. . . . . The captain said it was the most dangerous storm he had seen this winter—waves rolling forty feet high and the wind a cyclone.* . . . . It was a comfort to feel that every drop of the ocean and every atom of air was in our Father's hand, doing his will, and that nothing could touch us except as he wished.

The last three days have been as bright and spring-like as those five were dark and gloomy. Sunday was a splendid day, sun out bright and clear, sea smooth, health returning, service in the cabin in the afternoon, E—— reading and conducting the service, and I preaching. At noon there was a beautiful rainbow, forming a semicircle and stretching its broad base a mile apparently across the waves.

In the evening there was something still more beautiful. As we were walking the deck we saw little skimmers of auroral light flashing up to the zenith. In a few moments, however, they were all gathered in what you might call an electric cloud, stretching from the northeast to northwest, so thin that you could see the stars through it, while along its whole length the most beautiful colors chased each other in swift succes-

* One of the sailors was swept overboard and lost.

sion. Now it seemed to be the pearl-keyed finger-board of some great organ over which celestial fingers were flashing, and whose music could be heard had we only a sense to catch it. Anon it seemed as if troops of angels, clothed in rainbow hues, were flashing in alternate squadrons far across the heavens. You may think me enthusiastic. But when I tell you that our captain said that in all his voyages he had never seen the like, you can realize it was something really magnificent.

Our captain, by-the-way, is a genius. He is a great linguist, speaking French, German, Swedish, Russ, Italian, Arabic, Spanish, and I know not what. He is also quite a musician, playing clarionet, concertina, violin, and piano, all of which we have heard—as the steward says, "A good few" of instruments. He is, moreover, quite a writer and poet, and has entertained us with a rich fund of anecdote and adventure all the way over.

After spending a few days in Great Britain, stopping at Glasgow, Edinburg, and London, Mr. Payson and his brother hastened, by way of Munich, Innsbruck, Verona, and Florence, to Rome, where they met another younger brother, and made up a party for Egypt and the Holy Land. After spending a few days in Naples and its vicinity, they sailed for Alexandria, and visited Cairo, the Pyramids of Gizeh, Ismailia, and the Suez Canal. At Port Said they took the steamer for Jaffa, where they arrived upon a calm and sunny day, and, in spite of the proverbially rough sea and the yells and shrieks of the barbaric Arab boatmen, who, as every traveller testifies, are really quite as much of a hindrance as a help in reaching the shore, did get safely to land and secure a dragoman to conduct them to Ramleh. Here in the old convent they spent the night. The following day they reached Jerusalem, and his next letter is dated from this centre of Christendom, the dear and ancient city so sacred to every Christian heart.

TO HIS SISTER IN CHINA.

DEAR D——: In our journeyings among nominal Christians and superstitious heathen, I have thought very often of you and your laborious work. How much there is to discourage you! When you look at the teeming millions about you, and then at the little handful that you and others reach, it must weigh you to the ground, especially when you feel that your labors so little impress those whom you have reached. But be of good courage! Jesus worked here in a little land one-third of whose whole area I saw from the tower of Mizpeh the other afternoon. His work was only for three years in this contracted space, and yet to-day it fills the world. Work on, then, in his strength, for you know he works with you, and his word is leaven which shall leaven the whole lump.

I cannot tell you how vivid and intensely interesting all these scenes are, and especially those connected with the Bible. Those old names and places which we have known and learned to love, catch new life and power here, and it seems as if we could step into the brotherhood of the ancient patriarchs and prophets, and feel that they were indeed men of like passions and trials with ourselves, and that as they have conquered, so can we also.

JERUSALEM, March 24. 1873.

MY DEAR, DEAR WIFE: How long it seems since a word reached us from our homes. At London, Munich, and Rome, we were gladdened—since then nothing. Possibly to-morrow friends may bring us news. If so we shall be only too glad to see what we hoped to see at Cairo. It is only some ten days since we landed in Alexandria, and yet it seems an age. If I should write you only a part of what we see each day, it would make a book.

How I wish I could just sit down this evening and tell you and the dear children how we rode out to the Pyramids in a carriage, accompanied by two donkeys, on which we took turns in riding and being laughed at. It seemed as if we never could get to those huge piles that seemed always so near and yet so far. The air is so pure it deceives you completely as to distance. As we at last came up the sand plateau on which the Pyramids stand on the very edge of the desert, the Arabs came running together, and soon we were going up those steep steps at a great rate, with one Arab on each side and another behind pushing at the highest steps. When I tell you that most of those steps were like stepping from the floor to the top of the table, and that there were about three hundred of them, you can understand that it was some work to go up. The view was grand. On one side the desert stretching away towards the Atlantic as far as the eye could reach. On the other, Cairo and the huge hills behind it of sand—between the broad, beautiful plain conquered out of these very sands by the Nile. It was interesting to see the struggle going on between the desert and the great river. It is not strange that the Egyptians should have worshipped the Nile. It is to them a most glorious benefactor. . . . .

At noon we reached Jaffa. The sea was very smooth, so that we went into its ten-feet-wide port with safety; rode that night until eleven and a half o'clock to Ramleh; slept in the convent, and were off next morning to Beth-horon at six o'clock over such paths (they could not be called roads) as I never saw in all my life. We were intensely interested in the Valley of Ajalon, Beth-horon, Gibeon the Royal, and above all, Mizpeh, from whose lofty tower we could see across the land, from the mountains of Moab on the east to the waters of the Mediterranean, north as far as Ophra, and south to Jerusalem and Bethlehem. I cannot tell you my emotions as I looked over that wonderful scene. At my feet Samuel had gathered the people to elect their king; here he had erected Ebenezer; one half hour away at Gibeon the tabernacle had found a place for years, where Solomon offered so many sacrifices and received the wonderful vision promising him wisdom; then there was Jerusalem, that centre of the earth's worship, where the man Christ Jesus preached and suffered, died and ascended. I could not keep back the tears. It was the sublimest view of my life.

Since that I have stood at the foot and on the summit of the Mount of Olives, and I feel more and more there is no place like it on the earth. Yesterday (Sunday) we walked over the Mount to Bethany, and it was delightful to feel that we were looking on the same hills, valleys, and sky, on which Jesus looked when on earth. I know not why, but they are far more to me than Jerusalem itself. We expect to leave here for Hebron and the Jordan to-morrow, returning to Jerusalem to spend the Sabbath, then on to Nazareth, Damascus, Beirut, and beyond: shall leave Beirut (D. V.) the 21st of April for Smyrna, Constantinople, and the Danube. I wish I could tell you where to write next after receiving this, but I can say nothing more definite than Paris. I hoped to write the children, but fear I cannot to-night. May God bless you and keep you all. Love to all the dear ones at Orange, and at the chapel that ask after me.

Yours ever,   CHARLES.

In Camp, Joppa Gate, }
JERUSALEM, March 31, 1873.}

My Dear, Dear Wife: How I wish I could see all your dear faces to-night, and sleep under my own comfortable roof, spite of all I am enjoying. I have reached the last half of my time, and can hope soon, if the good Lord wills, to see you all again. It is so very long since either

E—— or I have heard a single word from our families. At Naples, Cairo, Jerusalem, the same cruel "*Nothing*" has greeted all our inquiries. And now we must leave to-morrow without the slightest prospect of a letter till we reach Beîrut. We must make the best of it, I suppose, and I will endeavor to drive it from my mind by telling you something of our tent-life and the strange experiences through which we are passing.

A week ago last Tuesday we started from Jerusalem for the pools of Solomon, about two and a half hours from here, to begin camp-life. Our dragoman, Esau Malook, had six horses ready for Messrs. N——, S—— of Dayton, Ohio, a young Englishman, E——, G——, and myself. The wind blew so fiercely that, just before we reached Rachel's Tomb, it sent my hat spinning across the fields, spite of the elastic by which it was fastened, and threatened to blow every garment I wore after it. About six o'clock we came to our camp, already prepared for us. We found three tents. They were about fourteen feet across. Two of them were sleeping tents, each of which contained three iron bedsteads for as many individuals, with beds and covering.... Rugs covered the ground within; a table fastened to the tent-pole adorned the centre, while nice camp-stools were arranged for seats. The third tent served as dining-room. We were hungry as bears, and you will sympathize with us when I tell you of the fare to which our cook subjected us: (1) Soup; (2) fish; (3) mutton roast, with peas; (4) birds, with salad, in sauce; (5) apricots, deliciously cooked; (6) oranges, nuts, dates, and raisins, with good tea and coffee. Don't you pity us?

For breakfast we have eggs, either boiled, fried, or in omelette, mutton chops and potatoes, with coffee, tea, or chocolate, as we may choose. At noon, by the wayside, under some shadowy tree, we usually have a cold lunch of chicken, mutton, sardines, ham, nuts, raisins, and oranges, on which we have thus far managed to survive till dinner came again.

When I tell you that the roughest roads in North Lyme are better than the best here, and that such a thing as a carriage is unknown, you will wonder how it is possible for these dragomen to carry so much comfort around with them. They do it by means of donkeys, on whose backs they strap not only tents, bedsteads, etc., but huge boxes full of crockery, so full that they can change the plates and knives and forks (the latter silver, the former Sheffield cutlery) between each course.

Wednesday morning at eight o'clock we were off for Hebron. Cook's party had three-quarters of an hour the start, but we caught them in two hours, and rode with them, in a dense fog or drizzling rain, all the way to Hebron. We soon came upon the vineyards of Eschol. The whole of this part of the country is given up to the vine. Hebron, lying in the midst of a beautiful valley, is a lively place of about eight thousand inhabitants. We rode along the narrow streets, about as wide as our sidewalks, jostling among the people, till at last we came to what seemed part of a house. It was all covered over, and so full of people that I should as soon have thought of riding into a large store. As I led the party, I came to an abrupt halt. A man, however, took my horse by the head, and led us along till we came to a sharp turn, when we saw the Mosque of Mach-pelah right before us. We could only look at the outside, as they do not permit Christians to enter.

We took our lunch in the sheik's house, and saw a woman with paint-ed eyes sitting on the floor grinding barley. The upper millstone whirled around on another hollow stone, which had a little trough by the side of it into which the meal rolled as it was ground. After lunch we rode about twenty-five minutes, and this brought us to the famous old oak of Abra-ham, under which, it is said, he entertained the angels. It is the only tree of the kind in this region, and if not *the* tree (!) appears more worthy of the honor than any we saw elsewhere. It rained very fast ; but, thanks to overcoat and shawl, which I wrapped around me, I was able to keep pretty dry. I have been a little prolix in my description of twenty-four hours, because it will help you to understand that during the next four days we enjoyed much in journeying to Bethlehem, Mar Saba, the Dead Sea, Jor-dan, Jericho, and Jerusalem.

I never felt better than I do now, and I can but hope that this tent-life will give me a vigor and energy I have not enjoyed for months. We had a most capital sermon from Rev. Mr. Aspinwall of New York, and a delightful communion-service yesterday morning, at the English chapel, under the care of Bishop Gobat. I send as much love as this little sheet can carry to all my dear friends in Orange and the chapel. Please remem-ber me most kindly to all who think of me.

Your good letter directed to Naples I have just received. It has been lying in the postoffice a week in an out-of-way place. We shall go from Beirut to Athens, and thence to Constantinople, where we shall be in about thirty-three days. We leave for Bethel in a few minutes now, and I have no more time to write. With much love,

Your own,   C——.

DAMASCUS, April, 1873.

MY DEAR, DEAR WIFE : You do not know how glad I am to feel that from this old city my homeward journey begins. This is our extreme eastern limit, and now " Westward the star," etc. It seems so very long since I saw all your dear faces.

This Damascus is a quaint old place, with a beauty all its own. Its abundant water is its greatest glory. Take away the Awaj and Barada of to-day, or the Pharphar and the Abana of the past, and Damascus is a desert, like the great waste of sand which surrounds it. As it is, you see a large city of fifteen thousand inhabitants (surrounded by one hundred villages, containing some fifty thousand more) buried in gardens and trees, vocal with running brooks and gushing fountains, and the whole set in a frame that adds not a little to the picture—a desert, and barren or snow-covered mountains.

I wish I could give you a sight of the moon as it rises night after night behind the minarets of the city and the minaret-shaped poplars which grace the gardens here. There is a peculiar golden tinge to the desert air that surrounds it which makes you feel yourself in dream-land at once, and ready to listen to the "Arabian Nights" or any similar entertainment. And if you saunter along down the banks of the river, and see the lights gleaming through the lattices, or weird processions coming out of narrow streets, guiding their steps by gauze, glass, or paper lanterns, you feel as though it was not reality, but a picture of the lotus-eater's imagination on which you were gazing. You will think I am just giving wing to fancies, but I assure you I never saw a city like this before.

Since I wrote the first page I have taken a canter with the rest of the party up to the sand-hill back of the city. The clouds which hung over us seemed made of desert sand instead of mist, and fell down about the hill in the most peculiar folds, threatening to break upon us at any moment. As we turned and looked back upon the city, I was quite unprepared for the scene. There it lay—Church's picture—with its white towers, houses, domes, and minarets, perfectly embowered in the greenest foliage—a beautiful pearl set in brightest emerald. As we came back we peered over walls six or eight feet high, made of mud, into the hidden beauties of gardens filled with apricot, quince, peach, orange, lemon, pomegranate, and various other fruit-trees, with grains, grasses, and herbs of every kind interspersed. Everything depends on the water; hence you find the people making what may be called sunken beds, from twenty-five to thirty feet long, and twelve or fourteen wide, which they surround with a little bank some six inches high. Into any one of these beds they can turn the many streams, which appear to gush forth on every side, until it is sufficiently moistened, when they divert them into some other thirsty bed.

Yesterday I preached for Dr. Patterson, one of the pastors of the United Presbyterian Mission, and had a very pleasant service. Most of the audience were travellers whom I have met from time to time as our paths have crossed in coming from Jerusalem here. To-morrow we leave for Beirut, and I will try to write you another page about the ruins and Lebanon.

Here I am, dear M——, up among these wonderful ruins of old Baalbec. I thought, from my reading, I was somewhat prepared for them, but the tenth part was not told me. At first sight you are impressed with the grandeur of the buildings. Think of one structure with an entrance or vestibule 180 feet wide and 37 feet deep, approached formerly by not less than 250 steps. Then comes a beautiful hexagon room 200 feet across ; then a large court, with several recesses and niches, 476 feet wide and 400 long ; then the temple proper, 300 feet by 160, surrounded by 54 magnificent columns, 6 standing, the remainder on the ground, or carried away. You can realize the size better when I tell you that, as I stood by the base of one of these fallen columns, it reached one and a half feet above my head, being about 8 feet through and 25 feet round. I know these words convey little, if any, idea of it to you. If you will look in Thomson's "Land and Book," vol. 1, p. 358, you will find a description of the ruins and a plan which will give you a better idea. I felt their grandeur somewhat as I rode in through a great vaulted archway, which must have been 150 feet long, built of huge stones and adorned with beautiful faces looking down from the ceiling ; but I felt it most of all when I stood by the side of the immense foundation-stones, which are so large that they gave name to the whole building, and it was called "Three-Stone Temple." They are each over 60 feet long and some 13 feet square. The three stones together are as long as a city block, and the whole structure would cover from Forty-second street to Thirty-eighth street, and from Lexington to Third avenue.

Adjoining it is another temple called the "Great Temple of the Sun," or Apollo. It is as beautiful as the other is grand, and is about 230 feet long by 117 wide. The great doorway is 21 feet wide and 42 high. It is surrounded by the most exquisite carvings of flowers, fruits, figures, etc., 4 feet wide on each side. The niches inside are also surrounded by carvings which look more like lace-work than stone. One, of which I made a little sketch, is a semicircle in shape, some 3½ feet in radius. The carved figures on the outer edge of the little arch come in this order : first, four stalks of wheat, then a grape or oak leaf, with six projections, then two seed-vesicles of the poppy. These are repeated fourteen times in this one niche, and I cannot give you the slightest idea of their exquisite perfection and beauty. Each niche has its own distinct design.

I wish you and all the dear friends were here to enjoy this admirable ruin, so beautifully situated between Lebanon and Anti-Lebanon, in the lovely valley of the Burka, which opens away to the south as far as the eye can reach. Thomson, you will see, argues strongly for this being the Baal-gad of the Bible, and thinks the ruins indicate the hand of a Solomon. It is singular that the Mohammedans attribute them to Solomon, son of David. A beautiful spring gushes forth into a stream half a mile from here and flows down past the temple, making a garden of beauty along its course.

I hope this has not wearied you. I cannot tell you how happy I am to face westward. Three days nearer home than when I left Damascus !

14

I shall expect to be with you early in June. We think now of going by Constantinople and the Danube, Vienna, Strasburg, Paris, London, etc. Love to all my dear friends in Orange and New York, Pray for me. Good-by. Kisses for the dear children from   PAPA.

TO HIS SUNDAY-SCHOOL.

MUNICH, 1873.

MY DEAR CHILDREN: Yesterday and the day before we were travelling on the banks of two of the most famous rivers in Germany—the Rhine and the Neckar. We were kept busy running from one side of the railroad-car to the other looking at the castles perched on the hills and cliffs on either bank. Every one has its own strange story, and they all remind me of one line in the Bible : "Their works do follow them." It is in the last book. See if you can find it.

I thought I would tell you a little about the most famous and most beautiful of these castles. That you may better remember it, I send you two things : first, a leaf picked off the walls, and next, the picture which stands at the beginning of this letter. You see the castle is built on the side of a high hill, called the "Königstuhl," or King's Throne. Below it lies the city, which has the same name as the castle—Heidelberg. It is on the left bank of the beautiful Neckar, and on the other side is another high hill called the "Holy Mountain," because many years ago a good man lived there in a cave.

A hundred years before America was discovered by Columbus, a man named Rudolph began this castle. He lived first in a strong place on the Rhine, but I suppose he thought this place more beautiful and just as strong, so he came here and built the first part of this palace-castle. He was a count, very rich and brave and selfish, I should think. I say selfish, for his castle shows that he was very much afraid somebody would rob him. Having robbed other men, he was afraid of them, and therefore built his stronghold on the side of this steep hill. I do not think you could climb up the path at all, for I saw strong men sit down and rest before they got even to the foot of the castle wall. Then, too, he made it of stone, very strong and thick. One tower, which he thought the strongest, has walls over twenty feet thick, that is, thicker than our house is wide. He cut narrow windows, called loopholes, through these thick walls on every side, so that he could put his guns out and shoot anybody that tried to get at him. Having dug a deep ditch all around his castle, he filled it with water, and over this ditch there was one narrow bridge, the only way by which anybody could get to the gate of the castle. This bridge was pulled up every night. The gate was made of strong timber covered with iron. It could be lifted, and its sharp teeth would come down in a minute if the soldiers wished to crush any one passing under it.

Rudolph and his descendants lived here for more than four hundred years, and the people who gathered around these counts lived at the foot of the hill, and went out with them to fight against their enemies, and expected them to protect their homes. But do you suppose they always did it? No; spite of all their efforts, poor Heidelberg has been plundered three times, cannonaded five times, and twice burned up. If you examine the picture closely, you will see the castle is in ruin. More than one hundred years ago they had to give it up. Strong as it was, the French took it. Perhaps the count and his family escaped by a secret passage which leads down a long flight of stairs, runs under the city, under the river itself, and comes out more than a mile away from the castle. The French put powder under that strong tower of which I spoke, and it split into two great pieces. One remained where it was, the other slipped down into the ditch, and lies there to-day.

So you see these ruins tell two stories: first, they say how cruel and selfish these men must have been to need such castles to defend them; and second, how cruel and mean their enemies must have been to have burned and ruined the beautiful building and city it took so many hundred years to finish.

There is another part of the castle which tells a different story. It is a wing built of cut stone by one of these counts for the home of his wife, whom he dearly loved. Behind it was her garden full of fine trees and flowers. Wishing to surprise her, he had a very beautiful gate made of costly stones and finely carved. The stones were made ready, and one night the workmen came and put it all up in a few hours. In the morning the princess went out into her garden and was amazed to see the gate. Coming nearer, she saw some words on it which said it was a present from her husband to his dear wife. That was three hundred years ago, but there it stands to-day, and is called " Elizabeth's Gate," sometimes, " Beautiful Gate."

Children, your works will follow you. God help you to build in love, not in hate. Then before all the world he will put a crown on your head, and say, " Well done." My paper is filled, and I say Good-by.

From your affectionate Pastor.

CHAPTER VII.

THE OLD AND THE NEW.

It will readily be seen, from what has been said in previous chapters, that the attachment of Mr. Payson's flock to the old chapel must have been very great. That rough room, which, with its uncarpeted floor and un-cushioned benches and ugly wooden posts, appeared so little like a church, was nevertheless the spiritual birth-place and home of many a weary soul, who there found comfort and rest and joy such as no other spot on earth could give. To more than one member of the mission congregation that bare and desolate-looking room had become indeed a Bethel, where the very words and expe-rience of the patriarch were repeated in their hearts.

It was, therefore, with no ordinary emotions of regret, after all the preparations had been made, that they turned to leave the old chapel at last. When the final hour of worship had arrived, and the new, large edifice on Thir-tieth street, with its spacious and quiet auditorium and beautiful Sunday-school rooms, stood ready to receive them, the pastor preached a sermon* to his people in which he endeavored to give some expression to the min-gled feelings of joy and sorrow with which they stood upon the threshold of the old. His text was chosen in Ezra 3: 12, 13: "'But many of the priests and Levites

* Sabbath evening, March 21, 1875.

and chief of the fathers, who were ancient men, that had seen the first house, when the foundation of this house was laid before their eyes, wept with a loud voice; and many shouted aloud for joy; so that the people could not discern the noise of the shout of joy from the noise of the weeping of the people; for the people shouted with a loud shout, and the noise was heard afar off.'

"How thoughts and emotions wrought tumultuously in human hearts twenty-four hundred years ago in Jerusalem! A remnant of Israel's millions had returned from Babylon. Among the ruins of the sacred city the foundations of the new temple had been laid, and the people gathered to place the cornerstone. Young and old were there. Men who, between fifty and sixty years ago, had gone up to the temple of Solomon, and had looked upon that glorious building, which was one of the wonders of the world, stood among them. Is it strange that they wept as they contrasted the present weakness with the past glory, or that profound emotions stirred their souls as they recalled all of loss and trial they had passed through since last they looked upon that temple, going out in flames, and dying a ruin at their feet?

"These wept, and others sang and rejoiced. Those who had often heard of the past in the land of tears, rejoiced that once more the Lord had 'done great things for them.' The same God who had brought Israel out of Egypt with a mighty hand, had come and brought them out of Assyria; and more than this, he had touched the heart of Cyrus, so that he helped Israel with army and treasure, while Pharaoh, when he held

*

them captive, did all he could to prevent their exodus. Throughout this exile they had had neither temple nor tabernacle—a thing Israel had not known before for a thousand years ; but now they were to have their own temple again, and they shouted and sang.* . . .

"As we glance at the past, the best thoughts, it seems to me, are those which recall the good hand of our God upon us in all these years of our *growth—material, intellectual, and spiritual.*

"(1.) Let us look first at the *material growth* of our church. What hath not God wrought in this direction ! Twenty years ago, a lady, one Sabbath afternoon, saw idle boys and girls in the street, and called them into the basement of her house. The little Sunday-school there begun was soon moved into a room on Thirty-fourth street. In the fall that school divided, one part locating on the west side, the other on the east. The eastern school had in it the germs of this work.

"The first Sunday-school services were held in a rough, uncomfortable room in Twenty-ninth street. Then the school removed in a few months to the public school building in Twenty-seventh street, where it remained until its own building—this chapel—was completed, January 10, 1858.

* Both the sermons in this chapter, it should be said, are fragmentary and incomplete even in the manuscripts ; and they are selected for publication not so much because of their intrinsic value as specimens of Mr. Payson's oratory, as because of their intimate connection with the history of his church. Still they may serve in a measure as illustrations of his style, if only it is borne in mind that they are at best but outlines or sketches. It will be remembered (*cf.* page 89) that he always spoke extemporaneously.

"In two years, more room was needed; the wings on each side, and that part of this room from the pillar eastward, were added; and the same kind Hand which helped us to gain so many blessings then, has been with us all these fourteen years since. Once more we have had to lengthen our cords and strengthen our stakes. God grant that it may not be the last time. May the success of the past only stimulate us to nobler and higher endeavors in the future.

"Nor should we overlook the growth indicated by increased contributions. Thirteen years ago I find our contributions were less than one hundred dollars for all benevolent work in this church. Now they have risen to nearly four thousand as the regular average amount, and this year's receipts will be probably over $6,000. And this, dear friends, is only the reflection of a like prosperity which through this very work has come to many a home connected with us.

"(2.) *Intellectually* we have grown. How many will look back to this place as the school where their minds were disciplined. By lectures and sermons, prayer-meeting and Bible class, Sunday-school and library, have they been led to grapple with the grandest truths which ever stir the minds of men, the truths of revelation. [Sir Isaac Newton's testimony.] . . . Some, in preparing to help others, have helped themselves yet more. . . . Other some will recall with profound emotion the noble teachers who for almost a score of years, in and out of season, have labored for their good. . . .

"(3.) Best of all is the *spiritual growth* connected with

this sacred place.   What revelations of God's love and grace have we received within these sacred walls ! Some will say in the Psalmist's words, ' I was born there.' There my life really began. There God quickened me, who was dead in trespasses and sins. There.he wrought the greatest miracle in me, the miracle of redemption.   If there is a peculiar feeling connected with one's birthplace—if men will travel thousands of miles and make unnumbered sacrifices to die where they were born, what words can fitly describe the tender emotions that will move many a heart as they turn back in memory to the place where God first met and called them his, and how will they praise and magnify his name for those great gifts which he has here bestowed.   I believe that even in heaven this dear old chapel will be remembered with reverence and affection.

   " Again, others will recall that this for them has been a place of spiritual growth and culture.   Here they first began to pray, to work, and to give.   And as they look back over prayer-meeting, Sabbath-school, Bible class, sermons, and communions, blessed to them in this very room, they will say, ' This is my Bethel.   It is none other than the house of God, the very gate of heaven !'   Others, too, recall to-night with peculiar emotions dear friends who here plumed their wings for glory.   We saw them ripening fast, and knew not that it was because the King would soon call them to thrones and kingdoms with him for ever.   Hallowed are these memories.   But joy triumphs over sorrow, for we know our loss is to them eternal gain.   Part of the host is in heaven. . . .

" But note that God rebukes the sorrow of some on this very occasion, Hag. 2 : 4, 9 . . . ' Be strong, all ye people, saith the Lord, and work, for I am with you, saith the Lord of hosts. The glory of this latter house shall be greater than of the former, and in this place will I give peace, saith the Lord of hosts.' Do not limit me. I gave to you the ark, the tabernacle, yea, and the temple ; and I took them away for better things. You would have made idols of them as of Nehushtan ; I would lift you to a higher worship. . . .

" So in due time 'the Word was made flesh, and dwelt among us.' And it is said, ' Ye are the temples of God, and the Spirit of God dwelleth in you ;' . . . God ever drawing nearer, until he enters the very soul.

"Let us, then, beware of limiting our God. It is not these stained and dingy walls, these posts dividing our audience-room in twain, nor the ungainly and cumbered entrance, which has brought the blessing. No ! it is only because, in spite of these obstacles, God has been with us. Oh, limit him not ! If any one years ago had said, ' Keep the school in the basement, or had forbidden us to add this library, class-rooms, and German chapel,' would it have been well ? So let no one weaken the hands of his brethren by saying, ' It had been better to-day in the old place.'

" But, none the less, let us remember that God only can make these new courts glorious. As walls and seats here have not the blessing in themselves, so God must be with us, or all is vain and lost. . . . [. . . David and ark— Uzziah—Uzzah].

"Now we need to impress upon our hearts this solemn lesson. We are to feel that no building is of itself sacred. The pulpit, communion-table, seats, organ, are nothing in themselves. It is only as they become helps to spiritual life and worship that they can prove real blessings to our souls. Look at John 4:23, 24: 'But the hour cometh, and now is, when the true worshippers shall worship the Father in spirit and in truth; for the Father seeketh such to worship him. God is a Spirit, and they that worship him must worship him in spirit and in truth.' Through faith and prayer only can we reach after Christ and find him. 'My house,' says Jesus, 'shall be called the house of prayer.' It is a place to commune with God. . . .

". . . Above all other things, let us remember that love is the fulfilling of the law. Therefore may all hatred, envies, jealousies, evil speaking, be left behind us. May each, in the spirit of love and holy courtesy, seek not his own, but his neighbor's good. And thus may we show to the poor and stranger those divine fruits of Christian charity that have made this old chapel beautiful to many a weary heart. . . .

"By faith, dear friends, we can reach our hands to Christ. By prayer, through Christ, we can receive the Holy Ghost, and he shall be to each of us, wherever we may be, the Comforter and Guide to everlasting life. . . .

"In my journey through Palestine, we paused on the heights of Samaria. A glorious view opened before us. Below and to the south lay the beautiful plain of El-Mukhna, suggesting in its loveliness the precious

memory of sacred places left behind—Jerusalem, Bethany, Gethsemane. Before us lay the path to Nazareth
and Galilee, and other spots endeared to every Christian
heart by words and miracles of Christ ; while far beyond, to the eye of faith, appeared the borders of another
land. Should we then linger there ? We might well
rejoice to remain among such scenes for ever ; but to
the north lay our homeward way. Duty, honor, work
called us to go forward.

"So here we stand to-night. God calls us to a new
place and a new work for him. Hearing this word, let
us go forward, believing that he is able to make the way
plain to better things on earth and the glories of the
New Jerusalem hereafter."

The Annual Report of the Chapel Committee, read,
April 21, 1875, by Mr. David Wetmore, chairman, before a public meeting of the Madison Square Church,
contains the following reference to the Memorial
Chapel :

"It is doubtless known to all present that this church
decided to appropriate their Memorial Contributions to
the erection of a new edifice for the better accommoda-
tion of those worshipping at the chapel, feeling that, with
enlarged and more comfortable quarters both for Sunday-
school and church services, the numbers and efficiency
of the organization would be increased and the cause of
the Master promoted. It will also be remembered that
at the date of the last Annual Report the Chapel Committee announced that the land had been contracted for

in four lots on the north side of Thirtieth street, 100 feet
east of Third avenue; size, 100 feet front by 98 feet 9
inches deep.   The lots were delivered in June, and work
commenced soon after.   The cornerstone was laid on
September 14 by our pastor the Rev. William Adams,
and the chapel was dedicated to the service of the Master on Easter Sunday, March 28.

"It will not of course be expected that we in this
Report to you should describe the edifice, as it has spoken for itself to most of you, and certainly should to all.
Its praise already is in most of the churches.   We must,
however, be permitted to mingle our congratulations with
yours, sir, and our fellow-members', that we have been
permitted, in the good providence of God, to add another
temple to his praise, to open another sanctuary in his
name, whose word of invitation is, 'Whosoever will, let
him come.'

"The old chapel—also memorial—will soon pass from
our possession.   Can we take leave of it without the
liveliest emotions of gratitude to Him who hath led us
there in all these years.   He has been there in the midst,
and that to bless.   There men have been born again, and
little children have sat at His feet.   Its walls have echoed
the song of praise, and notes of joy have been carried up
to the temple not made with hands.   To it the Lord has
looked, and from it the heart-whisper has gone to his
open ear.   A little while some were with us there, and
again a little while and they were not, for they had followed Him who went to prepare a place for them.   Rich,
full, and hallowed are the memories that cling to the old

chapel. Richer, fuller, and more sacred may those be that shall cluster around the new."

The following description of the new church is kindly furnished us by the architect, Mr. J. C. Cady of this city.

This building is designed to meet the wants of a large and growing congregation for church and other services, to accommodate (separately from the church auditorium) one of the largest Sabbath-schools in the city, and to provide for the independent services of a German congregation, as well as the various organizations connected with the general work. It has been the purpose of its architect not only to meet these varied wants, but to infuse into the whole an artistic spirit appropriate to the peculiarities and arrangement of the building. He has designed the details involving ornamental effect with especial reference to this—the stained glass windows, the organ, the furniture, and appointments generally. The building covers a plot of 100x100. The front, to a depth of about forty feet, is three stories in height, and is used for Sabbath-school and kindred purposes. On the first floor the infant-classes have three large rooms, which may be connected or otherwise by sliding doors, and which can, if desired, be connected with the auditorium.

On the second floor and over the infant-rooms is the main Sunday-school hall, accommodating several hundred children, also the Library and superintendent's rooms. Over this story is one devoted to Bible-classes, having some fourteen rooms, each adapted to from twenty to thirty persons. A large class of young men have with great interest raised funds by which their apartment has been quite elaborately and beautifully furnished.

The various stories described face the south, having an abundance of light (and sunshine if desired). In the rear of these, covering about 68x100 feet, is the church auditorium, seating about eleven hundred persons. It is approached by broad, well-lighted halls at either end of the façade, as well as a spacious central entrance. This room is in form an elongated octagon, and gets light from seven of the eight sides, transmitted through large traceried windows that are placed quite a height from the floor, giving much dignity and loftiness of effect. The lighting of the room is further increased by a large panelled ceiling light, which will also throw the organ into bright relief when its decorated pipes shall have been added.

The seating is based upon a polygonal figure, and brings all the auditors easily within the influence of the speaker, and with cosey and social effect. The pulpit is placed at the centre of the rear wall.

The organ is bracketed out from this wall above the pulpit, and is

15

designed, by means of its richly-decorated pipes, to be the focal point of the room.

The roof is of the "open timber" variety, the spandrels of the large trusses being filled with ornamental work. The iron work is exposed to view and emphasized by decoration.

On the east side the series of large traceried windows is discontinued, (a necessity owing to the position of an adjoining building,) and there is an arcade of seven smaller windows.

A lofty clock, rising from the auditorium belt-course to the central window, will, when in its place, complete the grouping.

Two large light-wells, (one on either side of the building,) built of masonry, do the further service of receiving the smoke-flues, the ventilating and the rain-water pipes; so in case of damage to either, it would be limited to the masonry well. The ventilating-flues are built around the smoke-flues and heated by them, gaining a strong draft which draws off the foul air of the building. It is believed that thus grouping together these important, but sometimes troublesome and dangerous adjuncts of a building, will prove an advantage both as regards efficiency and safety.

The style of the building is the early French Gothic.

The façade on Thirtieth street is built of Philadelphia pressed brick, with trimmings of Nova Scotia stone and buff brick. A tower, with belfry, stage, and spire, terminates each end of the façade, while a large gable with a rose-window rises over the central portion. The many rooms of the front portion, all requiring plentiful light, have rendered necessary a large number of windows. These have been grouped and emphasized with reference to the general effect.

The building and furniture have cost about $60,000.

Upon entering the new chapel, Easter Sunday, March 28, 1875, Mr. Payson delivered a discourse, of which the following is a rough outline. The notes of this sermon were fragmentary, and this attempt at reproduction is in consequence very imperfect, but it may serve the purpose of indicating in a rude way his line of thought.

"'*THESE STONES SHALL BE FOR A MEMORIAL.*'
JOSH. 4: 7.

"'Can we ever forget?' some might have asked, as they stepped dry-shod out of the bed of the Jordan. To

Memorial Chapel of the Madison Square Church.

many an Israelite a memorial may have seemed unnecessary. 'This wonderful experience, this parting of the
spring-floods of Jordan, this passing with ease where our
enemies believed that we could not pass at all—can these
ever fade from memory?' Perhaps not.....

"But man 'cometh forth like a flower, and is cut
down; he fleeth also as a shadow, and continueth not.'
This generation and the next passed away, what will
have become of this story? Gone, gone for ever, or else
mingled with the myths of the past in a confusion worse
than oblivion itself. Why! Men to-day doubt the existence of Troy and Homer!.... Hence a memorial
was needful, and for two reasons: (1) to stimulate inquiry, and (2) to strengthen memory; so that (ver. 24)
'all the people of the earth might know the hand of the
Lord that it is mighty, that ye might fear the Lord your
God for ever.'

"God has surrounded us with memorials. The rainbow, the passover, the Lord's Supper, and the Sabbath—
all these are memorials; and God has thus endorsed that
feeling, which is almost instinctive in human hearts, to
rear some monuments of special grace..... So then
we have divine encouragement to make this building
serve a double purpose: that while we gather here to
learn new lessons of his love, we may at the same time
be reminded of the past and all the favors and the blessings it has brought.

"In the providence of God this building serves as a
triple memorial; and the very day when we are permitted to present this gift to him is the chief of all the days

of the year, for not only is it *a* Sabbath, but *the* Sabbath
of Sabbaths. Is it not Easter Sunday? and are we not
permitted to feel that this is one of the best-established
of all the memorial days? Before, the Sabbath marked
the Creation; from that first Easter it marks a greater
and more precious event, namely: the victory of Christ
over death and the grave, and through him the victory
of all whom he represents—the army of the redeemed in
every age and clime.

"And this anniversary of religious liberty is a fitting
time to recall that, one hundred years ago, our fathers
began their great struggle for freedom. Often, in the
course of the next fifteen months, I shall have occasion
to refer to this. Now I will only remind you that, but
for God's great goodness, we should to-day have no city,
state, or general government. Who that was a partici-
pant in the last war, who that saw the mob surging along
our streets a few years since, does not thank God that
we have a church in which to worship?

"There are, however, apart from these general consid-
erations, two objects for which this new building must
ever serve as a special memorial. The first is the reunion
of the Old and New School Presbyterian Churches; the
second, the united efforts of the two branches of the Madison Square Church for sixteen long years, which have
finally culminated in the erection of this new edifice.

"I. *The Reunion.* Surely, *we* ought to recall, with
profound gratitude, the reunion of the divided Presbyterian Church of America. To it, under God, we owe the

final erection of this building. All previous efforts had met with comparative failure. We were aground. But that grand tidal wave of benevolence which swept over the united church in 1871, bore us on to success. That this aid came from God, is apparent from the reports of the Committee who had the Memorial Fund in charge. Enthusiastically had the General Assembly in Philadelphia, in 1870, voted as a thank-offering, to be collected within a year, a fund of five millions. But ten and a half months passed away, and the Committee could only report part of one million contributed. Then it was that they went to God, and, in the striking language of their excellent chairman, gave all up to him, feeling that, if such was his will, they would gladly content themselves with two or three millions. And then it was that God appeared in power and seemed to move the churches as by a common impulse.

"How many here to-day remember that wonderful seven weeks when we raised more than $4,000, and the parent church ten times that sum. You will recall that the whole Presbyterian Church reported not five, but eight millions; and with the two which the Committee felt were given to other objects then on account of it—even ten millions. Thus under God we have reason to trace the erection of this church to the influence of the reunion.

"But this was only one out of many deliverances which He wrought at that time. Think what a work that reunion was. In the Old School branch there were some 2,700 churches, and 250,000 members; in the New

School 1,800 churches, and 170,000 members. What a body to harmonize! For more than thirty years they had been separated. The division had been felt not only in seminaries and in all educational and benevolent institutions, but in the churches themselves. Often in the same little village two poor organizations would struggle for existence till their life seemed a living death. So bitter was the feeling and so great the obstacles to be overcome, that wise men on the Committee said that, while they were willing to work for the reunion, they never expected to see its consummation during their lifetime. Think of the eight long years required to accomplish the work, and we realize the numberless difficulties to be met.

"There was one dark hour recorded which will illustrate our obligations to Him who has given us all. The Committee had been striving for several days to arrive at some statement which should harmonize all minds; but it seemed an utter impossibility. They separated for three or four hours for refreshment and rest, feeling that when they came together again it would be to decide that no way to union now seemed attainable. Dr. Gurley (who died soon afterwards) went away not to rest, but to fast and pray, and while in prayer the Gurley Amendment, so called, came to him. The Committee met, and with joyful surprise found that it covered the case. So again we were saved.

"But the hand of our God is seen even more strikingly in the removal of American slavery. Dr. Adams, in his interesting article on the reunion remarks, that slavery, as it caused the war, had also much to do with the division of the Presbyterian Church. This was not generally recognized in public debate. But large ships are turned about by that plank which is out of sight beneath the water. The entire extinction of slavery has been among the many causes which has made reunion more possible and more certain. What occasion for joy have we then to-day, as we feel that this beautiful building becomes a memorial of the extinction of American slavery, the foulest blot that ever rested on the fair name of our beloved land. May the lesson of those long years of suffering endured by the negro, and of the fearful four years of civil war, with all their sacrifices of treasure and blood, never pass from our minds. May it help to make sin more exceeding hateful. May it enable us to realize that the putting away of one sin will lead to the removal of a thousand other evils, and open the door to numberless blessings which perhaps otherwise we never could have seen.

" As a church we owe profound gratitude to God for permitting us in his providence to occupy so honorable a position in consummating this work. Dr. Adams was very unexpectedly called to take a leading position as chairman of the Reunion Committee. Here his wisdom and rare judgment did much to bring about the best results. The memorial says that his speeches at New York and Pittsburg contributed most powerfully to the conviction which seemed finally to become unanimous, that reunion was safe and right and most glorifying to God. So distinguished were his services that some have felt that we might depart from the usual custom, and rear this memorial to his honor, even while he is still with us. But we know that this would not be his desire, and that he would rather say in the words of the Psalmist, 'Not unto us, O Lord, not unto us, but unto thy name give glory, for thy mercy and for thy truth's sake.' How fitting however it was that the church which through God's providence has been so signally honored, should bring the largest memorial offering and lay it down at Jesus' feet. Of the four thousand churches of our body, the Madison Square contributed the greatest amount, obtaining over $182,000, (one hundred and eighty-two thousand dollars). . . .

"May this building then remind us of God's goodness in securing (1) the Reunion, (2) the Extinction of Slavery, and (3) that Generosity which resulted in so many blessed fruits both at home and abroad.

"II. In the second place these stones are a memorial of the *united efforts* put forth by the two branches of our own church towards securing the erection of this edifice.

"We are reminded first of all of an eventful evening in October, 1867. During the previous week I had attended a meeting of the American Board, and my heart had been stirred by the loving sacrifices of the converts from heathenism—especially the work done by the poor churches connected with the Harpoot Mission, which led me to inquire if I was encouraging my people to do all that they could. If those, whose means were as nothing compared with ours, could do so much, should not we be ashamed to do so little? That night I told you the

story of what I had seen and heard as best I could.
You were greatly interested. But when I asked if you
were ready to practically apply the lesson, if each one
would undertake the next three years to do your best to
raise $10,000 towards a new building, you were some-
what staggered, and I do not wonder. This was over
$3,000 a year, and we had never raised more than one-
half that sum in the same length of time.

"But each one was asked to give only as the Lord
blessed, and to give not for your pastor's sake, but to
God himself, and for Christ's glory. Then we united in
silent prayer. Then came the moment on which the
existence of this building under God depended. I shall
never forget that moment. Would you assume this burden, or not? Nor shall I ever forget that rising vote.
No man waited for his neighbor, no man looked right or
left ; but, as if moved by one spirit, every member of our
church, I think, and almost every member of the congregation arose. It was a glorious moment in our history,
and these stones are its memorial here. What memorial
God hath made of it above, eternity will reveal.

"In the first year you raised the sum called for, and
I doubt not the third year would have seen the amount
required, had it not become evident that the new church
would not then be built. At the end of three years,
however, we had $6,000 in bank.

"The following spring witnessed our extraordinary
efforts to secure the Memorial Fund. Then you were
asked to raised $4,000 in seven weeks. Could you pos-
sibly do it? .... Some gave fifty cents, some two dol-

lars, some five, twenty-five, fifty, one hundred, two hun-
dren, two hundred and twenty-five even ; and at the end
of the time allotted more than $3,000 were paid in, and
a conditional offer made the sum more than $4,000. Ah!
those were days of prayer and sacrifice! Who of us
that had a share in that work will ever forget what zeal,
enthusiasm, and devotion to the Lord, characterized it
from the first. Some gave their souvenirs of better
days. Some sold their jewelry and keepsakes. Some
promised money, and knew not where the work was to
be found by which it could be secured. They prayed
for work, and it came ; and their pledges given in faith
were redeemed. It is a remarkable fact that out of
hundreds of subscriptions, only between twenty or thirty
remained unpaid at the end of seven weeks.

"That $10,000 put at interest, became $12,000 ; and
these stones are for a memorial. They show what this
church, through God's blessing, has done in the past,
and what therefore we have reason to believe we can do
in the future.

"These stones too are a beautiful memorial of the
generous spirit which has ever ruled among our brethren
at the Madison Square Church toward those who meet
at Third avenue. From the beginning, twenty years
ago, they have shown the most liberal spirit toward this
work. But when we came to the memorial collection
for the erection of this building, an event occurred which
is not to be forgotten to-day. Instead of giving by collection or subscription as is their custom, they made it
a Freewill Offering. In accordance with the sugges-

tion of their pastor, each donor sent an envelope containing his contribution. . . . It was snowing as he
make the request; and with his wonted felicity of language, Dr. Adams suggested that their offerings should
come into his house even as the snowflakes were then
falling upon the earth. Thence came the name of
'Snowflake Offering,' which was given to that noble gift
of $40,000.

"It is one of my greatest joys connected with this
building to recall that it is built entirely of freewill offerings. There never has been a collection or subscription
in either church for this purpose. And when I remember how God loves these freewill offerings, and rejoices
in a cheerful giver, and what promises he has associated
with them in his word, I can but hope for unwonted
blessings to connect themselves with this House of
Praise. There was another feature of this 'Snowflake
Offering' which was especially pleasing. In looking
over the record we find the children associated with the
parents in this work, and even the very youngest of the
family have participated in the gift. May we not hope
that this may prove a beautiful augury that the children
will retain the same loving interest in this work in the
future which their parents have shown in the past and
in the present. . . .

"But it is not these stones alone which are a memorial. I am surrounded to-day with other offerings, each of
which is fragrant with pleasant memories. Permit me to
speak of two or three. Here is a small Bible; and yet
to me it is most precious. S ven years ago next month

an aged mother in our church lay dying. She was poor in this world's goods but full of faith and love. . . . She bade her son take a little roll out of her trunk. It contained four silver half dollars—his Christmas present to her. . . 'Give this to the new church,' she said, 'when I am gone.' Seven years have I kept that money sacred. Last week those silver half-dollars were exchanged for this book. Thus, though dead, she yet speaketh through the best of books for her Lord and Saviour on earth, whom she is loving and adoring in heaven.

"This platform and all the furnishing of this pulpit remind us of the efforts of our Bible-class. Ten months ago they began their good work, and, by many a sacrifice, have been enabled, not only to provide these things, but to make their own room so inviting, that almost every visitor seeks it out, though it is on the upper floor of this building. I allude to this with the more pleasure, because this effort has brought with it so many other blessings. It has made these young men to know and love each other. A year ago they scarcely knew each others' names. It has told them how much forty young men can do, when there is united purpose. Shall we not all pray that the lesson they have now learned of the blessings of giving may be sanctified to them in all the future? May this church and the cause of Christ throughout the world long be blessed through the gifts and efforts of those young men, who in a single year have secured probably not less than seven hundred dollars. May their example stimulate others to nobler deeds and loftier purposes.

"In a few days we expect to see a beautiful clock placed in this room to be called 'The Children's Clock,' since largely through their efforts it has been secured for the church. . . . .

"But I must not forget one other memorial to-day— those cushions, which add so much to the cheerfulness and comfort of the room. They are the results of one of the most pleasant works ever undertaken in this church— our Fair of last December. Many of you like myself were opposed to fairs ; but we found that it was possible to conduct even a fair upon Christian principles. How many with busy hands were at work all summer through ? Young and old, weak and strong, alike labored, and many, if not all, as they labored prayed. How much enthusiasm, what zeal and brotherly love were stimulated by it. How many pleasant acquaintances were made : how much of kindly feeling on the part of our neighbors found expression. A divine benediction seemed to rest upon it, and the results—eighteen hundred dollars—have been a wonder to us all. It only shows how much can be accomplished in any congregation when each one willingly does a part, no matter how little. . . . The building and furniture have cost not far from sixty thousand dollars ; the land fifteen thousand ; some fifteen thousand· are yet to be provided for. . . . ."

Mr. Payson concluded his discourse by unfolding and enlarging upon the following lessons, of which we have however, only this skeleton left :

16

"*Lessons.* 1. We see how strong, under God, united effort for a definite purpose becomes.

"2. That the highest joys and blessings here are those for which we have toiled and sacrificed ourselves.

"3. That the same God who guided the church for six thousand years is with us. Oh remember that dark Friday eighteen centuries ago when Christ travailed in soul. He shall see the result and be satisfied. May we travail with him here and rejoice there for ever."

In the providence of God it proved that Mr. Payson's work was almost done when he entered this new building with his flock. He was privileged to worship with them there scarcely two years, and then was taken from the midst of abundant usefulness and widely extending labors, in the fulness of life, with the best part of his ministry yet in prospect, and in the very prime and promise of his years, to worship in those other courts not made with hands, eternal in the heavens. But

> "Service there is rest,
> Rest, service: for the Paradise of saints,
> Like Eden with its toilless husbandry,
> Has many plants to tend, and flowers to twine,
> And fruit-trees in the garden of the soul
> That ask the culture of celestial skill."

CHAPTER VIII.

HOME LIFE AND PERSONAL CHARACTERISTICS.

THERE are a great many elements of character which can never be discovered in the forum or the street. They must be sought for in the quiet seclusion of the study or the drawingroom, an hour's frolic with the children, a summer's tramp in the woods, or the common routine of daily experience at home.

The unselfish love which Mr. Payson cherished for those who in the providence of God were brought to be in any way dependent upon him, made him at all times a most dutiful son and a helpful and sympathizing brother. Speaking of his care and thoughtfulness of their widowed mother in her declining years, one of his sisters says :

Most fond and proud his mother always was of this her eldest son. She being like him, warm-hearted, active, and energetic, their feelings were wholly congenial, and his annual visits to her home were occasions of much delight to both mother and son. What Charles thought, or said, or did, was always wise and right in her partial eyes, and during her eight years of widowhood she relied implicitly on his advice and judgment. He was indeed to her in every respect all that the eldest son should be to a widowed mother.

We younger brothers and sisters (she continues) looked up to Charles, our eldest brother, especially after he entered college, as to an oracle ; and when older grown, numberless have been the occasions when we have sought his kind advice or sympathy, and found it to be just what we needed. Going to him with burdened hearts, the cordial grasp of his hand and his cheerful words of welcome lightened our burden at once; and with this energetic older brother to aid us in our various plans and undertakings, we almost felt that there was no such word as fail. He had

such strong faith, and prayed so earnestly, that I have often been gladdened to know he was praying for me. I hope his supplications will not
cease now that he is gone from earth.

In a note dated January 3, 1855, he says :

MY DEAR SISTER: I wanted to write that "long letter" you asked
for, so that you should receive it New Year's, but, as usual, was too busy.
I see from the tone of your last that you are in what might be called the
desperate part of the moulting period. You feel as though you cared for
no one, and no one cared for you; that you are of no use to the world,
and the sooner you are out of it the happier you would be. You look
upon every one as a critic, and while you would like a kind friend, you
wish others to make all the advances. Every word and move is construed,
if possible, to your disadvantage. In fact, you feel generally miserable.

Now, my dear sister, while I pity, do n't think I shall give you one
encouraging word. I know just where you are, I think.· I have been
through the same battle, and know that every one must fight it for himself
some time. You have fought it younger than most ; but I think I can see
a little clear sky in your case. You say that you "are going to do just
what is right, and let people do and say what they please." A capital
resolution! And just as soon as, trusting in God, you can live it, you will
be happy. Till then all the letters of consolation and the volumes of
advice that could be bestowed will not benefit you a straw. So thinking,
I shall now cease my homily and take up the news. . . .

SEP'T. 6, 1859.

MY DEAR LITTLE SIS: I call you little, for I cannot realize that you
have become so old. I can't make you more than seventeen, and I do really
hope that my dear, cheerful, laughter-loving sister may always remain sweet
seventeen at heart, even though her hair should in the lapse of time turn
gray and her loving face be wrinkled with the cares of this busy world.
You know as well as I the best charm to drive dark trouble away. Oh, is
it not blessed to cast all our care on Him !

I was reading a sweet verse this morning, and I must tell it to you.
It is in Psalm 38 : 9 : "Lord, all my desire is before thee." He is a happy
man that can bring his every desire—all of them, and lay them down before Jesus, and say, "Lord, thou knowest my every wish; if it is best for
me to have them, it will make them tenfold more precious because thou
didst give them ; and if thou seest that I shall be better without them, I
am content, for thou art still my own, and in thee I am happy, though all
else be removed." Let us, my dear sister, make the most of our precious
religion, it is so full of joy. We can carry heaven in our hearts if we only
will. Why, then, stay so far away from Him that is altogether lovely !

You speak most affectingly your pathetic farewell, as though it was settled that I was to be married in four or five weeks. Spare your tears. It will be time to shed them when the direful event takes place, if at all, which seems extremely doubtful. Still, if my Father would send to me the "right one" to make my lonesome hours cheerful, to sympathize with me when I come in tired out—in fact, to make the solitary one a home, I should be very happy and very thankful; and yet even this I can leave with him. Just when Thou pleasest. I have never been so happy as during this last year, and all because I have lived nearer to my Saviour than ever before. Keep your hand in his all the time, dearest, and you will always be happy.

Forgive my long sermon, but my heart was full to-night, and I talked as I felt. I often think of you in your loneliness, and am very proud that I have such a dear, courageous sister, and one that is winning so many dear friends to herself and family by her energy and cheerful courage.

Yours,   CHARLIE.

No. 113 CLINTON PLACE, }
Sept. 6, 1859. }

MY DEAR MOTHER, SISTERS, AND BROTHERS: I received your delightful package of letters to-day, and a happy morning I had studying them out. By the way, D——, allow me to remark that a little lampblack or coal-dust would not injure the color of your ink. I was very sorry to learn of the serious illness of so many in Fayetteville. Do be very careful of yourselves, and especially of mother, as I feel very anxious about her delicate state of health. If any of you are seriously ill, inform me at once, for I can run home any time for a day for two, if it seems best. . . .

Everything is only too encouraging in my work. I am almost afraid when I see God beginning to bless me; I become instantly so proud, that I have to suffer fearfully in consequence. But he is very good. I never was happier, and hope I can leave everything in his hand to guide just as he wishes. Do pray for me. It is blessed to think you are prayed for.

Let me hear soon, as I feel quite anxious in regard to the prevailing epidemic.   Yours,

          CHARLIE.

His eldest sister was called, in the providence of God, to labor as a foreign missionary in one of the open ports of China, and her departure to that field in 1868, and faithful labors for many years among the perishing millions of that heathen city, became the occasions of an active sympathy and prayerful interest which only death could change.

"It has been sad work," he writes to a friend, "getting D——'s things together—sometimes even solemn, as I thought we might never see her again, China is such a long way off. Still the thought comes at once, 'It is God's work, and when he calls, blessed are those who obey.' I hope none of our House will ever be Jonahs, refusing to do his holy will. China is such a grand field. There is so much that is thrilling in the thought of bringing that vast empire to know of Christ and his salvation." . . . . To herself he writes: "We think of you and pray for you often, hoping the dear Lord will use you to his glory and the good of souls. And we will be willing to say, 'Thy will, O God, be done.'"

Nov. 17, 1868.

My Dear Sister: We were very glad to hear from you yesterday, and to learn of your safety thus far. When I heard the windows shaking Saturday night, as I had not heard them shake for months, and thought that the wind was blowing directly on shore, I felt no little concern for your safety. Monday and Tuesday morning papers, were eagerly scanned for any news of the Arizona, and, I assure you, that time no news was good news. My seasickness for ten days in crossing the Atlantic enables me to appreciate your trouble; I only think I had rather have it right sharp, as you did in the gale, than long drawn out to perfect weariness. You will be glad to know that our people remember you in their prayer-meetings. G—— says he was a little startled Sunday night to hear a young man in the prayer-meeting who had prayed for the church-officers, exclaim, "But we would particularly remember the sister of our pastor, who has just left us for China." If it is startling, nevertheless it is most delightful to him who believes in prayer, to feel that others who love God and whom God loves, are presenting petitions in his or her behalf. . . . . Your dear letters are a great comfort to us. Our people are deeply interested in them, and if there is any way in which you could wisely use $100 or $200 a year for the mission, I am sure it would be forthcoming. They have just sent an extra $100 to Mrs. Lloyd, of South Africa, making $260 for the year just ended. G—— has sent you a specimen of our new Prayer Register, from which you will see you are remembered especially, every Tuesday. . . . . I rejoice in God's goodness to you, inclining the hearts of your dear scholars to seek Christ. Our people prayed for them with much earnestness. It is remarkable that so large a proportion of them have shown such interest. . . . .

Ever yours,   CHARLES.

"Forgive me, my dear sister," he writes again, "if I seem neglectful ever. This is Monday, my rest-day. Yet I have a service at half-past eleven, and another at half past twelve. Presbytery meets at two o'clock, and I have an urgent invitation from Mrs. I—— to address a Woman's meeting this evening. . . . We have scattered 300 mite-boxes among our families, and have received some $200 in four months. I have asked the Sunday-school children to raise the money for the telescope you need. They gave me about $40 last Sabbath, and two months hence will bring their contributions again, so that I hope to forward the instrument to you before a great while."

NEW YORK, 1876.

MY DEAR D——: How fast the weeks speed away! until before we know it they have passed into months! You know not how often I re-proach myself for permitting so many days to pass before I write you. There are two reasons for this, I think. In the first place, I have no fac-ulty as a letter-writer; and in the second, I feel as though (you are so far off) I must write a very long letter to make it worth while to write at all. Perhaps if I did not see your nice letters to G——, I should write oftener, for the sake of getting hold of Foochow news. I was much pleased, as well as the rest of your friends, at the pluck with which you rescued your pictures from the "absorbing Chinee." We all laughed, and felt you needed no one to fight your battles. . . . . .

Our new building is every week more homelike, and we all enjoy it. Our people have raised about $7,000 this year, and there is at present an excellent spirit among them. We are beginning to count the years and months before we can hope to see you. I trust you will have an assistant in training, so that you can leave without anxiety.

With much love, yours,   CHARLES.

Mr. Payson's domestic life was as happy as his public life was useful. He was married August 6, 1861, to Miss Mary Lord Ely, eldest daughter of John Ely, Esq., of this city, who proved to him through all his remaining years a faithful and devoted wife. His children—of whom there were five, two boys and three girls—were as dear to him as the apple of his eye, for he was a man of ardent affections; and their early lives were blessed with the love of a father whose prayers for them each day at the family altar seemed to bear them up on eagle wings to the very shelter of the throne.

His entire life at home was pervaded by the same spirit which made him among his people and in the church so tenderly beloved. In a letter to his sister, written January 12, 1876, he says :

It often seems to me that it is not so much *for what we do* that God gives us work here, as to.see *what sort of characters* we shall develop in these duties; nay, rather, what spiritual wealth we may gather in and through them; and I do hope that all your trials of loneliness and care may make you very rich to all eternity.

Under the influence of this belief his domestic life was continually illumined by the cheerfulness of a sunny faith which, as one of his most intimate friends once said, "resolutely looked at everything in a bright light, and neither foreboded evil nor imputed it to others." His coming home was to his children like a burst of sunshine. The evening which he always spent with them, in fulfilment of his engagement with his people to be regularly "at home on Thursdays," was the happiest of the week. He usually had some story or game or interesting bit of information with which to amuse them, and the hour for retiring always came earlier in their judgment on that night than on any other. Nothing could attract or interest them in any degree as he did.

By instinct and experience a teacher, he was fertile in devices by which to impart useful knowledge to them, while at the same time he was giving them diversion and amusement. One method which he chose was to have them each bring him, at breakfast, the name of a familiar object (as knife or chair or book) in all the different languages they could find. The object was agreed upon the day before at the breakfast-table, and he himself took part with them in the work and the sport. Each one was furnished with a book neatly ruled in six columns, for English, French, German, Latin, Greek, and "Various," by which was meant Dutch, Spanish, or Portuguese, as the case might be. The words were always printed, because the youngest could not write ; and if the work was neatly done, at the end of the week each child received some slight reward. Following is an example of this exercise.

ENGLISH.	FRENCH.	GERMAN.	LATIN.	GREEK.	VARIOUS.
HOUSE.	MAISON.	HAUS.	DOMUS.	OIKOS.	CASA.
DOOR.	PORTE.	THOR.	PORTA.	THURA.	PORTA.
HALL.	SALLE.	SAAL.	AULA.	AULE.	SALA.

His children also greatly profited by his love of nature and science, especially of geology, of which he was very fond. He would call their attention to a common stone or flower, perhaps, and then, after reading a little from some book on the subject, which was far beyond their comprehension, would give them a simple lecture, explaining the laws of nature with apt and frequent illustration, and making it all so attractive that even older persons would stop and listen as interested as the children themselves.

He seldom went away from home without writing them letters, of which the following illustrate the readiness with which he could adapt himself even to the youngest.

Tuesday Morning

Dear Little Bess

Papa is very much pleased to get your nice
letters and know you do not forget him. He will here to see
to that flower bed as soon as he gets Home.

When Papa was up in the woods they showed him a little
Island in the middle of the Lake. Two weeks ago they
saw something swimming in the water They took their boats
and went after it. When they got close to it they saw it
was a Bear. He could not hurt them in the water So
they drove him on to the Island. One boat watched him
while the other went back for the gun and dog. When
they came back the Bear had run into the bushes. The dog
ran all round trying to find him. The two men went
after him one with the gun; the other with stones went
ahead. "Keep close with your gun so you can kill him if
he runs after me." he said. When he looked round the
man had not stirred. He was afraid. Then the man
threw a stone into the bushes. The Bear ran out. The
Man shot him with the gun but did not kill him
The Bear jump-ed in-to the Lake, the dog after him.

The men got into the Boats rowed after him. shot
him again and killed him. When I got there they showed me one of his great sharp claws.

Kiss the Baby + Eddy + Sarah + Mama + give my love to all
                                                    Papa

Monday Morning.

DEAR CHARLIE AND SARAH AND BESS: It rains very hard to-day, so I will take time to tell my dear children what I have been doing. The cars took me by Mr. Brown's house, South Orange, and Morristown to Dover. There I took the Boonville cars. These are wide cars like the Erie's, and I had a very good seat. When I reached the Delaware river Mr. Jessup came into the cars. He told me all about the great river that runs in the deep gulf so far below.

Then we rolled across a high bridge and passed into another state. Geography class! please tell me what state it was. Then we climbed up to the top of the Pocano mountains. Here was a great sawmill and thousands of huge logs belonging to Mr. Dodge of New York. A little beyond we came to a large town named Scranton, where we got a lunch. Mr. Jessup left me pretty soon after at Montrose. It is up here that our coal comes from. They dig it out in big pieces, then put it into a kind of mill called a Breaker, which makes it of the sizes you see in the cars. At five o'clock I was at Binghamton. Tell mamma the first person almost that I saw was Mr. Joseph Ely. He wished me to come back and preach Sunday. . . . .

Then we rolled across the country to Syracuse. When I found that there was a train at nine o'clock to Manlius, I was very sorry I did not bring Sarah with me. Aunt Amelia was very glad to see me. Willie was so sorry Charlie did not come. He had a pony and rode him very nicely, "because he was seven years old and was strong." In the afternoon I took the cars to Auntie Lou's. Fanny was in bed, but wanted me to come and kiss her. Now, where are your letters? Write soon. Give love to all, and a kiss to mamma and Eddy from

Your own dear   PAPA.

Nothing touched him more deeply or gave him greater joy in all his intercourse with his children, than even the slightest evidence of their being drawn in any degree towards a Christian life. His daily prayers for them at the hour of "worship" were very remarkable. Each schoolboy temptation and childish want were remembered at the throne of grace with a fervor and reverent familiarity of faith which seemed to plead that no want could be small in the sight of God which was a real want. His reference to the changing experiences of their daily lives—the separations, reunions, sorrows, joys, and providential blessings, which come and go perpetually in life, was often most pathetic, so that even casual visitors who worshipped with the family were deeply moved and led to own the power of simple faith to make a Christian home the very house of God and gate of heaven.

A marked characteristic of his daily life was prayerfulness. "Every morning after breakfast, before beginning his studies for the day," writes Mrs. Payson, "he had an hour to himself for prayer and meditation which he never missed when at home. While he was ill, I read to him, at his request, from Bowen's Meditations* and a short passage from the Bible. From the time we were married I never knew of his having anything to decide that was of any importance that he did not ask me to pray with him. He always prayed over his sermons, and asked me, if I did not go to church, to remember him in prayer at home. He never went to any committee-meeting without praying with me, and I do not remember of our going out to make calls or visits together, especially if it were at a time when what he said might be of influence to others in a religious life, that he did not ask me to pray with him.

"He did not go out to his afternoon visiting among his own people without prayer, if only a moment or two in the study before leaving. He often took some one person and made him an especial subject of prayer. Such

* His favorite book of devotion during the last years of his life.

he would commonly remember at bedtime when we were alone. He would pray for any of those near to his heart either by ties of blood or friendship at our family morning worship. I rejoice to remember how very often he has prayed with me in every trouble, and in every cause of thanksgiving, in our own especial cares and troubles as well as those of his dear people. And the same spirit of constant devotion made itself felt in all his relations to his friends. You recollect that when Mrs. M—— asked him to remember her sons at the Fulton St. Prayer-meeting, he said to her, 'Why not here and now?' So he then knelt with her, and she will never forget his earnest, loving petitions for her and hers. Often when anything came up that especially disturbed him he would spread it out before the Lord, and then as he said '*he would leave it*,' and not suffer himself to be wearied or troubled by it. I shall never forget the day he left us, how the same little grace was said over his cup of beef tea or glass of milk: 'God bless this food and may it give me strength to recover.' He desired to have the doctors prayed for as his friends, and to give them the assurance of his trust in their skill."

His confidence in prayer was remarkable. Nothing that gave him any trouble was too small for him to spread before the Lord, and when he had done this he expected to receive an answer. Speaking of moving from O—— into the city he says :

I do not know whether we shall get into the city this summer or not. Am trying to leave it all in our Father's hands. What a blessed thought that we are His *loved* children, and that He so tenderly cares for us because we are his children, Joshua 1 : 7 to 9 has been a great comfort to me of late. Read it, and may God help you to be strong and of good courage.

About the erection of his new chapel he writes, " Pray for us that God would send us the right place, the right building, and the right kind of people to fill the building." The architect, Mr. J. C. Cady, sends us the following reminiscence :

Some three years ago, when the movement for building his new church was pressed forward, I had an appointment to meet the building committee and pastor, and for the first time exhibit the studies prepared for it. As they assembled there was some pleasant conversation on various topics, when finally one member said, "Well, I think it 's time we entered upon our evening's work ; suppose we have the portfolio opened and begin to consider the design."

Before any movement was made Mr. Payson said very quietly, "I feel it is a very serious matter that we enter upon this evening. Shall we not look to our Heavenly Father for his divine guidance and wisdom?" There was a general assent, when he offered a short, fervent, and pertinent prayer.

Although meeting frquently with church committees upon such business, I had never before met with one whose proceedings were opened in this proper and reasonable manner. Some time after, when the plans were drawing near completion, I met a mechanic—a member of Mr. Payson's church—with whom I was acquainted. Said he : "Mr. Payson prayed for you the other morning in church." " Prayed for *me!* What do you mean?" said I. " Why he prayed that the Lord in his wisdom would bless and guide the mind and hand that were arranging and designing their new house of worship, that it might be to the glory of God and their own best advantage."

Mr. Payson's religion pervaded his whole life, as these incidents illustrate. One could not be with him five minutes without feeling this, and realizing the genuineness and sincerity of his piety.

Yours sincerely, J. CLEAVELAND CADY.

In this connection may be also mentioned the following incident related by a member of his church, which illustrates the fact that religion not only pervaded all his life, but that it bore its natural fruits in a loving and forgiving disposition.

In the summer of 1872, while Mr. Payson and his family were absent from the city for a time, two boys of 16 or 18 years of age were seen to enter the basement of his residence and remain long enough to create suspicion. The police were notified, and upon opening the house found the two boys endeavoring to secure valuables. They were arrested and were believed to be in league with professional house-breakers.

That same evening Mr. Payson returned to the city, and after attending the prayer-meeting invited me to spend the night with him.

The earnest prayer he offered before retiring I shall never forget. He remembered his absent family most affectionately, and the church people in all their vicissitudes in life, and asked that God would bless them and cause all out of Christ to early seek his salvation. And then came the part of the prayer which impressed me most. He prayed God to forgive those boys that had sought to rob him, and to lead them out of darkness into his marvellous light, that they might be changed from their evil ways and that this experience might prove a great lesson to them and prevent their going on in sin. . . .

Another incident is recalled by a friend in the following words:

One of his church-members accidentally broke her looking-glass, the only one she had. Distressed at her loss, and, on account of her poverty unable to replace the article, she took her trouble in prayer to God. She had heard from the lips of her pastor of God's loving fatherhood, and that although nothing was too great for his power, neither was anything too trivial for his notice. So she prayed in faith and very soon, the next day it may have been, the answer came. A wealthy gentleman having heard of the poor woman's loss, made her a present of the desired article.

This gentleman meeting her pastor soon after, referred to the broken looking-glass and expressed some doubts as to the propriety of troubling the Lord with such a trifling matter. "But," said Mr. Payson, "it was no trifle to the poor woman. Her one mirror was perhaps as valuable in her estimation as a whole cargo of mirrors would be to you. And I think if you had a ship loaded with costly mirrors just nearing the harbor, and a fearful storm should arise driving the vessel out to sea, you would not think it out of place to ask God to preserve the vessel and its valuable freight." The gentleman's reply indicated that he should feel quite justified in offering prayer concerning an affair of such importance.

This feature of his character, it should be said, greatly affected his influence upon his people. Not only did it lead him in his pastoral visits to pray with and for them with an impassioned fervor and directness which enabled them to realize the divine sympathy, but it moulded all his intercourse with them, and especially his friendly counsels and advice. More than one has testified since his decease that throughout the seventeen years of his ministry, nothing impressed them so deeply as the uniform earnestness and sincerity with which, after they had conferred with him about some doubt or trouble and he had given them sound advice, he would invariably add, " Now take the matter to the Lord. Lay it before him and ask what he would have you do. You cannot go astray if you are following his voice."

Next to his prayerfulness should be mentioned the *cheerfulness* of Mr. Payson's life. The hearty enthusiasm with which he engaged in every good work for the Master was carried into games and recreations as well; and in the dull routine of common life there was seldom found an hour when he could be surprised by his friends in anything like despondency. His cheerful faith in God was at all times sunlit and bright, gladdening his own personal experience and sweetening his intercourse with men.

One secret of this, perhaps, is to be sought in the singular purity of his character. Nothing impure ever secured a lodgment in his mind ; it was like a magnet, which draws the clean bits of shining metal from the heap of sand. He abhorred that which was evil. Obscene and vulgar things might come to his notice day by day, as they must come to every man engaged in work like his; but no sooner were they met and recognized, than they were indignantly cast out of mind and heart with the same sort of repellant energy with which the pith-balls of an electric machine are touched and tossed. His language and conduct, as the mirrors of his thought, were pure.

"Although," says a most intimate friend, "it was his lot to often see and know much that was vicious, he never was tainted by it. He was always distressed if a story or a joke were told in his hearing which would not bear the light of open day, and was not perfectly pure. This was very lovely in him; it was like Christ. He was truly among those blessed ones who are 'pure in heart;' 'blessed, for they shall see God.'"

The Rev. Thomas Street, formerly of this city, writes:

My intimacy with him was very close ; but I never heard from him an expression which he would not have the whole world hear. Full of vivacity, sprightly, cheerful, ready to join in the heartiest merriment in the very boyishness of abandon, he never departed from the most delicate purity, nor would he tolerate it for a moment in others. He carried with him constantly the conviction of God's presence and his own accountability. "Lord, what wilt thou have me to do?" was the question of his life, and to do God's will was his inflexible purpose. In this, if possible, he was morbidly conscientious.

Such purity of mind must have its influence on the life. It leaves it sunlit, like the sky from which each earthly cloud is brushed away. And Mr. Payson's life was full of cheerfulness. ⁂

"There was nothing long-faced or straight-laced about his religion," writes a sister ; "not the slightest tinge of melancholy. By nature cheerful and buoyant—more so, I think, than any of the family—he carried the same enviable disposition into his religion. But it was his strong faith and childlike confidence in his heavenly Father, inducing him to bring every trouble and anxiety of life to the Father's feet, and *leave* them there, which served, quite as much as did his natural temperament, to keep him so light-hearted and untroubled. There were assuredly very few days in all his ministry when he was not able heartily to respond to the words of the hymn,

> "Careful without care I am,
>   Nor feel my happy toil,
> Kept in peace by Jesus' name,
>   Supported by his smile ;
> Joyful thus my faith to show,
>   I find his service my reward ;
> Every work I do below,
>   I do it to the Lord."

In a letter to one of his sisters, he says :

There is a good deal of religious interest among our people. Our prayer-meetings have been well attended—indeed, better than ever before, and many are anxiously asking, "What must we do?" On Monday last we had an important meeting of our Committee, in which they decided not to attempt the raising of the funds necessary for our chapel till times look more auspicious. I came home quite disheartened, and when I awoke the next morning and recalled the unwelcome decision, I hardly felt ambition enough to dress. . . . But just then a little voice began to whisper in my heart. I would not listen at first; but it grew louder and stronger, till I could not but hear, and it said, "Why art thou cast down, O my soul, and why art thou disquieted within me? hope thou in God, for I shall yet praise him who is the health of my countenance and my God." I need hardly say, my dear sister, that with that precious word out of the wells of salvation my anxiety took wings, and I went forth to my duty to spend as happy a day as I have known in a long time.

"On Christmas last," writes a member of his church, "we had the customary festival for the children. The writer was requested to see that the organ and pulpit were decorated with evergreens, and Mr. Payson was desirous that it should be done on Saturday evening to be ready for Sabbath morning, as his sermon treated of Christmas, and Monday was Christmas day. The evergreens did not arrive, however, in time to admit of their being hung ; and when I sought Mr. Payson the next morning (Sabbath) to explain to him the reason, with a heavenly light on his countenance he replied, ' It is all right. If the dear Lord wanted them, he would have arranged it so ; but as it appears he did not so ordain, it is just as well.'

" To our dear pastor," he adds, "everything was right, when guided by the Lord ; and that Sabbath day was full of heavenly thoughts to me, caused by those few golden words about the evergreens."

It appears from this fact that "little things" as well as great felt the impress of his cheerfulness. His whole life, indeed, was pervaded by the sentiment that that is an unpardonable conceit of men which makes them look upon some things as little in the sight of God which they call little, and that, if it pleases God to think of us at all, everything we care for is His care. So common life and trivial wants were touched and gladdened by his faith.

He had a great love for nature too, which appeared at times to attain the strength of an absorbing passion. From childhood he was a most enthusiastic fisherman, and in summer vacations would roam for days together by the side of a little stream or mountain lake, delighted whenever he caught a "shiner" or "had a bite." He loved the wild woods, and the crags and peaks of rocky hills. Switzerland and the Tyrol remained an inspiration in his memory long after he had been among their peaks. And "camping out," whether among the streams and forests of his own free land, or in the barren, desolated plains of Palestine, became a mode of life congenial to his tastes and grateful to his love of nature. He was a welcome visitor in any camp of fishermen or hunters, entering heartily into all their sports, and never failing in such an intercourse with friends to leave the impress of a cheerful, sunny, glad, and buoyant faith, which sanctified whatever he might meet, and threw a halo over hours which sometimes are distained by rudeness or impurity. At the risk of a slight anticipation of the narrative, we cannot refrain from adding here the testimony of a friend and brother minister, the Rev. William J. Erdman of Chicago:

My memories of him are peculiarly pleasant and delightsome. We always met in late years in a vacation among the hills and streams, until within four or five years past; and between enjoyment of nature and fellowship in divine experiences, our days were wont to pass in light and peace and deep mutual joy.

A week we once spent among the hills of New Hampshire is especially dear to memory. Other men might be remembered for some transient experiences in such a vacation of a summer week; but his form and cheery laugh and springy step are for ever associated not only with wild hills, and cold, clear, mountain streams, and the peaceful meadows of the Connecticut, but far more with deep spiritual discourse on diviner things, and the great unseen world he now has entered. Hereafter, should I again revisit those scenes, I know how instinctively I shall recall his image and his words. An unseen form will move through light and shade, unspoken words will sound over running brooks and along the rude footpaths and sheepwalks of the hills, and a light that never shone on land or sea will illumine all.

I speak of this, because at such times of freest fellowship, the best and brightest, the most true and real, comes to the light; and I can say of Charles Payson, I loved him. His self-denying work, continued perseveringly, patiently for waiting years, found in me at least an appreciating admirer, and I am glad to remember how I always spoke of him to others. And while writing these things I can hardly keep back my tears, for no death for years affects me so.

These testimonies to his purity, his cheerfulness, his love of nature, and his trust in God, are witnesses that Christian principles do not depress or sadden human hearts, nor cast a gloom upon the daily life. The native charms of an affable and sympathetic nature, sobered by experience and disciplined by care, are none the less great when Christian faith and love and glad obedience to God have thrown their grace upon the character. Like clambering vines in autumn, crimsoned by frosts and glorified by age, these common principles of Christian life make yet more beautiful what God in providence or nature may have made attractive in itself. And though it would not be denied that Mr. Payson's character like that of every other man was incomplete, and unsymmetrical in parts, and certainly not "perfect" in the ideal sense, it is no less a truth that his experience confirms the teaching of the past that Christian virtues give an added beauty to a character which in its native traits is fortunate.

A single word may well be added here concerning his free and generous hospitality. It was genuine. No one that ever stepped within his door and sat beside his well-filled board could think himself a stranger there again. There were a heartiness and a spontaneity about his conduct as a host which made one feel at home with him at once; and every resource of a well-stored mind and heart, as well as every comfort of the pastor's house, was freely placed at the disposal of his guests. For more than one, who had no special claims upon his thought or care, the cheerful welcome which he gave, and the kind intent which breathed through all his conduct towards his guests, made the metropolis, which otherwise was drear and cold to them, a resting-place. There was one spot at least amid its thronging multitudes and stony streets, where kindliness of heart and courtesy and glad self-sacrifice for friends had thrown the charms of their attractiveness, and where the native goodness of a generous man, and all his Christian thoughtfulness, had made the atmosphere of home.

His cheerfulness was just as marked a feature of his *social life.* Here, too, it was enkindling. It "melted the ice all out of the air." It dissipated coldness and formality. It made the scene a charming one for those who came within the influence of his words. And the secret of his power here, which was certainly far more than ordinary, is to be given perhaps in the word *personal.* His social life was personal. He had no faculty at entertaining a whole roomful of guests at once. The grace and charm which have distinguished other men in such a sphere of influence as that, he did not have. But there was something engrossing about his way of conversing with a friend in society, so that for the time being the individual with whom he spoke was made to feel (what was most true) that for that interview at least, Charles Payson was thinking and living for him alone.

His social gifts were magnetic. A fine enthusiasm pervaded all his intercourse with men. A short acquaintance with him would suffice to show that he had carried Christian principles and Christian motives of action into this more common but important sphere of life. A stranger soon discovered that

> " 'T was his ambition, generous and great,
> A *life* to life's great end to consecrate ;"

and in that end as an essential past he placed unselfish love for man, which sought the good and happiness of all he met. His courtesy was real. The affectations of society he despised. He hated duplicity. What was merely "polite" but insincere, he could not tolerate. With all the indignant scorn of an honest heart he repudiated what society too often is quite willing to endorse. But what was generous and kind and true was sure to find a ready recognition in his heart.

"With a fine presence and engaging manners," writes a friend, a member of his church, "he had the instincts of a gentleman, combined with culture and refined tastes. Few men had such a faculty of winning the esteem, confidence, and affection of others. He carried a full heart in an open hand. That soul must have been downcast indeed that did not find itself lightened and cheered by coming into contact with his warm and generous nature. He was peculiarly the friend of the poor, the erring, and the sorrowing. Many influential associations brought him into circles of affluence and social eminence, but his great joy was to be among the poor, and to go about like his Master doing good."

His fondness for society was as great as his faculty for making others happy. He loved to be among his friends, and his readiness for forming new friendships which became at once "a part and parcel of his life," and remained a constant source of happiness, was quite as marked a feature of his character as the constancy with which he cherished them. A few days' visit at Edinburgh in Scotland, where he rested from his journeying, sufficed to make of utter strangers there some of the warmest friends of his whole life. In Montreal, in Toronto, in Glasgow, in Rome, in Cairo, in Damascus, the interview of a day or two with Christian friends whom he there met for the first and only time, endeared him to their memories, and became a source of lasting pleasure to himself. In many a humble home, hidden among the hills and forests of our own land, where a summer's vacation gave him intercourse with "common people," and rest or recreation for a day, his name is remembered still with undisguised affection. Everywhere, as has been said, " he carried a full heart in an open hand." His nature was transparent, and being pure and wholesome and affectionate, attracted men to love and honor him.

The broad *catholicity of spirit* which tempered his public life should not be overlooked in any estimate of his character. He worked for men as men. He was a philanthropist in the grandest sense of that word—a Christian philanthropist. He loved all those who loved his Saviour's name or sought his Saviour's grace with a peculiar affection ; but he sought the good of every one he met with an honesty and directness of purpose which no man could deny. During the protracted meetings at the Hippodrome, held in 1875 under the direction of Mr. Moody, he labored with an assiduity and devotion which were remarkable ; and several cases of peculiar difficulty among the inquirers—such as reformed inebriates—were intrusted to his special care. Strangers were attracted towards him by the kindliness of his manner and by his just consideration of the views of others who differed from him; while his "energetic and often ardent way of presenting his own views upon any subject which he considered vital," impressed all those who heard him with his unmistakable sincerity.

One of the members of his church thus speaks of her experience :

If I had time I should like to tell you what he did for *me*, and I must tell you a little. After having been prayed and labored with for many years, and all to no purpose, except to make me more stubborn than ever, if possible, I happened (?) one Sunday evening to hear him at the Young Men's Christian Association. I had never seen or heard of him before, but he made such an impression upon me that I felt that I must see him and talk with him and ask him "what I should do to be saved." . . . . Consequently the next day I found his address in the Directory, and called upon him. I need not tell you how kindly he received me, nor can I tell you what he did for me, save that, humanly speaking, I feel that I owe my conversion to him. . . . After this I took a class in the Sunday-school, and generally remained to the morning service, which I enjoyed very much.

Another, who was never a member of his church nor in any way connected with his work, writes from Italy, after receiving the news of his decease, as follows :

Ever since I first knew Mr. Payson, I felt I could talk with him as I never have been able to do with my own pastor, and so I used often and often to speak to him as my pastor, for he had made plain to me some dark places; and that winter when I was sick in New York he did more to help me to be patient than any other friend. The memory of those visits to my room are very precious, when, from his own nearness to the Saviour, he made me almost to feel the presence of Jesus in my sick-room, and I used to think, after one of these visits, that I had been on holy ground.

Speaking of his success in the work to which he gave his life, a brother minister writes to "The Evangelist":

The secret of it is not hard to find; it was the enthusiastic devotion of his whole being to the field where the Master had placed him, and his implicit reliance upon the presence and the power of the Holy Spirit. The same characteristic that fitted him so well for the special work in which he was engaged greatly endeared him to all who knew him.

Charles Payson was as honest, as truthful, as transparent, as it is possible for a man to be. He never reached his ends by side movements, by concealment, by *finesse.* Every one might freely know just what he thought upon any subject, and exactly what he wished to do. He did not hesitate to lay bare his heart, and he never dreamed that such frankness could give offence, and it very rarely did.

He was a very enthusiastic, and at times impulsive man. This gave him force at all times and in every undertaking. He gave himself wholly to everything that he had to do. It was remarked by a friend, at his funeral, that he made less distinction than most men between great things and little. Nothing to him was a little thing if it was in the line of duty....

Above all, it is to be said that every power of mind, body, and soul, was consecrated to the service of the Master. The grand characteristic of his life was his personal piety. Every question was looked at with reference to his duty as a servant of God. In conversation this thought was always manifest; in debate the subject was considered with reference to its bearings upon personal duty; in his public addresses there was always the same earnest enforcement of complete submission to the will of God. It was this characteristic that gave him personal influence with all his companions, that explained the power of his preaching, and that made his own life peaceful and happy. It was this same complete submission to God's will, and unquestioning faith in the Divine love, that took away all fear of death, and enabled him with perfect confidence to leave his people whom he loved, and the family that clung to him, to the care of Him who doeth all things well.

Another friend, a member of his church, says : He believed that "the Gospel should be preached to the poor," and to this end he did not shrink from any labor. The visiting among them he did not delegate to others; he went among them himself, visiting in their humble and wretched homes, and carrying the light of his own beaming presence into many dark places. For twenty years he had made the subject of City Missions his earnest study, and had become so familiar with all its aspects that hardly any detail escaped his notice. Hence his counsels in Session and Presbytery were always valuable. In his speech and in his action he had almost a boyish enthusiasm. This, however, was balanced by such solid and discreet judgment, that his opinion carried weight with men much older than himself. In discussion he proved a man of positive convictions, yet studiously tolerant and even tender towards brethren whose opinions constrained dissent.

The Rev. Thomas Street, formerly of this city, in a letter to his brother, dated January 25, 1877, pays the following tribute of affection to his memory:

In my ministry of over thirty years I can scarcely recall an acquaint·ance whose memory is so full of pleasure and profit to me as his. He was so pure, so strong in Christian qualities, and so simple-minded. He had a wonderful comprehension of the Scriptures. He would, as by intuition, strike the very heart of its meaning. I have had from him some remarkable revelations of beauty and power in his impromptu exegeses which I shall never forget. They were the result of that good common sense which strongly characterized the whole man. He always touched the spiritual key, opening up rich harmonies of divine tenderness. He not only loved, but *venerated* the word of God. He never questioned the possibility of inspiration. "Thus saith the Lord" sounded all through his studies of the Book. It was God speaking to his inmost soul.

I said he was simple-minded. He was a child in this regard—a child in full companionship with his Father. His faith was absolute. No one could hear him pray without feeling that he was wholly absorbed with the presence of God. His prayers reminded me of the pleading of Abraham in behalf of Sodom. They were familiar without being irreverent, confident without presumption. His earnestness was specially marked when he bore upon his heart the church of which he was pastor, which he so dearly loved, and of which he was so justly proud. Many times have I bowed with him in the little room adjoining his chapel in Third avenue, and felt that his faith was literally the evidence of things not seen as yet, while he poured forth his soul in yearning for his precious flock. . . .

In giving he was generous to a fault. In working he was untiring. In preaching, in revival and Sabbath-school labor, in the Temperance and other reforms, he threw his whole force, and in everything he was *manly.* In the pulpit and out of it he never lost his manhood. His splendid phy·sique was typical of his character. He utterly despised the conventional effeminacy of the pulpit. Broad, liberal, decided in his Christian views, he expressed them clearly, fearlessly, and manfully. His sincerity, his honesty, his entire consecration to his work, the evident purity and nobility of his purpose, gave him a hold upon all who knew and heard him that never relaxed.

I write these words to you, my dear brother, from my honest conviction of his worth and from the warm love I bore him. If Charles had been permitted to live I believe he would have attained the highest position of responsibility and usefulness within the gift of the church, for he had in his character all the elements of the grandest results.

The following appreciative words are from a member
of the Memorial chapel :

Although my infirmity of hearing denied me the privilege of listening
to Mr. Payson on the Sabbath, I have had, through weekly reports of
members of my family, a good account both of the manner and matter of
his discourses. I always had the conviction that he wielded no little power
in the pulpit. His manner was reverential, highly nervous, and often impassioned. His style was lucid and familiar, and no one ever thought him
perfunctory in the pulpit, or indeed elsewhere. Sometimes there were
flashes of irony or sarcasm, which, although not inconsistent with a proper
humility and warm affections, might, I feared, give a stranger reason to
think him less amiable than every one else knew him to be. He was a
diligent student of the Word, and unfolded its truths in the spirit of one
who had himself been taught by the Great Teacher, and held a great commission from his Master. He attached little importance to those aspects
of truth which are non-essential to salvation and Christian culture, and
which only remotely touch Christian obligation. Whatever value such
truths may have in the schools, he deemed the discussion of them unsuit-
able for his people. Hence, when he saw the impenitent and ignorant
perishing around him, he had no time or taste for the subtleties of theology.

I well remember once asking him if he had read a work of a polem-
ical character which had interested me, and seemed an important treatise
for both ministers and laymen. The terms of his reply I cannot recall,
but I shall not forget the spirit in which he deprecated the controversies
which, in his judgment, promised no good results, fomented strife among
brethren of a common faith and hope, and paralyzed Christian labors. . . .
He ever felt, what Paul taught the Corinthians, that "knowledge," of a
certain kind "puffeth up," but Christian "charity" or love "buildeth up;"
that, "intellectually, we can know little of God, and that Christian knowledge is this : to know by love." He felt, in all the intensity of his large
emotional nature, that he must preach Christ, the wisdom of God—through
his atoning death, our righteousness; through his Spirit, our sanctifier;
and in his spotless example, our model. And so our pastor handled the
word of God, and preached to every man's conscience, as one who had felt
in his own soul its power and grace.

I suppose few pastors ever had the wonderful versatility of gifts which
in the last century were conferred on John F. Oberlin, and, together with
rare Christian graces, were all consecrated to the instruction and guidance
of that little flock near Strasburg. His life and labors among the humble
peasantry not only made the hamlet of Waldback famous, but have made

his name the theme of admiration and delight in far distant lands. Our pastor had so much healthy common sense, and such a fund of resources at command for the benefit of those Mr. Lincoln termed "plain people," that I have often thought of Oberlin when observing how easily his flexible character and faculties could meet their various wants. It would be untrue or extravagant to say that he had Oberlin's almost intuitive knowledge about education, medicine, and surgery, the construction of good highways and strong bridges, the processes of agriculture, and of almost all secular business, which made him so invaluable as adviser and helper; but I am convinced that the same circumstances and exigencies would have developed in Mr. Payson in large degree the same executive powers and fitness as a leader for the masses. He seemed always to have what I must term the knack of being helpful to poor, distressed, and discouraged people, in just the times when assistance was most needed, and in the ways where it was most valuable. In our own chapel his brain was ever teeming with plans for their relief and support; and all were so wholesome and practical, resulting from a fertile common sense and sound judgment, that the manhood and self-respect of beneficiaries were guarded and encouraged, and almost never forfeited. His whole nature seemed a fountain of active kindness, bubbling up and running over in quick, warm, and active sympathies for dependent and suffering humanity. It seemed almost a conviction with him that he must endure in his own life and experience every circumstance of privation, discomfort, and sorrow which befell this flock of Christ over which he was the under-shepherd. No ease or self-indulgence stood in the way of his taking inventory of their material and spiritual wants. These known, "he remembered the forgotten;" he visited and relieved the widow and fatherless; his cheery tones made a cordial for the despondent; he hastened to counsel and bring back the erring one, to pray with the sick, to clear the way of obstacles from before the weak, and to lift up those who but for his kind sympathy had despaired of help from themselves, from others, or from God.... He knew in a measure unknown to most of Christ's professed followers the burden which weighed down One of whom the prophetic historian wrote, "Surely he hath borne our griefs and carried our sorrows;" and this great burden he assumed and carried bravely, resolutely, even joyfully, through the constraining love of his Master.*

I well remember my first interview with him, in 1862. He then impressed me as having, with a becoming clerical dignity, a most genial and

* His deep interest in the welfare of his church was shown by the fact that *out of a total membership of nearly 700, he knew where all but four could be found, and what their new relations were if they had changed their residence.* He was greatly indebted in this matter to the invaluable aid of his associates in Christian work.

amiable temper, and he seemed at that time, as he ever afterward proved to be, the most accessible of men. His fine magnetism was electric, and operated stronger than argument in making him at once attractive and never repellent. Very soon after an introduction one felt that he had made a personal friend in Mr. Payson's acquaintance—that the good man was interested in *him,* although a stranger. He soon learned that he was a true man, and, without cant or ostentation, an advanced Christian, and that the name, person, and work of Christ were engaging themes, stirring to its depths a heart full of Christian and human sympathies. He knew that the man before him believed life to be real and earnest, and that with heroic ardor he was sharing its labors and conflicts—a man who, like Nehemiah, was doing a great work, and could not come down to the trifles and baubles of the hour. More than this, he evinced by word or manner, or both, that he earnestly desired that his visitor should be engaged in the work of carrying up the temple of God in his own heart, and in restoring the moral wastes around him. And all this seemed the ordinary life-work of a man without vainglory or hunger for applause, or the consciousness of doing more than other laborers in the Master's vineyard. He seemed conscious only of remembering and obeying the injunction, " Whatsoever ye do, do it heartily as to the Lord." ...

One living a life so consecrated to God and Christ, and so full of love for man, is always ready for death, and at the end of forty-five years has lived long, because he has lived to make existence noble. Our pastor was true to God and for God. His life was spent in loving loyal service for the Master, and he loved his race with a breadth and ardor that proved that he felt debtor to all who bore the name of man. And being dead, his works do follow him.

> " Thy works and alms, and all thy good endeavor,
> Stayed not behind, nor in the grave were trod,
> But as faith pointed with her golden rod,
> Followed thee up to joy and bliss for ever."   A——.

It need hardly be added that the influence of such a man upon the people of his charge was very great. They loved him, To-day they mourn for him as for a friend—a personal friend—in many cases as for a father or a brother. His whole soul had gone out towards them and he had become almost identified with their lives.

"In imitation of his Master," as has been truly said, "he aimost literally 'himself took their infirmities and bare their sins.'" To him they came for counsel and sympathy, not only in spiritual things, but in temporal anxieties and fears. Said a member of his church, as she spoke of him with tears running down her cheeks, "For ten years I have gone to him with every trouble!" What wonder that he was tenderly beloved?

When he went abroad to Palestine, in 1873, and it was discovered just on the eve of his departure that he was himself to defray the expenses of the journey and also of supplying the pulpit during his absence, this poor people, who were compelled as a rule to live by the day, immediately raised $200 to relieve him of the burden of supply. One good woman on whom the committee called—the widowed mother of a large family of children, all of whom have joined this church—was just leaving her room to purchase the meat for dinner, when the question was asked, "Can you afford to give us anything to help supply the pulpit while Mr. Payson is in Palestine?" "Yes," she replied at once, "I will give you the fifty cents I was about to spend for dinner. We can go without our meat well enough if it will only help to raise this sum." And it may be added that $200 contributed in this way measures a vast amount of genuine affection and very strong attachment.

It was said by the members of the delegation that waited upon the Chapel Committee of the parent church in 1870, when Mr. Payson's resignation was accepted, that so great was their love for him that fully two-thirds, if not more, of the people would have followed him to another church if he had been compelled to leave.

And to-day in many a happy home whose Christian principles and faithful service of the Lord have been established by his life, the mention of his name will bring the instant hush of sorrow; and the softening tone and tearful eyes of such as mourn "in hope" reveal the depth and strength and genuine worth of that affection which a Christian pastor wins.

CHAPTER IX.

THE LAST DAYS.

"'Death has made his darkness beautiful with thee.'

"THINKING of our dear brother sleeping sweetly now and dreamlessly beneath the violet-sprinkled sods of spring, the sentence quoted above seems to be just the one to describe what his life and death were like... God has a plan for every one of us, and I am not vain enough to imagine that I know better than He what is best for me, or what was best for that dear brother. He was needed in heaven or he would not have been called up there. Perhaps there was work up there which had been waiting for him from his earliest days, and God had been preparing him all these forty-five years to engage in that work.

"'So many worlds! so much to do!
How know I what had need of thee?
For thou wert strong as thou wert true.'"

Such were the thoughts with which an absent sister endeavored to console herself and others in view of the affliction to which they were unexpectedly called by the sudden decease of Mr. Payson. His work was ended here abruptly, in the full prime of manhood and by a brief and fatal illness which no physician's skill could stay; but it is continued in another world beyond, as we have reason to believe, almost as it was interrupted, in the praise and adoration of a Saviour's love. Few Christian ministers even have been privileged to say with greater truth, "When I go down to the grave I can say like many others, 'I have finished my day's work,' but I cannot say I have finished my life. My day's work will begin the next morning. The grave closes on the twilight to open with the dawn." In a letter dated Sept. 24, 1872, Mr. Payson writes:

MY DEAR BROTHER: Here we are high up on the hills of old Lyme at the beautiful home of Mrs. E——, in sight of the old church where father preached in 1838-40, and of the valley where I went to school. There, opposite, are Essex and Old Saybrook, and the lighthouse, and the Point where I lived so many other weeks, all full of pleasant memories that come trooping across my mind as each peculiar scene passes before me. As I look, they bring to my mind that passage in Stanley's Egypt where he tells of the tombs of the kings with their many chambers, on whose walls are pictured the mementoes of each monarch's life, so that when he wakes he shall be in the midst of the scenes in which he lived.

Will it not be one of the joys of heaven to sweep the horizon of memory, and pass once and again and again through vistas made inexpressibly beautiful by the associations of life? Oh what a place will heaven be, with all that is lovely, and noble, and grand, of old earth, the glory of the nations brought in and all the vile and bad and deceiving left out for ever and ever!

The last public service in the chapel at which Mr. Payson officiated was the sacrament of the Lord's Supper. Upon the evening of January 7, 1877, he gathered his beloved people for the last time before the communion table of the Lord, and there spoke to them of the Saviour's love with all his accustomed fervor and pathos. Neither he nor they had then any thought of the sad separation which was so soon to follow, and they now recall his words on that occasion with peculiar gratitude that in the kind providence of God they were permitted to sit down with him at this last interview in "heavenly places in Christ Jesus." He dwelt upon the theme of the Saviour's love most fondly, in his own warm, earnest, happy way, pleading tenderly and eloquently for the blessed Redeemer, and urging the acceptance of His grace by souls unsaved.

After the service, as was his custom, he kept the new communicants for a little while and addressed to them a few especial words in view of their new relations to the church.

Monday, the day following, was the first of the Week of Prayer, an anniversary which was always observed at the chapel by services in the evening. During the first part of the day Mr. Payson was down town attending to some necessary business, and appeared to be as well as ever until early in the afternoon, when he complained of a sick headache. With his usual determination, however, he put this aside, and went down to the evening prayer-meeting, when he spoke upon the topic for Monday.

Tuesday morning found him still uncomfortable with headache and pain, and that afternoon he consulted Dr. Andrew H. Smith, who lived near by, and whom he greatly esteemed both as a physician and a friend. No serious cause for alarm was discovered at this interview, and some simple remedy was prescribed. During Tuesday night, however, he suffered extreme pain, so that the physician was summoned as soon as it was day, and gave him anodynes. On Wednesday, Thursday, and Friday, he still suffered, and, as there appeared no immediate prospect of relief, he became at last content to abandon his active labors for a time, and to bear this sickness which had been laid upon him so unexpectedly as from his Father's hands. Saturday morning the disease was pronounced to be a clear case of pneumonia, and Dr. Smith requested that the family physician, Dr. John L. Campbell, should be called in consultation, having given very strict orders that no one was to see the patient but those who were called to nurse him, and that all exciting topics were to be avoided.

The immediate cause of the disease may be traced to Mr. Payson's exposure to the terrible storm of Saturday, January 6, although his health for several months previous to this had not been as firm and vigorous as usual. He was greatly favored in having for his physicians two personal friends, both medical men of high standing and long experience in the metropolis, in whose skill and judgment he had the utmost confidence—Dr. Campbell having been for many years his family physician ; and he remarked during his illness that "if he had been a prince he could not have had more devoted attention or untiring service."

The kind thoughtfulness of his many friends also was a great source of comfort to him. They proved most loving and faithful and devoted. Every day and almost every hour brought him some new assurance of their interest and sympathy. Delicacies for the sick-room, flowers and fruits, and all the little gifts which affection prompts loving hearts to offer, came in large measure to him and never failed to give him pleasure.

The constant inquiries of many anxious friends, as

soon as it became known that he was really ill, were remarkable; and in addition to those made at the house, word was sent every night and morning to the sexton of his church for the information of his devoted people. His brethren in the ministry called and inquired after him, and prayed for his recovery, if it might please the Lord to spare his life. The prayers of his people, and of all those who loved him, were daily offered in his behalf; while in many of the churches of the city and its vicinity he was publicly remembered upon the Sabbath. Every-thing was done which the fondest and most tender affec-tion could devise; and his physicians were unremitting in their care. Favored by a naturally strong constitution and a vigorous hold upon life, it did seem that he must be spared for many years to his family and to the church.

But Providence determined otherwise. Amid the alternations of hope and fear, with sometimes a promise and sometimes a threat, his friends saw the dreadful progress of the disease continue from bad to worse. On Sunday, January 21st, there was an apparent change for the better, and frequently from day to day there would appear some gleams of light. But upon Monday, January 22d, a most unfavorable change occurred, and on Tuesday his friends were filled with the gravest fears. They saw that there was only the barest possibility of his recovery. Throughout the day and night the most powerful stimu-lants were administered once every hour; but nothing availed to check the steady progress of the disease. Early on Wednesday morning his wife said to him, while busily engaged in making him more comfortable, " You have

19

been very brave to get through this dreadful night ;" and he replied, " I am not through yet, dearest."

The physician was sent for at daylight, in the hope that something might be done to relieve his labored breathing, and a quantity of pure oxygen gas was procured and given to him constantly as long as he could breathe. But it only served to delay the event. Nothing could save him then. He died very peacefully at the last, breathing his life out calmly and quietly, as though he were taking rest in sleep, and with an utter absence of all fear. He rose once and again to struggle with the disease, and seek to regain his failing breath ; but, just as an expiring flame dies almost away, then rises fitfully and flashes brightly for another instant, and so, surely and steadily, passes away, he fell asleep.

> " What did we ask, with all our love for him,
>   But just a little breath of fuller life
>   To float the laboring lungs ? And God hath given
>   Him life itself—full, everlasting life !
>   What did we pray for ? Rest, even for a night,
>   That he might rise with sleep's most golden dews,
>   Refreshed to feel the morning in his soul ;
>   And God hath given him His eternal rest."

From the very commencement of his illness the beauty and brightness of Mr. Payson's character were most apparent. It was a great pleasure to be with him in the sick-room. He put aside all care and earthly anxieties, and was cheerful and composed when not in actual pain ; and then he was patient and fearful of troubling others. During the first few days, when he suffered most, his gentleness and patience were remarkable. And towards the close of his sickness, when the loneliness of death, the separation from friends and from work which he dearly loved, and the desolation and need of his family must have come before him in their dreadfulness, he was sustained and cheered by a constant faith in God, which enabled him to leave his wife, his children, and the church he loved so much, in the hands of Him whose changeless love he never doubted even while so sick.

As might have been expected of him, he could not rest content without holding family worship each day, both morning and evening, with his wife and as many others present as his failing strength would permit. Frequently he called one of his brothers to the bedside, and asked that he would kneel and pray with him that God would be pleased to bless the medicine used, and to insure his recovery, if it were His will. It was most affecting to those who were with him upon the last day, to notice how his faith reached down to common things. The powerful stimulant* which he was obliged to take on Tuesday night was very distasteful to him, as brandy always had been, and he only consented to take it as a prescription of the doctor. But his faith in the power of prayer was shown in the unaffected earnestness with which he asked his brother to kneel and pray that God would bless this stimulant to his recovery; and again, when the next time came for taking it, said, "I think that our prayer the last time helped us a great deal; wont you ask the Lord to bless us again ?"

* A mixture of brandy and ammonia.

He did not lose hope of life until a very short time before he died. Indeed, he did not seem to consider it likely that he would die, until the physician plainly told him so at eleven o'clock on Wednesday. Then he said, " I cannot understand it. It does not seem possible. I cannot think my work is done. One word from Jesus now and I shall still live on and work for him." And then he asked his brothers to pray for him, that if it were the Lord's will he might be spared and permitted to labor longer for the church on earth. He was a strong man stricken down in the very prime of life, and seemed to cling to life just as was natural; and he evidently cherished a very great attachment for his work. Repeatedly during that day he asked that, if it was the Lord's will, he might be spared to labor on. But there was not the slightest suggestion in any tone or look of anything like a rebellious or uncheerful spirit in submitting to the Father's will.

He felt no fear whatever of the future, but was enabled peacefully to trust his family, his little children, his dearly-loved church, and his own soul in the Saviour's hands. Once he said that, " in the faith that he had preached and that he loved, in that faith he could die." It was triumphant. There was no exultant outcry, no ecstasy of intoxicating emotions such as dreams or visions might bring; there was no parade of faith. But there *was* VICTORY, and death was no more to him than sleep. He left the dearest treasures that he had on earth —his wife, his children, and his church—in the hands of a covenant-keeping God, as quietly and with as evident satisfaction as though he had seen Him and heard Him say, "I will provide for them now." There was no dread or doubt—not the slightest trace of either of them in all that he said. With an unclouded intellect and a perfectly clear understanding of what his danger was, his faith was firm and constant to the very end; and he fell asleep at last as fearlessly as though it were no other than the daily rest from toil of which he knew the end—refreshment, strength, and new, fresh life.

When his wife brought the children to his bedside early on Wednesday morning, he spoke to them each at length, with broken words and sentences, as his breath was failing him, but most impressively. It would be sacrilege to repeat the words he uttered to her and to them at such an hour; but none that heard them can ever forget the fervor with which he commended them one and all to the love of God, invoked His special blessing on their lives, exhorted them one by one to a loving, faithful service of His will, and assured them that "to live near Christ was the only true happiness;" while with a pathos none of his children can recall without a tear, he added, "And as you have loved your father, remember these words." When the baby was brought wonderingly to his side, he said, "Let me kiss the darling!" and then, as he clasped her in his arms, he added, "How can she do without her father? But God knows best."

Not long after this he said to his wife and friends that "it was his desire to do the will of the Master, wherever it might lead." He sent the most affectionate assurances of regard to the father and mother of his wife begging her to thank them for all their kindness, and said that "he wished to bear testimony that he had found among Episcopalians as warm and earnest Christians as any in his own church."

To his absent sister, a missionary, he sent, as his parting message, "Tell my dear sister D—— that I had hoped to live and see her here again. Tell her, that when she comes to die she will feel that her work is deathless."

After sending affectionate messages to all his immediate friends and relatives who were not present, he said with extraordinary emphasis, as though he could not forget his absent church and his life-work, "AND TO ALL ELSE I SAY, CLING CLOSE TO JESUS."

Frequently during his illness he desired Mrs. Payson to read his favorite chapters, the fourteenth, fifteenth, and sixteenth of St. John ; and it comforted and rested him not a little to have her pray with him. When wearied out with pain, he was oftentimes relieved and refreshed by her reading an old familiar hymn, such as "Rock of Ages ;" and for any such little attention or kindness in the sick-room he was most touchingly grateful. It was a very great pleasure to be with him there.

He was deeply interested in the "Life of Norman McLeod," which had been given him at Christmas, and oftentimes would have a little of it read aloud when, in the early stages of his illness, he wished to sleep or to rest.

"His was a kindred spirit," writes one of his friends, "in his ardent love of nature and all beautiful things, in his patriotism, his catholicity of spirit, his energetic, ardent way of presenting his views on any subject which he considered vital, and in his devotion to the common people."

Upon the last day of his life his friends who were present sang to him (when their feelings would permit them to do so) his favorite hymns. He asked to have them sing, "I need Thee every hour," and endeavored himself to join them in it, but his labored breathing would not permit him to sing more than a word or two at a time. "We are on our journey home," "How firm a foundation," and "Rock of Ages," seemed very grateful to him, and at times his expressive face responded to them with a glad, bright look which told how much he rested in their comfortable truths. One of his brothers attempted to repeat the hymn which was a favorite of their mother's, "For ever with the Lord;" but his voice faltered before he reached the end, and he was compelled to stop. Mr. Payson then took it up and with broken utterance and most fervent emphasis continued:

> "Knowing as I am known,
> How shall I love that word,
> And oft repeat before the throne,
> 'For ever with the Lord.'"

Once he said "Brighter" with great earnestness. Again, not very long before he ceased speaking, and after the doctor had told him plainly that he could not recover, he said, "It seems strange that perhaps before night I may see father and mother and Jesus."

To a very kind and much valued friend who stood by his side he said, "I suppose the Lord saw that my work was done." And at another time, after seeming to be lost in deep reverie for some moments, he leaned quickly forward and said very distinctly and earnestly, " Thy will be done, Thy will be done. Amen and Amen."

About twelve o'clock he ceased speaking, though once when his wife asked him, " Dear C——, is the Lord Jesus near you ?" he answered by a movement of his head, and again not long after seemed to hear what was said, though he did not respond. But within a brief half hour he had gone beyond the reach of human voices, and remained unconscious till about three minutes after one o'clock, when with two or three deep breaths he passed away. And so he rests in Jesus, for evermore at peace, full of joy and holiness, free for evermore from all infirmity or hindrance in serving the Lord with perfect liberty.

"It was deeply touching to me," writes one of his brothers, "to hear him once refer to himself in a prayer he offered, half audibly. I was standing near his bed and partly bending over him while arranging some medicines by his side, when I overheard him say in this half whisper, 'Lord Jesus, thou knowest all my great infirmities, but thou wilt keep me thine.'"

Such was the end. And as we follow him in our thoughts away may we not hear the angelic interpreter saying of that " great multitude which no man could number," " These are they which .... have washed their robes and made them white in the blood of the Lamb. Therefore are they before the throne of God, and serve him day and night in his temple : and He that sitteth on the throne shall dwell among them. They shall hunger no more, neither thirst any more, neither shall the sun light on them, nor any heat. For the Lamb which is in the midst of the throne shall feed them, and shall lead them unto living fountains of waters: and God shall wipe away all tears from their eyes."

"The fond parents and their dutiful son!" exclaimed his sister in a letter written not long after—"what a joyful meeting theirs must have been! Now for ever united, how must the three rejoice together and praise God as never before for all the way along which he has led them!

"This recalls to my mind," she adds, "the last words father ever wrote me: 'How exhilarating and transporting the forethought that (as we have often prayed) we as an entire family shall at last gather around the throne.' May it not be that they will have 'morning and evening prayers' together, or some such united service, when they will pray in behalf of us who are left to struggle on below?

"'At one dear knee we proffered vows,
  One lesson from one Book we learned
  Ere childhood's flaxen ringlets turned
To black and brown on kindred brows.

"'The face will shine
  Upon me while I muse alone,
  And that dear voice I once have known
Still speak to me of me and mine.

"'Known and unknown, human, divine,
  Sweet human hand and lips and eye,
  Dear heavenly friend that canst not die,
Mine, mine for ever, ever mine.

"'Far off thou art, but ever nigh;
  I have thee still and I rejoice;
  I prosper circled with thy voice;
I shall not lose thee though I die.'"

Mr. Payson's directions were that the funeral should be from his own church among those who loved him and cherished his memory; and he wished that everything should be as plain and inexpensive as possible, as was befitting one whose example was uniformly consistent with his teaching.

It need hardly be said that the loss of such a man was keenly felt and tenderly lamented not only by the

large congregation to whom he had ministered for so
many years, but throughout the church and city, and
especially in the Presbytery of New York, of which he
was an efficient and active member. Letters of sympathy, containing many expressions of personal bereavement as well as of condolence, were received by Mrs.
Payson and her family from a very large circle of friends,
from not a few churches and public organizations in the
vicinity, and from every religious society with which Mr.
Payson had been connected.* One friend writes :

> We all loved him; and as my mind reverts to the scenes of the last
> sixteen years in which he was an actor, his presence lends a light pecu-
> liarly his own—whether it was in religious service or in games in our
> hours of recreation, he was the same enthusiastic man, the same cour-
> teous Christian gentleman. Ah, our human loves have suffered a sad
> loss; but he is our friend still, and is now a new link to bind us to the
> heavenly and better world. . . . . I saw many weeping women stoop down
> to kiss the marble brow at his funeral ; and well might they weep, for in
> their pastor they had lost their best earthly friend. Few men could have
> died in New York at whose funeral so many tears would have been shed.
>
> Says another : He was such a *grand man*, so good, so true, so manly,
> yet as simple-hearted as a little child. I knew of no one whose society
> did me so much good, who I feel was living so completely for God and
> His church. Many sweet hours have we spent together, many times on
> bended knees gone to the throne together. I can never forget the fer-
> vency of his prayers, and the wonderful, faith-full, heart-trust he had in
> God's promises. If ever there was a soul ripe for heaven it was his. Yet
> it seems hard that he should be taken right in the prime of his life, in the
> full tide of his usefulness. It may be that God saw that his death might
> preach louder than his life. He did his life-work well, and the richest
> reward that a true soul can crave he has attained.
>
> There was that about him that made every one love him. When he
> visited me some time ago he took such an interest in everything, even lit-
> tle things concerning my children, that their hearts warmed up to him at
> once. We all loved him dearly ; our house was a scene of mourning
> when we heard of his death. I never expect to find another with so many

---

* Some of these papers may be found in the Appendix, note C.

good qualities. I know that I have never found a friend so true and loyal.

But what is our loss to yours ? We have thought so much of you with your orphaned children around you. We have thought of that home which was always so bright and cheerful, the scene of so many delightful gatherings, now darkened with sorrow, and have asked our Father in heaven to comfort and support you from the very depths of our hearts. You have the sweetest memories of the dear life. You have much to live over again. Your children have an honored name to bear, and above all you have God to lean upon—your God and his. I remember once Charles gave me this text to write a sermon from: "His lovingkindness is better than life." Lay that text to your heart, my dear sister. I shall always associate it with him. I wish it were in my power to see you and try and bring comfort to you. I can only write words that are cold to what I feel. My wife sends her heart full of love to you, and I assure you that I fully join her in it. May God bless you, and "as one whom his mother comforteth," may he comfort you. If it is in my power to serve you in any way I will only be too happy to do it. Again, God keep you in his arms and surround your little ones with his covenant care. He will.

Believe me, my dear Mrs. Payson, affectionately and sorrowfully yours.

It is with inexpressible grief and pain and amazement, (writes another) that I have heard of your beloved brother's death. On the human side it looks untimely, but we must be still and know that God is God.

We loved and admired him far more than he knew, and reproach ourselves that we did not give more expression to these sentiments, now that it is too late. As for you, the loss is irreparable, and nothing but faith in God can carry you through it. And it seems as if the church of Christ could not spare him. And then his poor wife—my heart aches for her—and your sister in China, coming home to such bereavement, so different from what she was expecting ! I feel deeply for and with you all.

It is no time to talk of comfort. This is the time for tears ; God grant us peaceable fruit *afterward*. You are overwhelmed with visitors, so I dare not add to your fatigue and care by coming to you, save in this way. When you feel that you *can* see me, come and let us talk together of the other side ; *his* joy, his *beatitude*, in the presence of the One he loved and lived for.

With tenderest sympathy and affection.

One of his brethren in the ministry says:

My DEAR MRS. PAYSON : I see by this day's paper the notice of our brother Payson's death, and hasten at once to write and tell you how my heart aches for you and your children.

If ever there was a godly man, and one thoroughly devoted to his work, it was your husband. I have often felt that he set me an example that I should copy. His knowledge of God's Word was a matter of constant surprise to the Philotheans,* and many a time have I heard it mentioned with admiration. In his pastoral duties I do not believe he had a superior in this city. What a loss to his church and congregation!

May the God who brought him all through his life and gave him so many tokens of his favor, comfort your heart now when most you need his gracious support. Yours most sincerely.

NEW YORK, Jan. 25, 1877.

The following is from a friend not connected with his church.

MY DEAR MRS. PAYSON : .... God moves in a mysterious way, his wonders to perform; and truly it seems to us a mystery that one so good, so holy, so perfectly fitted for his work as your beloved husband, should be removed in the midst of his abundant labors.

I cannot believe it yet, and it seems to me I never before realized so fully the perfect certainty of an immediate translation to glory as in the case of this dear friend. What must the trial be to those who have lost such a husband, father, brother, and guide, as he was. Quite lately he spent an evening with us, telling us all about his journey to Canada, and, with the Bible in his hand as his text-book, explained to one of my sons the wrong points in Professor Huxley's lectures. Never did he pay us a visit without breathing the spirit of the Christian pastor, and making us feel the better for his advice and consolation, and sometimes by prayer strengthening us.

He followed my dear boys through life with his best wishes and prayers, and would ever have done them good. The inexpressible comfort he gave to us all at the time our beloved M—— died can never be forgotten, and we feel bereaved in your bereavement.

May we walk in his footsteps, treasure his advice and example, and so live that we may one day meet him where no suffering, no sorrow will ever enter. May the Lord bless you and comfort you, and enable you to say, "Thy will be done," and may your dear children be a blessing to you and grow up in the steps of their sainted father.

---

* The name of a company of ministers with whom he met every Saturday.

Mrs. R—— unites with me in affectionate sympathy, and believe me, dear Mrs. Payson,

Your sincere friend.

Orange, N. J.

Another writes from Italy:

It seems so strange that one so more than commonly useful should be taken away; but "He who doeth all things well" had a "need be" for him, perhaps to do a greater work that we do n't know anything about. I wonder and wonder why so many of us are left who are of so little use in the world; but He knows.

The Pastors' Association of New York City and Vicinity, composed of representative men from various denominations, forwarded to Mrs. Payson a copy of the following paper, expressive of their sympathy in her bereavement :*

In the removal of our brother, Charles H. Payson, from his earthly field of labor, the Pastors' Association has lost one of its most faithful and efficient members. We desire to record our sense of his devotion to the Master's service, of his well-defined convictions, coupled with a large-souled charity towards those who differed with him, of his untiring industry in his pastorate, of his active sympathy with the poor and suffering, of his warm affection for his brethren, and of the Christian consistency of his entire life. We give this testimony to our dear brother's work on earth in the blessed and assured hope of rejoining him in the heavenly rest.

New York, Jan. 29, 1877.

Very many more such testimonials might be given; but these may suffice to indicate the widespread and general sorrow which was occasioned by the news of his death. They are the garlands which accompany his bier.

Seldom is a more impressive or solemn scene to be witnessed than that at the funeral services of this beloved pastor and friend. At an early hour of Saturday,

---

* Other similar papers may be found in the Appendix, Note C.

January 27, the beautiful Memorial chapel was crowded to the utmost with those who came to pay the last tribute of respect and affection, while many turned away unable to gain admission. Besides his own congregation, there were present large numbers of personal friends, including almost all of his brother ministers of the Presbytery of New York, and not a few prominent laymen, who testified by their presence to the high esteem in which he was held by the church at large. A conspicuous feature in the audience was the Payson Bible class, consisting of ninety-one young men. The class was named after the pastor on account of the deep interest he always evinced in their welfare.

The services, as he would have wished, were very simple. Familiar hymns were sung, short passages of Scripture were read, and prayer was offered. Brief addresses descriptive of his character as a man, a Christian, and a pastor, and expressing the deep affection with which he was universally regarded, were made by the Rev. Drs. William J. Tucker, William Adams, Howard Crosby, Charles D. Helmer, and Erskine N. White, the latter two his classmates in the Union Theological Seminary. A deep and tearful solemnity rested upon every face throughout the assembly, and at times the forced suppression of feeling, both upon the part of the speakers and hearers, was "almost painful." Several of those who spoke remarked, after the exercises were over, that they never before had seen an audience which seemed so deeply moved by their own personal grief and sense of loss. " There was a sensation of tenderness," as one of them said, "throughout the house. It seemed as though only one word was needed from the speaker to lead the whole congregation into convulsive grief and lamentation. It required an almost painful effort on the part of all who spoke to restrain the strong emotions that were everywhere visible."

Most admirable and affectionate tributes were paid to Mr. Payson's character by those who addressed the assembly, and in such honest, earnest words, that the service, though very long, was exceedingly consoling to all who sorrowed for his loss. His frankness, his whole-souled devotion to the cause of saving men; his decision of character and strength of principle, coupled with rare kindness of heart and unfeigned charity for those who differed from him in their views of truth; his self-denying service of the Master; his rule of making no distinction between what men call little and great things, if only he could serve the Lord and His people: his unfaltering faith and practical views of every phase of Christian life—these and other prominent traits of character were dwelt upon most lovingly by men who had known him long and intimately, and who, it was plain to see, revered his memory.

The most pathetic scenes occurred while those who loved him paused beside his bier and took their last farewell. Poor men and women, old, decrepit—friendless now—broke down in sobs and tears as they gazed upon his dear dead face. Very many of them lost in this man the truest friend God ever gave them, and they could not restrain their grief.

"For more than an hour they passed by the bier, to the number of over a thousand, young and old, rich and poor; and I never saw in my life," says an eye-witness, "such a large number of sincere mourners. The most affectionate tributes to his memory were borne by many and many a poor old widow and lonely one whom this good man, by his true sympathy, had helped to bear life's burdens; and nothing which his friends could wish has been withheld to comfort them as they recall his faithful work and his rich reward—nothing, I mean, of outward testimony to his worth."*

The following addresses were delivered on the occasion.

The Rev. William J. Tucker, D. D.,† said:

We are brought together by such an unexpected sorrow, that our first thoughts are hardly those of faith, but rather of doubt and defeat ; even as our Lord and Master once exclaimed in the presence of his enemies, "Verily, this is your hour and the power of darkness."

Well nigh every circumstance is present to give meaning to death. A life broken before it had felt the strain of years, an unfinished work, of which everything about this place speaks to us, a people with heavy hearts, waiting if there be any words of comfort to which they may listen, and a home with its earthly loves and hopes shattered and fallen—what are these but reminders to us all that we live and love and do our work under the eye of the great enemy!

"But thanks be to God, which giveth us the victory through our Lord Jesus Christ."

---

* A graphic description of the services at the chapel, together with a glowing tribute to Mr. Payson's character, may be found in the article of the Rev. John Hall, D. D., of this city, written for a contemporary weekly, and published herewith in the Appendix, Note D.

† Pastor of the Madison Square Presbyterian church, New York city.

As I sat a little time ago beside the heart that knows more than we all the meaning of this hour, and heard from her lips the words of triumph in which our brother laid down his life, and saw in her eyes the reflection of his own faith, I felt, as it is rarely given us to feel, the reality of the promise that "death is swallowed up in victory." And, surely, brethren of the ministry, if one of our number has thus died, lifting up those about him into something of his own spirit, we ought not to withhold at this time the full response of our faith, "We believe in the resurrection of the dead and in the life everlasting." Let us speak with one another and to this people under the inspiration of our beliefs. Let us also make this an hour of grateful remembrance. There are very many things coming to us, by the grace of God, out of this life for which we may thank Him, and take heart.

For myself, though so recently a fellow-worker with Mr. Payson in this church, let me say that the impression which he has made upon me is clear and strong. I saw from the first that I had to do with a consecrated man. And the more I saw of his purpose and methods, the more evident it became that the whole man was in his work. Indeed, I never knew one who gave himself out more freely, lavishly. There was apparently no distinction in his mind, such as men are wont to make, between things great and small. All things to him were great, as having to do with the service of his Master; so that, whoever came to him in the name of Christ, was sure of receiving whatever he had to give, whe her of sympathy, or instruction, or time.

*

Here, I think, lay the reason of his success. Certainly we have here that last thing, which if men lack in their work for Christ, they will fall short of success. There was not only no confusion in the purpose of his life, there was absolutely no reserve in the expression of his life. His love for men was manifestly deep and genuine, and through it he poured into their hearts the energies of his nature and the riches of his faith.

What we see, therefore, in the sorrow of this congregation is the simple response to a love which through long years had been freely given. These hearts are saying to us through their tears what God permits to be said, in measure, of a true servant, as of Himself, "We love him because he first loved us."

Such is the impression which an acquaintance of less than two years gave me of Mr. Payson, and which will pervade all my remembrances of him. It is that of a man who had given himself to Christ years before I knew him, but whom I knew in the daily endeavor of his life to use himself most generously for Christ.

We can ill afford to lose a worker like him out of our ranks under the necessities of to-day ; but neither may we withhold a worker like him from early entrance into the Master's joy.

REMARKS BY THE REV. WILLIAM ADAMS, D. D.*

No spectacle is more suggestive or impressive than the funeral of a Christian minister. Often has he in-

* President of the Union Theological Seminary, formerly pastor of the Madison Square Presbyterian Church.

structed his people concerning the great mystery of death. Often has he taught them the only method by which they could be prepared for that event by faith in Him who has disarmed death of its sting. Frequently has he administered consolation to the bereaved, as he stood with mourners at the open grave. At length his own appointed time has come. There is no official exemption for any from the necessity of dying. He who has been so long familiar with the sight of death, in his turn is brought to experience it for himself, and now he lies still and lifeless in front of the pulpit where for years he had preached the gospel of Jesus Christ.

In the present instance it is not an aged servant of God seeking rest at sunset after a long and laborious life. It seems, as we might say, according to the course of nature, that such a one as " Paul the aged," having finished his course and accomplished the work given him to do, should fall on sleep. But here is one cut off in his prime and promise, falling prematurely, as man expresses it, with the best part of his stewardship yet in prospect. The suddenness of the event, moreover, is appalling. In the very midst of youthful vigor, of abounding health, with every reasonable expectation of length of days, in "an hour when we looked not for it," the summons has come, and the young minister of Christ is taken away when he could not be spared by the reapers.

This is no time for eulogy. In the presence of death the words of man seem poor and paltry. Little need is there of our speaking to one another concerning our departed brother, when he is speaking to us in such tender tones by his cold and pallid lips. Less we ought not to say, ere he is borne by devout men to his burial, than this : never was any man more earnest, more self-forget-ful, more faithful in the work of the ministry, than he. We might well and honestly borrow for his epitaph the words in the Sacred Annals descriptive of Barnabas : " He was a good man, and full of the Holy Ghost and of faith ; and much people were added unto the Lord." When Dorcas died at Joppa, the widows whom she had befriended gathered weeping about her bier, showing one to another the garments which she had made for their comfort. Many are there in this assembly who mourn to-day the loss of a true friend who had often vis-ited and helped them in times of sickness and want and loneliness and widowhood. It is right to "make lamen-tation" over such a one, removed when he was most needed and most useful. His best eulogy is that his death must be and is regarded as a public bereave-ment.

It is recorded of Dr. Edward Payson, the illustrious kinsman of our deceased brother, that, by his own direc-tion, a paper was laid upon his breast in his coffin, hav-ing this inscription : " REMEMBER THE WORDS WHICH I SPAKE UNTO YOU WHILE I WAS YET WITH YOU ;" so that as his people passed by in long procession to take the last look of their pastor, they might receive another ser-mon from him who, living and dying, evinced this as the desire of his heart, that they might be saved. If these lips now sealed in death could break this strange silence

and resume their articulate language, who can doubt that
their testimony would be the very same as before when
he entreated men to look unto the Lamb of God which
taketh away the sin of the world. If there be any in this
assembly who have withstood the persuasions of their
pastor when living, let them yield to his last, tender, post-
humous appeal, as they shall see his face no more. *Last*,
did I say? I recall and qualify the word. The influence
of a faithful Christian minister does not cease with the
vibrations of the air which gave his thoughts and words
a voice. His thoughts have quickened the thoughts of
others. His words will echo on in the memories of living men long after he has gone from their sight. Being
dead, he will still speak ; and the comparisons and judg-
ments and resolutions which he has stirred in the minds
of his hearers will reproduce and multiply themselves in
long succession in many others whom he will never see
on the earth. A good man may depart, but he never
dies. Had in "everlasting remembrance," his influence,
in the best sense, attains an earthly immortality.

The example of our Lord, when visiting the family at
Bethany at the time when Lazarus died, is our best model
on occasions like the present. That He wept at the
grave of his friend is proof that there is a place, in our
bereavements, for the expression of our natural sensibili-
ties. But nothing was said by our great Teacher in the
way of exciting this class of emotions. His divine act of
consolation was in holding forth those sublime truths of
our religion which by their very weight were sure to
overpower and moderate all fainter impressions. " Thy

brother shall rise again." "I am the Resurrection and
the Life. He that believeth in me, though he were dead,
yet shall he live ; and he that liveth and believeth in me
shall never die." Were we to follow only the "sorrow
of the world," we should dwell altogether upon those
aspects of death which move us to tears : the abrupt ter-
mination of a useful life, the irreparable loss of a young
family, brightness and buoyancy turned in a night into
widowhood and orphanage, the disappointment and grief
of an affectionate congregation, and all the varied circumstances, public and private, which impart to this
event so much of gloom and depression. But, after all,
these are only the extrinsic and casual associations of
death. As for all which is essential and instructive and
consoling, we fall back upon the great and calm articles
of our Christian faith. Now is the time to lay hold, as
with an anchor sure and steadfast, of those immovable
truths which were announced by Jesus Christ to Martha
and Mary when their brother died. There is a place in
our grief for hope as well as for memory, for congratula-
tion as well as for mourning. Death has a twofold
aspect—the one towards those who survive, than which
nothing can be more terrible, the other towards those
who go to be with Christ, than which nothing can be
more attractive. Let us congratulate our young brother
that his work is finished and that he hath entered into
rest, leaving to those who mourn his departure the priceless legacy of an untarnished name, a good Christian
character. "Weeping with them who weep," let us all
find, as the wisest lesson of the hour, that impulse to a

simpler faith in Him who is the conqueror of death, which will be our best preparation for our own departure.

REMARKS OF REV. HOWARD CROSBY, D. D., LL. D.[*]

It is an April day of commingled cloud and sunshine with our hearts when a Christian friend leaves us for his heavenly home. Sorrow and joy are strangely blended. When we think of the promotion, the glory, how can we help echo the cry of praise and thanksgiving for the salvation completed in the triumph of heaven? Ay, this is all so sure, that we can afford to give way to the sorrow which sees the disaster which has befallen us. . . . And then, again, this very sorrow bears a fruit of joy. Our affliction *works out* for us the weight of glory. There is an organic connection between our tears and our pæans of victory.

Dear Charles Payson! now where Christ is! absent from the body and present with the Lord! We greet you as anticipating us in the realizations of our glorious hope. We could not wish to call you back to the toils and trials of this preparatory life.

But what a loss is ours! I belonged to a company of ministers who met each week to converse on Bible themes, of which circle our brother Payson was a conspicuous member. We loved him with all our hearts; with no *if* or *but;* it was an entire affection. How we shall miss his manly counsel, his earnest exhortations, his faithful testimony in those weekly reunions!

[*] Pastor of Fourth Avenue Presbyterian Church, and Chancellor of the New York University.

And this flourishing church, how can it ever supply the place of its large-hearted and indefatigable pastor? For nearly a score of years his energies and prayers have been concentrated on this spot, and here the Spirit has put His seal to his consistent labors by building up an active and zealous people, the influence of whose example cannot be calculated for its extent and power. Oh what heart-wounds are caused here by this departure of one so beloved!

If I were asked as to the distinguishing traits of our dear brother's character, I should say, first, *truthfulness.* He had no concealment. He said what he felt. If he pressed your hand in friendship, you knew there was no contempt or sarcasm or doubt lurking behind. His character was transparent. He entertained no guile. . . . . Secondly, *single-heartedness.* I never knew a man who seemed so utterly free from all worldly notions in his ministry. This was made very clear to me as we often walked together those Saturday evenings and talked of the interests of Christ's kingdom. He had the one aim to glorify the Lord by his ministry, and to this he brought all his talents and energies with a heartiness that was enthusiasm. . . . . . Thirdly, *gentleness.* With fixed opinions of his own, and profoundly conscientious in their bold maintenance, he nevertheless treated opposing opinions with respect, never failing in his kindness and courtesy towards those who differed with him. This was the more a credit to him, as his own views upon any important question were always very decided. It is no special credit to be amiable towards those who differ from us if we are not positive ourselves ; but strong in his own convictions, his gentleness towards his brethren created a new bond of love.

Such a character was one to be loved. And he *was* loved, tenderly, devotedly. Oh, what a joy it is to know that we are not done with him ! No ! no ! no ! The apostle, in the thirteenth chapter of Corinthians, after leading us upward far away from earth to the bright, golden future of the heavenly world, cries in a holy ecstasy, "And *now* (in this heavenly glory) . . . abideth faith, hope, love, ... and the greatest of these is love."

Yes, these tender affections, consecrated in Christ, will never cease. The love that bound us and Charles Payson together is still potent, and it shall be stronger than ever when we join him in the dear home above.

REMARKS BY THE REV. C. D. HELMER, D. D., A CLASS-
MATE.*

The sympathies and desires of my heart to-day would place me in the group of those upon whom the stroke of this great affliction falls most heavily. But my long and intimate acquaintance with this lamented brother furnishes also a reason for a few words to be spoken at this hour of farewell over his mortal remains. I knew Mr. Payson in his boyhood; I knew him in his excellent Christian home, where a godly father and a saintly mother filled the household with the pure and genial atmosphere of an earnest piety and consecrated life. I knew him as a

* Pastor of the Tompkins Avenue Congregational Church, Brooklyn, New York.

young man in his earlier and preparatory studies ; and I knew him in the whole course of special training for the ministry. We were members of the same class in the Theological Seminary.

It was my pleasure and good fortune, also, at the close of our Seminary studies, to be a travelling companion with him for many months of daily and hourly intercourse, and with all the peculiarly close intimacy of fellow-travellers, making everywhere the same journey and with the same plan and purpose. Since he began the active work of his ministry in New York, our acquaintance has continued; but there are others here more competent to speak of this later part of his career.

And knowing Charles H. Payson thus intimately over a period of thirty years and more, I can speak of him with the delightful confidence of uttering the truth, as always and everywhere a positive and genuine Christian. I have been with him on many and various occasions, that would naturally disclose the qualities of his character, and never knew him to flinch from what he believed to be right and duty. He was eminently conscientious. Whether in study or work or recreation, in private or in social relations, he had one rule of life, which was the law of uprightness. So strongly was this quality of his character impressed upon my mind, that I never expected under any circumstances to see him swerve from what seemed to him the path of duty.

This conscientiousness showed itself, not only in the ordinary affairs of every-day life, but was quite as conspicuous in his studies and his work as a minister. He

could tolerate no sham, no make-believe in anything.
What he believed and what he taught as a preacher of
the Gospel was the result of his own honest and earnest
study of the word of God.

Mr. Payson was a minister of the Gospel by blood,
by inheritance of nature, and by all the shaping influences
of his home and early life. He came of ministerial
stock. The piety, culture, refinement, and moral development, of his ancestry, on both the paternal and maternal
side, left him a grand inheritance. These forces of the
past did much to shape his brain and give depth and
strength to his religious nature. He became a preacher
of the Gospel by a positive bias almost irresistible. And
at the same time his own personal feelings, desires, and
aims, all were in harmony with the controlling influences
of his life. So that he knew something of what Paul
meant when he said, " Woe is me if I preach not the
Gospel."

No one could come in contact with our beloved brother, without being impressed by his singular whole-heart-
edness in his work. His services were as far as possible
from the dreary and cold style of the perfunctory perfor-
mer. His soul was in his words and deeds. I should say
that he was a man of fire. His was a burning zeal, coupled
with practical discretion and good sense. What a fine
enthusiasm pervaded all that he did and said! How it
blazed out in everything, warming the whole atmosphere
that enveloped his kindled and enkindling life! Not
inaptly nor irreverently may these words, sanctified by the
holiest application, be borrowed for him : " He was a

burning and a shining light." Beneath the glow of his
nature the chill fled out of the air, the ice ran away in
singing streams, and the very rocks were melted. This
peculiar warmth and fervor of soul rendered him great
service in his work as a pastor. It bound others to him
with strongest ties; grappled his friends close to him;
made it easy for strangers to approach, and paved the
way for all burdened and troubled souls to bring him the
secrets of their suffering lives. His sympathy was cap-
tivating and contagious; and was an exemplification of
that divine compassion for mankind, which so wonderfully characterized the life of Jesus.

And now, with all these excellent qualifications for
the work given him to do for the Lord and for man, he
has wrought for eighteen fruitful years. With studious
retirement from every kind of notoriety, always shunning
most instinctively whatever might seem to be self-seek-
ing, he has labored zealously and faithfully, doing all
things as unto the Lord. And in the very zenith of his
usefulness and power his career has suddenly ended.
We bow before the unexplained will of God. To us it
must seem a great and, in some respects, irreparable loss.

But while he has ceased from his labors, his works do
follow him. What he has accomplished is not to be regarded as in analogy with the unfinished productions of
the artist. Many a painter has died with an unfinished
picture on his easel, which no one coming after could
complete for him. But this godly minister, working for
moral and spiritual character, has left behind that which
will be carried on to perfection. The word of divine

truth, the sanctifying Spirit of God, the gospel means of grace, will continue to fill in and fill out that which has been begun, even unto "the measure of the fulness of the stature of Christ." Look at that regiment of young men yonder standing along against the walls of this sanctuary, a strong and earnest band that had gathered about their leader who now lies here in the pallor and silence of death. These are evidence in part of the good work accomplished by our lamented brother. And they will go forth still to the glorious warfare, "the good fight of faith," to do what he has taught and incited them to do, to win victories for the gospel of Christ in the world, and so to continue his power, his influence, his labors among men. How much this involves and signifies will never be perceived till the harvest shall be measured in the heavens where all things are known. But these remarks must not be prolonged. I am here chiefly to join with others in the tender and solemn service of burial, to offer my tribute of honor and affection.

REMARKS BY THE REV. ERSKINE N. WHITE, D. D., A CLASS-
MATE.*

It is very hard for me to realize that the comrade of many years, the tried friend, the Christian brother, this fellow-laborer in the gospel of Christ, is gone. It seems almost impossible to believe that I shall never again hear his cordial greeting, never again feel the warm clasp of his hand, never again reply to his affectionate inquiry

* Pastor of the West Twenty-third Street Presbyterian Church, New York City.

*

as to how it fares with me and my work. Doubtless
as time passes we shall all of us appreciate more and
more keenly the great loss we have sustained in this
sudden, unlooked-for departure of our brother : to-day I
stand here simply to express in as few words as possible
my own sense of personal bereavement, and to add my
tribute of respect and love to those already paid.

I have known and loved Charles Payson for more
than twenty years—from the time that we were classmates in the Union Theological Seminary. Since then
we have been in constant communication, laboring much
of the time side by side as members of the same Presbytery, and our relations to one another have been fraternal and intimate in the highest degree. As I have
looked back upon our long association, I have asked myself what was there in his life that now in this retrospect
seems most prominent and characteristic. I can think
of nothing that so entirely marked his words and acts as
that to which reference has been already made—his *self-
consecration.* He was eager, enthusiastic, self-denying in
his work; he was fertile in expedient, untiring in execution, sympathetic and gracious in manner ; but he was
always and above all a *consecrated* man. In conversation
he brought every question to the touchstone of God's
will and our duty as Christ's servants. In any discussion in ministerial circles I always expected to hear from
him a reference of the subject to its bearings upon our
Christian work and Christian life, and I was rarely disappointed. In public address the same spirit was manifest ; his object was always to impress his hearers with

their personal responsibility to God. This it was that made him such an enthusiastic, sympathetic worker in times of special religious interest. This it was that gave him such power to influence men to seek the Saviour whom he loved. He spake that which he knew, and his utterance commanded belief.

To our poor human wisdom it seems sad and inexplicable that such a man should be cut off in the midst of his days, at the very meridian of his strength. We had supposed that his mind was maturing, his powers enlarging, his life ripening for still better work awaiting him here, and to the pain of our bereavement we are tempted to add the fear of loss to the kingdom of Christ. Is it not then a precious privilege that we can turn to God's word and be assured that such service is interrupted by death but for the moment?

"What are these," asked John, "who are arrayed in white robes?" And the answer was, "These are they who have washed their robes and made them white in the blood of the Lamb; therefore are they before the throne of God, and *serve* him day and night in his temple, and he that sitteth on the throne shall dwell among them." Thus the work of our brother continues; it is only the *field* that is changed. All the joy that there is in faithful service is still his; it is only the trials, the anxieties, the temptations, the disappointments that have ended.

As I have sat here to-day my thoughts have gone back to the last occasion when I stood in this pulpit. Then he was by my side. It was at the meeting for praise and thanksgiving held last summer at the close of special services, and after the ingathering of the harvest of souls. Then as now the house was crowded, and the chorus of praise was full and grand. You know whose face seemed most radiant with joy, whose voice most earnestly led that song of thanksgiving. Doubtless few who were then present but are here again to-day, but he, the leader, is gone. While we are gathered here with heads bowed in mourning, he is with that far greater company gathered out of every kindred and tongue and people and nation who, redeemed by the precious blood of the Lamb, are singing the new song. And, my dear hearers, although our eyes are dimmed with tears and our voices choked with sobs, shall not we, too, in view of our brother's Christian life, successful work, and triumphant death, unite in saying,

"Blessing and honor and glory and power be unto him that sitteth upon the throne and to the Lamb for ever and ever."

At the close of the exercises the benediction was pronounced by the Rev. Martin A. Erdmann, pastor of the German branch of the Memorial Chapel, and an opportunity was then afforded the congregation to take their last farewell of the pastor whom they loved so tenderly, and who had served them with so faithful and devoted a spirit. It is impossible to reproduce in any words the pathos and the eloquence of scenes which followed in that hour. They formed a "monument of praise" which any Christian man might covet, and were an earnest of that rich reward which all shall have at last to whom it may be said, " Come, ye blessed of my Father, inherit the kingdom prepared for you from the foundation of the world : for I was a hungered, and ye gave me meat : I was thirsty, and ye gave me drink : I was a stranger, and ye took me in : naked and ye clothed me : I was sick, and ye visited me : I was in prison, and ye came unto me."

After the congregation had taken their farewell, the remains were borne to their final resting-place at Wood-lawn, a beautiful cemetery on the border of New York. It is not far from the city, and the many friends who loved him there have already learned to think it nearer than it is. The plot of ground selected lies almost at the summit of a grassy knoll which gently slopes towards the rising sun, and has beneath its feet a little sheet of water where the clouds and sunshine and the stars are mirrored peacefully. In the midst of beauties which he loved, where God and nature speak to man of death and life, he rests from all his toil. And as we turn away from this sweet resting-place, we can but repeat the words of a member of his own church who loved and honored him :

" ONE LIVING A LIFE SO CONSECRATED TO GOD AND CHRIST, AND SO FULL OF LOVE FOR MEN, IS ALWAYS READY FOR DEATH ; AND AT THE END OF FORTY-FIVE YEARS HAS LIVED LONG, BECAUSE HE HAS LIVED TO MAKE EXISTENCE NOBLE."

"Servant of God, well done! rest from thy loved employ;
The battle fought, the victory won, enter thy Master's joy!

"The cry at midnight came: he started up to hear;
A mortal arrow pierced his frame; he fell, but felt no fear.

"His spirit with a bound left its encumbering clay,
His tent at sunrise on the ground a darkened ruin lay.

"Soldier of Christ, well done!   Praise be thy new employ;
And while eternal ages run, rest in thy Saviour's joy."

JAMES MONTGOMERY.

APPENDIX.

NOTE A, (Page 85.)*

MISSION WORK IN NEW YORK PRES-BYTERIAN CHURCHES.

BY REV. WILLIAM J. TUCKER, D. D.,

PASTOR OF THE MADISON SQUARE CHURCH.

THE success of Mission work in New York City un-der the Chapel system, has brought about a state of things for which there is no provision in the Presbyterian order. Presbyterianism recognizes simply the church and the regular pastorate. No place has as yet been found for the chapel, or for those who do pastoral work in connection with chapels. The difficulties in the way of full recognition of this work and of these workers are greater than those unfamiliar with church work in this city would suppose. It ought to be stated that the whole matter is under almost constant discussion in the New York Presbytery, with a view to its right adjust-ment.

The first difficulty is in the arrangement of church statistics. The column of church statistics in the min-utes of the General Assembly is designed to give a fair

* Compare also page 65.

exhibit of the work and benevolence of each church during the year. But the churches of New York city are divided into two classes, those which gather the results of their work into one place, and those which gather the results of their work in some permanent form at the various places where it is carried on. The churches of this second class differ from the first, not that they alone do work outside themselves, but in the fact that they build chapels, gather there permanent congregations, and make provision for the ordinances and sacraments of the church.

The amount of church life which flows into these chapels varies somewhat. Perhaps a fair statement of the present relation would be that the churches furnish about one half the workers and about two thirds of the means for carrying on chapel work. It will thus be seen that it would be very difficult to divide, in any table of statistics, between church and chapel. And it will also be seen that any comparison among the churches would be unjust, which should fail to credit the churches which do so large a part of their work through chapels, with the results gained there.

On the other hand, the injustice is evident as seen in the case of Mr. Payson, in that there is no official recognition of those who do pastoral work at the chapels, and to whose leadership the success of the various enterprises is so largely due. And none deprecate this injustice more than those pastors whose names are at present used to represent the whole work of the church.

It is questionable whether any better adjustment can

be made *at this point,* than that proposed by the last committee appointed by the Presbytery to consider this subject, of which committee Mr. Payson himself was a member. The plan proposed was that the names of those doing pastoral work, whether at church or chapel, if members of the Presbytery, should be bracketed together, and placed against the name of the church, the statistics of the church, which follow, remaining as at present, undivided. This plan allows the unity of the church to remain unimpaired, and at the same time recognizes those who do pastoral work without the pastoral title.

As to the *ministerial standing* of those working as pastors at the chapels, there comes in a second difficulty. The plan just proposed, which recognizes them in their work, does not meet the question of their official relation to the church. Any plan which shall meet this question must be matured in the General Assembly, as it might affect the order of the churches everywhere.

As has been said, Presbyterianism now recognizes only the regular pastorate in connection with the local church. Ordained ministers, not in the pastorate, are known as Evangelists or Stated Supplies. The regular pastorate allows a Colleague, but a Colleague would not represent the duties and relations of a chapel pastor. Here, then, lies the real and essential difficulty, if the chapel system is to become a permanent factor in the church work of New York city: to provide a pastoral office which shall correspond to it and meet its requirements.

It was the misfortune of Mr. Payson—which all who know him and his work deeply regret—that he wrought while everything was in the formative stage, or at least, before the system itself had taken shape. It is even now a question in the New York Presbytery whether what is known as the Chapel system shall or shall not be accepted as permanent and final. And while this question is pending, it may not be wondered at that the Assembly fails to provide a special pastoral relation for which there is little or no demand outside the city of New York.

The following letter is from the Rev. Thomas S. Hastings, D. D., Pastor of the West Presbyterian Church of this city.

NEW YORK, August 20, 1877.

THE REV. GEO. S. PAYSON—MY DEAR FRIEND: You asked me to put on paper some things which I have said about your lamented brother in the peculiar relations which he sustained as a Presbyter. It is a delicate and a difficult task to treat of those relations, because they were confessedly abnormal. Your brother was really, but not technically, a pastor. He was compelled year after year to see his name appear in the statistical tables of the Minutes of the General Assembly with ominous blanks opposite to it, as if he had done no work and gathered no fruit for the Master he so faithfully served. Sometimes he was entered in those tables as a "Stated Supply," and sometimes as a "City Missionary," and sometimes as holding no official position. Yet in the twenty years of our Presbyterial association, I never heard from him one word of complaint about this anomalous condition in which he lived so long and worked so well.

There have been and are marked differences of opinion in the Presbytery on this subject of "Chapel Work." Not a few of the pastors have complained openly that the brethren in charge of the chapels are not fairly treated in the General Assembly's Minutes, and they have claimed that the statistics of their work should be put to their credit instead of being absorbed in the statistics of the churches supporting these chapels. They have held that the technical difficulty in the way of recognizing and recording these brethren as pastors, and their chapels as churches, should be disregarded.

Others have insisted that it is the duty of the Presbytery to organize churches at these chapels and to install the incumbents as pastors. If this could be done, it certainly would be the proper way to remedy the present injustice. Those who know little practically about "chapel work" are very confident that this is the proper and only solution of the difficulty; but the pastors who are engaged in maintaining these chapels in connection with their churches find it quite impracticable to carry out this idea, and that because in many of the chapels there are not found suitable persons to ordain as elders and deacons, while those in the parent church who could be transferred to the chapel to fill these important offices are not willing to make the sacrifice of leaving their church home with its manifold ties.

Another secret of the difficulty is, that many of our most judicious laymen, whose sympathy and support are necessary to the maintenance of this mission work, and who have done and are doing excellent service in it, are honestly convinced that it is not at present wise or safe to organize separate churches at these chapels. They have seen the experiment tried in some notable instances, where the results were every way disastrous, and so their convictions are very strong, and are fully shared by a number of our wisest and most experienced pastors.

This whole subject has been frequently and earnestly discussed in the Presbytery of New York, and during such discussions I have often admired the discreet and patient silence of your brother under provocations which he must have keenly felt. My own position on this difficult subject has been so pronounced, that it would have been quite natural that at least in the intimacy of personal intercourse he should speak to me freely if he had any disposition to complain. But he has never said one word to me in a way to indicate that he was annoyed by his anomalous position, or that he was concerned about his personal interests. It would seem that others have moved in this matter, when it was supposed that he inspired their action, and so he was subjected to misapprehension. To me it is a pleasure to bear testimony, that, so far as I know, this was never the case. He seemed to me too thoroughly absorbed in his work to care for the technicalities to which I have referred. His whole heart was in the work to which he so nobly consecrated his life. Some of his brethren have been jealous for him, but he seemed jealous only for the cause of the Master he served. Very truly yours,

THOS. S. HASTINGS.

The unfriendly influence of this record of General Assembly upon the reputation of mission pastors in New York, and the practical injustice which any one of them

*

may suffer in consequence, may be illustrated by the following fact. A few years ago a prominent church in
one of the largest cities of the West, was in search of a
pastor, and among the many names commended to their
notice, that of Mr. Payson was mentioned, in terms of
such high praise, that they turned at once to the Minutes
of General Assembly for the record of his ministry.
They at once dismissed all farther thoughts of him as a
candidate for their pulpit. One of the church officers,
when afterwards questioned as to the reason, replied,
" We looked at his record, and found nothing but blanks
after his name for six long years, and we concluded that
he was not the kind of man we sought. . . . The *W.
C.'s* and *S. S.'s*," he added, " in our church are a drug."
(*W. C.* is the abbreviation used in the Minutes of General Assembly to designate ministers who are *without
charge.*)

NOTE B.

(Page 136, foot note.)*

It should be stated here that Mr. Payson was never wholly satisfied with the present system of Presbyterian church mission work in New York. For many years previous to his resignation, he had been ill at ease in his own field. He could not reconcile the state of things existing there with his views of what was right, and his judgment as to the best spiritual interests of those committed to his care. The chapel people, *as such*, were not represented in the Committee by which their affairs were administered. In his judgment it was both "unscriptural and un-Presbyterian," that a church of from 600 to 1,000 communicants should have no voice in the councils which determined what should be done for them ; and he lost no suitable opportunity of expressing his views clearly and emphatically upon this subject. He was especially desirous that at least a deacon or an elder, or one or two of the Chapel Committee of the parent church, should be elected from the chapel people themselves.

It is true this people were consulted with reference to any important step in which their interests were involved, and as far as possible their wishes were gratified ;

* Compare pages 128 and 133.

but still, the power of governing and directing the affairs of the chapel remained exclusively with the parent church.* This state of things did not commend itself to Mr. Payson's approval, and was one of the most efficient reasons, though not the immediate occasion of his resignation.

With reference to their prompt acceptance of Mr. Payson's resignation, it should be also stated, in justice to the Committee, that there was an intimate connection between this step and the action referred to in the article for the "Evangelist," quoted on page 129. Some allusion has already been made to this matter on page 128, but in addition to what was there stated, it should be said that "in proposing to his people to raise $10,000 towards the cost of a new building, Mr. Payson, without consultation or authority, took a position far in advance of the Committee, and one which they could not see their way clear to approve. The Madison Square Church had no definite plan or purpose with regard to the erection of a new edifice, and the Committee saw clearly that unpleasant consequences might ensue in case the church should decide not to build. The money could not be returned to the donors, for they were unknown, and it could not rightfully be used for any purpose, except that for which it was contributed. Hence the Committee felt constrained to decline the custody of the money, or in any way to commit the church to the undertaking;"

* Compare page 72.

and their views in regard to this matter may serve as at least a partial explanation of their action in this case.

It would reasonably be inferred, after all that has been said of Mr. Payson's life and labors, that he must have reached some important conclusions concerning the nature of mission work in New York City as hitherto conducted within the bounds of the denomination to which he belonged. And it is only doing justice to the truth to say that his convictions upon this matter were as decided and well-defined as they were individual. He had his own views of the problem of city evangelization, to which on proper occasions he did not hesitate to give the fullest and freest expression.

And perhaps there is no more suitable place than this, where the reader will have obtained a fair view of the whole field, to record his clear and pronounced judgment of the system under which he labored for so many years, and in which his patience and self-devotion were often taxed to the utmost.

At a meeting of the Pastors' Association of the city of New York, held March 21, 1875, at the special request of his brethren in the ministry, he opened the discussion for the day by remarks upon "*Mission Chapels as related to Christian Work.*" The bare abstract herewith given is only an abstract, and served merely as an outline for his address on that occasion, but it is sufficiently full and clear to furnish an index of his views.

The great problem of this missionary age, (he said,)

is how to reach the masses with the gospel. Scotland,
with Glasgow at the head, attempts it by sustentation;
Philadelphia, by colonization; New York, by the so-called mission system, commenced, so far as I can ascertain,
some twenty-five years since.

First came the Sunday-school, to which prayer-meetings and church services under theological students or
ministers were added as the necessity for their assistance
arose. Sometimes at the parent church, oftener at the
chapel, the sacraments were administered. All support of
the work as a rule came from the parent church; the
entire management of church, school, and the associated
work, was in the hands of the session, or, oftener, of a
committee appointed by the parent church. They appointed all officers, even to a pastor, and removed them
without any action *pro* or *con* on the part of the mission
congregation; but food and clothing were dispensed with
a liberal hand until, too often, on the part of those assisted, it was deemed a favor to become recipients of these
largesses and to indicate their approbation by condescending to attend the services. The results of the system after trial for a quarter of a century may be briefly
summed up as follows:

Of the three schools first established, one always remained without distinct organization or the administration of sacraments at the chapel. After a long and painful illness, continued through most of its existence, it
died some eight or ten months since. The second grew
into a distinct organization, but so cramped and hamper-
ed in every direction that it also miserably perished

within the past year. The third, after losing hundreds of converts who had united with a church which has since moved up town, has taken a new lease of life in Emmanuel Chapel. Under the faithful labors of its pastor and the sympathetic coöperation of the parent church, it has, we hope, great and good things in store.

Of the chapels since organized we may simply add that just in proportion as they have been granted church privileges and taught to do the utmost for themselves, have they advanced towards a success. Still it must be acknowledged that after twenty-five years of trial the mission system in New York is yet to produce its first self-supporting church. When we contrast these results with those of the colonization system of Philadelphia, and especially with those of the sustentation in Glasgow, we may well ask whether New York has attained to the best possible.

Let me conclude with presenting a summary of the advantages and disadvantages of the mission system.

(I.) The ADVANTAGES are: 1. This system is better than nothing. If churches can only exist on the high lands in the centre of the island, let us rejoice that there is at least some remembrance of those less-favored thousands who live upon its borders.

2. It provides a field of labor for the members of the parent church. Some of the noblest workers in New York to-day have been developed under this system.

3. It has saved souls not a few; it has given guidance

to the young and ignorant, has truly aided many a family in destitution, and has added hundreds to our church roll.

(II.) DISADVANTAGES. 1. It is contrary to the genius of Presbyterianism. This appears in the fact that for hundreds and thousands of church-members there is to-day no representation. . . . . It is shown also by the position of pastors in these chapels. Presbyterianism, after twenty-five years, has no name or place on her records for them. General Assemblies, Synods, Presbyteries, and Sessions, have striven sometimes by subterfuges to avoid the dilemma, but it still presses.

2. Too often this system is against the very Bible itself. . . . . In some of our chapels no contributions will be received for the support of home work. . . . . Not infrequently they even foster pauperism and deceit. Only the most abject of Americans and foreigners will attend places where they are regarded as recipients only.

3. It prevents colonization. Our Methodist and Baptist neighbors are continually establishing self-supporting churches in the very midst of our missions. Could not Presbyterianism do the same if managed aright?

4. It sacrifices the middle classes so far as our church is concerned. The rich men of New York, twenty years hence, are poor men to-day. They are the industrious, ambitious boys and girls of our public schools, and the young people coming from homes of industry and intelligence in the country. They will not, as a rule, go to our chapels. They cannot afford seats in our churches, and so they drift away into indifference, or, possibly, into

some church with which, by education and feeling, they have little fellowship.

5. It is breaking down the weaker churches of our city. Churches that for years have done a splendid work, that occupy excellent positions, are dying to-day for want of assistance comparatively trivial. Since the Reunion five Presbyterian churches have died. Six, out of thirty-eight remaining, are to-day without pastors. . . . .

(III.) CHANGES. 1. Set the premium on virtue, not vice. Help only those who will help themselves. Enforce the Bible rule, " If a man will not work, neither let him eat."

2. Work *with* these people instead of *for* them. Paul became all things—a Jew, a Greek, a Roman, even " weak"—if thereby he might only save some. Make these people helpers and workers in all that is good.

3. Establish a Sustentation Fund that will give a fair support to the pastors of any church that regularly contributes to this fund, no matter where or what that church may be.

NOTE C.

(Page 226.)

———•———

EXTRACT FROM MINUTES OF THE PRESBYTERY OF NEW YORK, MARCH 5, 1877.

The Rev. Charles H. Payson, for eighteen years a minister of Jesus Christ, died in the midst of his work, January 24, 1877. He was from the time of his ordination a member of this Presbytery, and his entire work was within the limits of this city.

Mr. Payson possessed in unusual degree the qualifications for the ministry of Christ. He was responsive to the truth. His whole nature kindled under the truths of revelation. He watched for the "light to break out of God's Holy Word;" and whatever he saw and felt, that he declared with an increasing joy. The pulpit was to him never a burden or a weariness, but always a delight. And he was a lover of men. Recognizing in all the possible image of the Lord Jesus, he endeavored to make the work of Christ real and evident in character. He knew no distinctions among those to whom he ministered, but gave himself with an equal energy and love to all.

With these qualifications, which are everywhere the signs of the ministry, he would have been in any field a successful minister. The peculiar success, therefore, which attended his work among us was the result of adaptation. He fitted himself—it may reverently be said "he straightened himself"—to the end before him.

His consecration was so complete that he knew no conflicting purposes, and to the work to which he had set himself apart he brought all his energies and enthusiasm, all the acquisitions from study and travel and the growing resources of his faith. So that his ministry, though quickly told in years, has left the impression and the power with many of the results of a finished work.

Mr. Payson was a man of marked individuality. As the end which he proposed to himself was distinct and personal, so were his convictions, opinions, and habits. He held firmly to his own principles and methods, though in a large spirit of charity towards those with whom he differed.

He went in and out among us in all ways of genial companionship, always revealing the sympathies of a large, true-hearted man. In his death he bore witness to the faith in which he lived. He went out from us, as he had lived among us, bravely, and in a great trust in his Redeemer.

It is therefore with heartfelt gratitude that we put upon the records of this Presbytery our estimate of the services and the life of our brother. Conscious of our loss as we still work for Christ, we thank God for the example which is one of such consecration, fidelity, and trust in Christian service. And in our sympathies with those most bereaved, the church to which he ministered, and specially the household of his care and love, we do rejoice in those comforts of God which gather about these and all remembrances of our dead.

WILLIAM J. TUCKER,
ERSKINE N. WHITE, } COMMITTEE.
WILLIAM ADAMS,

RESOLUTIONS OF THE PHILOTHEAN SOCIETY.

At a meeting of the Philothean Society, on Saturday,
January 27, 1877, it was the unanimous desire of the
members to convey to the widow of our dear brother,
Charles H. Payson, some expression of our high appreciation of him, of our grief at his loss, and of our sympathy for her in her great bereavement. By one of the
paradoxes of sorrow, his departure has made him unusually prominent; and as his character passes before the
regard of loving eyes, he seems grand and noble and
true; a scholar whose most delightful study was God's
revealed word; a minister who plead for the reconcilia-
tion of sinners to God as though he stood indeed in
Christ's stead; a pastor whose charge was any who
needed or asked his counsel; a Christian who was seeking continually a deeper consecration; a brother friendly,
faithful, charitable, beloved.

His decease flings our thoughts back upon the promises of God, upon the words of our Master touching the
resurrection, upon the benediction of the Voice from
heaven: "Blessed are the dead who die in the Lord;"
and we are comforted in the thought that "absent from
the body" is "present with the Lord." Our sorrow may
lead us to sympathize with her whose grief reaches
depths that we cannot sound, and whose loss is the loss
of a husband, pastor, guide, support—all in one. And
our comfort in Christ will lead us to pray that the everlasting arms may be about her, and that she may be
taught to say with simple, affectionate faith, "The Lord
is my husband."

It was resolved that a copy of this minute be forwarded to the widow of our deceased brother.

S. B. ROSSITER,
E. D. MURPHY.

RESOLUTIONS PRESENTED TO MRS. CHARLES PAYSON
AND FAMILY BY THE SOCIAL BIBLE-CLASS.

It having pleased our heavenly Father to remove from his active labors in our midst our beloved pastor and friend, Rev. Charles H. Payson, we, the undersigned, desire to sympathize with you in your deep bereavement, and to express our sincere love for him, and the deep loss all have sustained who knew him as a teacher, guide, and counsellor. But our loss is his gain.

> " None knew him but to love him,
> None named him but to praise."

We never shall forget the great interest he manifested towards us at all times, but especially how, upon the last Sabbath in which he was engaged in the Master's work on earth, he visited us, speaking words of delight and encouragement, and leaving his heartfelt wishes for our good. The soul of our pastor overflowed, and our souls were reached. He spoke truly, and his words have been fruitful seeds in our hearts. He was the voice of Christ speaking to us words of warning, counsel, and tenderness ; and his last words, " Cling to Christ," will long be remembered and cherished as the motto of our lives.

Seldom can the bereaved heart reject an expression

*

of grateful remembrance in which the departed are held by those in whom their past attention and kindness have wakened a deep interest and attachment. Therefore we are fully persuaded that you will acquit us of all intention of intruding upon your deep grief, when we endeavor to console you in a measure by directing your attention from your great loss to Him who afflicteth not willingly, and enableth us to say, in the exercise of our pastor's trust and confidence, " It is the Lord's will ; let him do as seemeth good in his sight."

Never was he so dear, so true, so noble, as when you now think of him as having but reflected the love of Him who is the true Husband of the widow, the Father of the fatherless. Through the wonderful grace of God it is your portion and ours to rejoice in a blessed hope that while he cannot return to us, we all may go to him, thus clinging to Christ.

$\left\{\begin{array}{l}\text{Signed by A. R. COLTON, Teacher,}\\ \text{and every member of the class.}\end{array}\right.$

RESOLUTIONS ADOPTED BY CITY MISSION SOCIETY, NEW YORK, JANUARY 29, 1877.

The missionaries of the New York City Mission and Tract Society, at their regular meeting held on Saturday, January 27, 1877, hearing of the death of their friend and brother, Rev. Charles H. Payson of the Memorial Chapel of this city, passed unanimously the following resolution : that having often been associated with the Rev. Charles H. Payson in missionary work, we

heartily unite in testifying to our sense of his high Chris
tian character and of his eminently successful ministry
among the people for whom he labored; and we do
hereby tender our sincere sympathies to his bereaved
church and his stricken family, and pray that the God of
all comfort may console and sustain them in this afflic-
tive dispensation.

In behalf of the missionaries,

JOHN RUSTON.

We cannot forbear adding here a part of a letter of
sympathy from one of the leading members of the Memorial Chapel. It breathes a spirit which we hope and
pray may become the prevailing spirit among a people
so deeply bereaved and so greatly blessed.

MY DEAR MRS. PAYSON: . . . Yesterday at our female prayer-meeting, Mrs. —— prayed for you and your children with so much earnest and
tender feeling, that it did me good, and I thought—it does not always re-
quire learning to make eloquence. These meetings have begun well and
now we want the answers to prayer in a church fully united, and a large
ingathering of precious souls. I think I mentioned to you that a verse in
Isaiah was very forcibly impressed upon me, soon after Mr. Payson's
death, "This people have I formed for myself; they shall show forth my
praise," and how it comforted me in view of the mysterious blow that took
our dear pastor away. Then I realized, too, *that the best way I could show
my loyalty to your husband would be to stay in the church he so loved, and
seek its peace and advancement.*

We have very much to be grateful for in the faithful ministrations of
Mr. E—— both in the pulpit and out of it, and very soon, he and the people will know each other for their mutual comfort, I am sure. . . .

I have written all this because I know that your interest in this church
can never cease, and that you and your husband are identified with it beyond all time. This thought is very sweet to me. How many ways the
Lord has of broadening and deepening our best affections.

NOTE D.

(Page 232.)

— ◆ —

The following tribute to his worth appears in an article upon the public services at the funeral of Mr. Payson, and is from the pen of the Rev. John Hall, D. D., of New York city.

FALLEN ON THE FIELD.

The day—it was in January—was bright overhead. The sun sent his kindly rays down on a frozen land, and in the streets of the city, where the pure snow cannot long escape the contamination of city life, the walks had become damp and muddy. It was all fair when you looked up—it was slippery and comfortless when you looked down. It was like enough the race now ended, that had been run in difficult and often disagreeable places, but over it, ever shining and warming, all the light of an uncreated Sun. The day and our thoughts harmonized—all below was unlovely—all above was sunshine.

For we are going to his funeral. He was a minister—it matters little of what denomination. That is the reason that the building is already crowded, though there is hardly a carriage about the door; and though no word has yet been spoken, nor the casket been carried in, many faces are tearful, and many eyes are red with weeping. They have left space for brother ministers on one side, and as they, with many names, crowd

into it, they too, catch the spirit of the scene, and their
greetings are silent and sorrowful. The assembly is far
too great for all to have seats. Round that farther wall
is a line of young men—such young men as earn honest
bread with their hands. They too, look as if their
brother had died. And on the other side, and all around,
are troops of weeping women; and mingling with the
children, here and there, their fathers—not so many of
them, for they in most cases had to work. Not often
does one see fifteen hundred persons so moved by one
feeling; so hushed in the presence of one great sorrow.
Why is this? Who is to be buried? A popular leader?
a large employer? a famous man? No: the pastor of
the congregation. That was his pulpit—his throne.
This goodly, even stately building (for though it was not
for the rich, why should it not be rich to lift up the
worshippers?) this fair church was his work-room. These
were his people—more than fellow-citizens, more than
neighbors, more than acquaintances, more than friends,
more, even in some sense, than family — *his people.*
Those sad-faced youths he called "my young men."
Those young women he called "my Bible-class." Those
sobered boys and girls he called "my children." They
all loved him, for he loved them all, and they knew it
well. And now they were carrying him into his own
church to lay him down in death-silence before his own
pulpit, that devout men might make lamentation over
him, before they carried him out to his burial. No wonder that they wept.

He was a minister among the poor, and to them.

That man whose ungloved hand is furtively wiping a tear as if he was ashamed of it, used to drink, while his wife wept and prayed. The pastor used to go to the house, cheered the mother, took the children into the infant class, (they found some garments on the way,) and they learned hymns and verses and bright, good child-ways that lightened their mother's darkened lot and room; and one day the pastor happened to see their father, who got to trust him and like him, and at length he must needs go and see how all this thing is done; and as he got into the habit of going, he dropped out of the habit of going to "the corner;" and now he is a man, with a lovely family. He will never trouble the police, nor be a charge on the state. He knows to-day that all he is, and all his children are, he owes to the brother-man whose body is to be carried past him there to the front of his pulpit.

There is a woman in faded mourning, crying as if her heart would break. Her son was her support. You see him yonder in the line; and when work could not be had, the minister went round to an employer and told the story, and said, "I don't want them to lose their self-respect by getting charity;" and the boy got work, and felt that he ought to do it well, for the sake of him who procured it; and that boy never will beg nor let his mother want. There is something in him that disinclines him to dependence.—And next to the widow you may see a homely face, young, but full of distress. She is a domestic, from the north of Ireland. While her father was strong she had not "to go out," but when he lost his health she came to America. The minister was her best friend—her counsellor, her confidant. When she had ten dollars to send home, he put her in the way to do it ; when she was out of place she consulted him, and he found her a safe lodging ; she called to tell him her new address when she was engaged again. By his advice she had put a little money in a savings-bank. The one sermon she could hear on Sunday brightened her week. And now he is gone, and she feels lonely as the day she landed. " Next to my father," the simple creature says in her grief, " I loved him the best in all the world."

Surely, surely, far beyond what Board or Committee can give, there are rewards to the workers in the tenements and lowlier homes of the people—present rewards in the priceless love of grateful hearts, coming rewards from Him who says, " Ye did it unto Me?"

A stir and a rustle behind, and a deeper stillness for a moment—and then the people rise, not now to praise God at the pastor's call, but to receive his silent form. The casket is laid down . . . . The minister was a man—with his own home-joys and cares. They realize how near he came to them. Mothers there remember how he bent over their dead children. Widows, whose stay he was, look in pity at that sweet, wondering baby-face that father shall not kiss again, and their tears flow amain. Minister and people—they are one, according to God's blessed plan—one household, an extension of the family, with common joys and sorrows ; and he was a great, strong, loving elder brother among them, who led them, and comforted them, and helped them, and loved them— and he is dead ! They are sorrowing most of all for this, that they shall see his face no more.

What need of any words now, but of "Resurrection of Life?" Fathers, brethren, classmates, companions in labor—what can they say so eloquent, so touching, so softening as is said by his people there? No need to tell us he was brave and true, and tender-hearted, and that love to his Master made him love his charge. *Their* faces, their tears tell it. They in their homes, lives, hopes, tell it, and as one studies the scene, his mind travels beyond it—beyond the bowed widow and her orphans—beyond the fair structure—out into the crowded thoroughfares, and over the land, and one longs to cry out—O men and brethren, reforming and bewailing crimes, and corruption, taxation, and all unlovely things that mar our freedom and block our difficult way—get men like him to work, and give them room ; and sooner and cheaper and better, than by all your statutes and commissions and costly machinery, will you make our city—ay, and our town and country life—pure and sweet and noble. Charles Paysons, ministers of the Gospel, blessed peacemakers, wise teachers, good friends, are more and mightier than your costliest array of police and your best balanced legislation for pacifying, purifying, and elevating the people.

www.ingramcontent.com/pod-product-compliance
Lightning Source LLC
Chambersburg PA
CBHW031332070726
47496CB00018B/1825